Intelligence and Academic Achievement

ABOUT THE AUTHOR

PANNEER SELVAM is born in Salem - Valappady of Tamil Nadu. He started his career as school teacher in New Delhi in the year 1991. He joins as lecturer in DIET, perundurai of Erode in 2000. Bharathiyar University were gave the Philosophy in Doctorates in Language and Education. He is the seventh diploma holder from National University of Educational Planning and Administration (NUEPA), New Delhi in 2002. In 2005, the Tamil Nadu government was given the 'Excellence Award' for his unrivalled teaching activities and some organization also. He has published more than hundreds of Research Papers and books in the field of Education. At present he is working in the department of Education, Bharathidasan University, Tamil Nadu.

ABOUT THE BOOK

Society is a significant medium where certain quality of life and certain types of activity and occupation are provided with the aim of securing child's development based on the social needs. Since it is a stem of growth characteristics of an adolescent period by which every student should adapt to the society in which we live and to which he is expected to adjust and contribute, the social intelligence and maturity receives importance at the present context. The conduct of many individual in the society tells about his intelligence and social maturity through which he can respond right according to situations. Intelligence is the general mental adaptability for new problems and new situations of life. It is the power within a person to analyze what to do and act accordingly. It also emphasis the ability to learn, that is one's intelligence is educable. Intelligence is the important aspect of an individual. Through intelligence one can know his abilities and capabilities. Intelligence test is used to categories people into different group. Person having intelligence is capable of doing all things. Teaching is an interactive process, involving four aspects teacher, student, learning process and learning situation.

❐

Intelligence and Academic Achievement

Dr. S.K. Panneer Selvam
Assistant Professor, Department of Education
Bharathidasan University, T.N.,India

AMIGA PRESS INC.

AMIGA PRESS INC.
H.O:- 28-A, Indra Park, St.No-9
Near-Chander Nagar, Krishna Nagar
Delhi: - 110051 (India)
Tel: - 011-22504028, +91-98736-57000
Email: - amigapress@gmail.com
info@amigapress.co.in
amigaeditorial@gmail.com
amigapub@gmail.com

Website: - www.amigapress.co.in

This edition is published by Amiga Press Inc.

ISBN: 978-93-84533-62-5

First Published 2020

Printed and bound in India by Replika Press Pvt. Ltd.

Contents

❐

1

Intelligence and Teaching Competence of Teacher Trainees

Thers should be the living incarnation of the great trinity of truth, goodness and beauty. They must have a deep sense of reasoning, non-violence and objective outlook towards everything and they must appreciate beauty and orderliness. Teacher must have robust optimism and free from frustration and compassion; his personality will be dead wood without tender feelings for anybody. His vision of life must be based on love sympathy and affection for all in general and for the needy and deprived classes of the society in particular.

According to Viswakavi Rabindranath Tagore "A lamp never lights another lamp unless it continues to burn its own flame. A teacher can never truly teach unless he is still learning in himself"

IMPORTANCE OF EDUCATION

Education is an exclusively human activity. Man inherits his cultural heritage from his elders in society, through education.A person without education is really like a blind. In the words of Rousseau, "Plants are developed by cultivation and men by education" Education nourishes us like a mother. It directs us to the proper path like the father.It guides us to reach our destination like a teacher.

According to John Dewey, "True education comes through the stimulation of child's power by the demands of social stimulation in which he finds himself".

CONCEPT OF INTELLIGENCE

Intelligence is the general mental adaptability for new problems and new situations of life. It is the power within a person to analyze what to do and act accordingly. It also emphasis the ability to learn, that is one's intelligence is educable. It also emphasis on effective use of concept and symbols in dealing with situations. Intelligence is an inherited capacity of an individual. It is the capacity to improve upon native tendency in the light of past experiences. This is manifested through his ability to adopt and to reconstruct the factors of his environment in accordance with his group. Most psychologists accept the idea that learning capacity is an essential aspect of intelligence. There are instances of pupils who face special fields like art and mechanics. Intelligence is the general capacity of an individual to consciously adjust his thinking to new requirements

INTELLIGENCE

Intelligence is the capacities to acquire and apply knowledge. Intelligence is the general ability Intelligence is assumed to be basically a matter of relationships. Many psychologists observe the positive relationships between different types of performance. There are various definitions given by the psychologists as follows

According to Colvin "An individual possess intelligence in so far as he has learned or can learn to adjust himself to an environment".

Freeman states "An individual is intelligent in proportion as he is able to carry on abstract thinking".

Gates observes, "Intelligence is a composite organization of abilities to learn, to grasp broad and stable facts especially abstract facts with alertness accuracy, to exercise mental control and to display flexibility ingenuity in seeking the solutions to problems".

Rex Knight notes, "Intelligence is the ability to discover the relevant qualities and relations of the objects or ideas that are before us and to evoke relevant idea; in other words it is capacity of relational thinking, directed to the attainment of some end".

CHARACTERISTICS OF INTELLIGENCE

According to Woodworth, "An intelligent person makes use of his past experience to an immediate problem or seek a goal. He can adopt himself to a novel situation and face to solve a new problem or master a complex situation. He tries to understand the cause of the problem before trying a solution for it.

Thinks ahead of time, keeps a brooder outlook and tries to be different from others.

TYPES OF INTELLIGENCE

Intelligence is the aggregate or global capacity of the individual to act purposefully to think rationally and to deal effectively with his environment. Philosophers and psychologists developed various types with regard to nature of intelligence; they classified intelligence into various categories.

CONCRETE INTLLIGENCE

This type of intelligence is applicable when the individual is handling concrete objects or machines. The person uses this intelligence in the operation of tools and instruments. Engineers and mechanics generally have this type of intelligence.

ABSTRACT INTELLIGENCE

This type of intelligence is acquired after an intensive study of book and related literature. It is mostly literary in content. Mostly good teachers, lawyers, doctors and philosophers have this type of knowledge.

SOCIAL INTELLIGENCE

Persons having this type of intelligence have a dynamic personality. They know the art of winning friends and influencing them. They present their views in an attractive manner and generally seek the approval of their friends and associates. Leaders, ministers, members of the diplomatic sources and social workers have it.

It is difficult to say about the distribution of the above three types of intelligence. Some may have more of concrete intelligence though he may not be an engineer. It is also possible that an engineer may have more of abstract intelligence and less of concrete.

Howard Gardner classified the intelligence into nine types based on multiple intelligence theory, they are:

- Naturalist Intelligence
- Musical Intelligence
- Logical Mathematical Intelligence
- Existential Intelligence
- Interpersonal Intelligence
- Bodily-Kinesthetic Intelligence
- Linguistic Intelligence
- Intra-personal Intelligence
- Spatial Intelligence

MEASUREMENT OF INTELLIGENCE

Some of the basic expressions for the measurement of intelligenceare mental age, chronological age and intelligence quotient.

1. Chronological Age

Chronological age is the physical age of a person, counted from the date and time of his birth. It is counted in terms of years, month and date etc.

2. Mental Age

Mental age is an index of intelligence rank. Mental age means that a given child's performance of a test is like the average performance on the same test of children of a given chorological age.

3. Intelligence Quotient

Intelligence quotient is synonymous with intelligence. Intelligence quotient (I.Q) means a child's Mental Age (M.A) divided by his Chronological Age (C.A) multiplied by IQ=(MA/CA)100.

INTELLIGENCE AND EDUCATIONAL IMPLICATION

Mental development is influenced by both heredity and environment. A very little change can be alone to change the influence of heredity. But the parents, the teachers and the school can provide a healthy and motivating intellectual environment for the child. In this regard, the combined efforts of the child, the family and the society can do a great deal of work. The cultural and social experiences, learning opportunities and discipline, which he receives in the learning environment contributes significantly towards his mental development in contrary to the notion that many students who fail in examination do have sufficient intelligence, but are unable to progress because of certain personality inadequacies, family problems and social factors.

TEACHNG COMPETENCE

The teacher has a major role in the educational development Gandhiji remarked that "no country can make any progress without good teachers" The quality and standard of education depends on the quality and standard of teachers. Teacher is the torch bearer of the race and guardian of the feature of the mankind.

According to Humagun Kabir: "Teachers are literally the architects of a nations destiny " Mrs. Indira Gandhi stated, "The nations well being depends upon the teachers well being our teachers are the 'custodians' of future. No society can afford to neglect them".

"Competency" ordinarily is defined as "Adequate for the purpose; suitable, sufficient, or as capable". In a sense it refers to adequate preparation to begin a professional career, and has a direct linkage to verification requirements.

Cooker (1976) defined "competence is seen as the ability to cope with a certain class of problems encountered on the job. A teacher who can deal with problems in certain area is said to be competent in that area a fully competent teacher is one who can cope successfully with any "propositional problem." Competency in teaching stems forms the capacity to reach out differing children and to create a rich and multidimensional environment for them (Joyce and Well 1985)

To study the effectiveness "competency based teacher training (CBTT) Strategy" for developing following basic teaching competencies among pre service teacher;

1. Cognitive- based teaching competency
2. Performance -based teaching competency
3. Affective - based teaching competency
4. Consequence - based teaching competency
5. Managerial - based teaching competency

CONCEPTS OF TEACHING COMPETENCE

A competent teacher has good command of subject matter and solid core of teaching skills. They have excellent instructional strategies supported by methods of goal setting, instructional planning and classroom management. They know how to motivate, communicate and work effectively with students. The teachers play an important role in molding and shaping the attitudes, habits, and manners and above all, the character and personality of the students. The teacher with competency does the planning, organization, reading and controlling of teaching. He is free to perform various activities to provide a learning experience to the learners

DEFINITIONS

In the words of Murthy and Lulla, "Competence based teacher education is that type of professional education of ãlassroom teachers that takes the pre-determined competence of teaching behaviors as the base of teacher education programs".

The Education Commission (1964-66) observed, "Of all the different factors, which influence its quality of education and its contribution to national development, the quality, competence and characters are undoubtedly the most significant".

COMPETENCIES TO BE DEVELOPED

Competence in the use of any methodology involves being able to choose intelligently with the knowledge, experience and skill to make chosen methods work effectively. This can only be acquired by experience, which requires confidence, risk taking and reflection on what happens, so the competencies that are to be developed among the teacher trainees are as follows

1. Competence to understand the sight process of learning, including learning, learning by doing, learning to be, learning to do and learning to become.
2. Competence to devise dynamic methods in the day-to-day situations based on the needs and interests of children
3. Competence to organize the classroom in such a manner that different kinds of activities may be organized in it so that children may receive required guidance from teacher.
4. Competence to become an example of qualities that he/she wants to develop among his/ her students, realizing that example is superior to mere instruction and preaching.
5. Competence in regard to language, delivery of speech and other method of communication.
6. Competence in regard to the contents of the subject that he /she is supposed to teach. The teacher should be able to answer questions that belong to the immediate reason or even to some remotely related subject matter, which may occur in subsequent reason.
7. Competence to engage children in a meaningful manner so that children my develop capacity to ask question and may be inspired to find out the answers by themselves.
8. Competence to innovate so as to create proper environment in the classroom to enable children to develop wider horizons of perceptions.
9. Competence to develop among students a scientific temper, which is often confined to cultivation of various attitudes, includes objective observation, experimentation and consideration of every point of view relevant to the enquiry in a logical manner.

The competencies mentioned above suggest that the school teacher in the developing countries may inspire a change in the impulses of the pupils growing personality so as to have a balanced blending of knowledge, power, love and skills that are required for his/her development as a good individual and useful member of the society. The teacher has to develop competence to innovative methods oriented and learner's need based. The teachers may be apprised what they are supposed to teach.

COMPETENCY AREAS

National Council for Teacher Education (NCTE) has identified ten competency areas in teacher preparation:

1. Contextual competencies including development of education in society and teacher's role in it.
2. Conceptual competencies comprising various concepts of education and learning and psychological, sociological and physiological aspects of education.
3. Curricula and content competencies relating different stages of education like primary, upper-primary and secondary.
4. Transitional competencies as regards general subject-wise and stage-wise dimensions.
5. Competencies in other educational activities such as planning and organizing morning assembly, etc.
6. Competencies relating to teaching-learning materials
7. Evaluation competencies including preparation, selection, use of tools, justice etc.
8. Management competencies including organization of classroom, school and community activities.
9. Competencies related to working with parents understand the role; discuss the problems; active co-operation; organize parent teacher meetings; explore and utilize educational resources etc.,
10. Competencies related to working with the community and other agencies through understand the importance; contribute for improvement; realize the objectives; develop wholesome relationship; explore and exploit community educational resources activities etc.

A to Z OF TEACHING COMPETENCIES

Teaching is an interactive process involving many aspects of teacher, student, learning process and learning situations. So, in order to be a competent teacher one must have competent in the following dispositions.

'A' is for alertness.
'B' is for business like attitude to keep busy in worthwhile tasks.
'C' is for clarity and co-operative teaching learning.
'D' is for devotion and discovery.
'E' is for enthusiasm, expecting children to learn and evaluation.
'F' is for feedback for the guidance of the learner and evaluation
'G' is for goal setting and achieving.
'H' is for hard work, honest work, humility and humor.

'I' is for involvement of children.
'J' is for judicious attitude and just action.
'K' is for knowledge of the students, subject-mater of oneself.
'L' is for linking learning with daily experiences and life.
'M' is for motivation.
'N' is for need-based learning.
'O' is for objectivity and providing out of classroom learning experiences.
'P' is for practice and praising children when needed.
'Q' is for quiz organizing for monitoring learning progress
'R' is for relationships and review.
'S' is for stimulation.
'T' is for tolerance and the technology of teaching learning.
'U' is for unbiased attitude and unexpected encounters and situations.
'V' is for a variety of learning experience.
'W' is for warmth and wisdom.
'X' is for x-ray of the learning process.
'Y' is for yearning and eagerness.
'Z' is for zeal.

ESSENTIAL QUALITIES OF A COMPETENT TEACHER

In order to be a competent teacher, he must possess certain special qualities such as

1. Qualities relating to professional requirements
2. Qualities relating to character and personality.
3. Qualities relating to human relationship.
4. Qualifications relation to professional educational/ training

SIGNIFICANCE OF THE STUDY

Intelligence is the important aspect of an individual. Through intelligence one can know his abilities and capabilities. Intelligence test is used to categories people into different group. Person having intelligence is capable of doing all things. Teaching is an interactive process, involving four aspects teacher, student, learning process and learning situation. A competent teacher possesses all the necessary qualities to interact with the school and community. Teacher with intelligence will be able to teach students with all capabilities. So the present study has been conducted to verify how intelligence is correlated with the teaching competency of the B.Ed teacher trainees. It is must that every teacher trainee should have minimum intelligence to be perfect in his teaching competency. Hence this study has been conducted to verify these interesting aspects.

CONCLUSION

The first chapter is chiefly concerned with the conceptual framework of the problem chosen for the present study. The descriptions on teaching competence and intelligence among the teacher trainees have been presented to highlight the conceptual position with which this study has been planned and conducted. ❐

2

Review of Relaterd Literature

The key to the vast store house of the published literature may open door to source of significant problems and exclamatory hypotheses and provide helpful orientation for definition of the problem, background for selection of procedure and comparative data for interpretation of results. In order to be truly creative and original one must read extensively and critically as stimulus to thinking good (1959)

Review of related literature gives a broad idea to the investigator to carry out his research work in a successful manner. It also helps him get thorough knowledge in his research work. Review tells the researcher what has been done and what needs to be done in a particular topic.

The related literature available on the proposed study is presented in this chapter under the following heads.

1. Studies related to intelligence.
2. Studies related to teaching competence.
3. Studies on intelligence and teaching competence.

FOREIGN STUDIES ON INTELLLIGENCE

Ann (2000) conducted an investigation on, "The influence of preference for novelty and gender on intelligence." The purpose of this research was to further investigate the link between preference for novelty and intelligence. A total sample of 86 children in grade V was selected. The result showed positive effect of cognitive novelty preference on intelligence.

Asthana (2000) made an attempt to assess the differences in some cognitive variables of general intelligence in rural and urban children. The study was conducted on 60 rural and 60 urban primary school children. Alexander along pass Test was used of measure general intelligence. The findings of the study showed that the rural children were to less intelligence into comparison to the urban primary schools children.

Hoenig (2002) conducted a study on the relation between memory and intelligence in children with learning disabilities. Memory of the ability to retain information was evaluated using the Test of Memory and Learning, a recently released test that gives a comprehensive measure of global memory functioning. Winchester's intelligence Scale for children used to assess intelligence. The tests to 80 students (aged 6-12 years) with learning disabilities. The correlation between global measure of memory and global measure of intelligence was significant indicating that the memory should be viewed as an important component when evaluating children with learning disabilities.

De.Smedt (2003) conducted a research on pre-academic and early-academic achievement in children with relocardio facial syndrome of borderline or normal intelligence. The study focused on pre-academic and early -academic skills in borderline to normal intelligent children within the last year of kindergarten and first grade of a primary school in Flanders. In the Kindergarten group, meta-linguistic awareness and counting skills were examined. In the group of first graders, children were tested on reading, spelling and mathematics.13 children participated in this study. There were no differences in intelligence and academic outcomes between boys and girls, and no differences in IQ and academic achievement between children with cardiac defects or severe velopharyngeal insufficiency (IPI) and children without these deficits. With regard to pre-academic achievement in general, a characteristic profile with clearly better results for meta-linguistic awareness in comparison with counting skill was found, but this difference was not statistically significant. However, at an individual level –especially within the domain of counting skills and mathematics, there is wide variability, with some children showing remarkable learning difficulties already at an early age.

Demethiou (2003) conducted research on, "The Missing link in the relations between intelligence and personality". The researcher studied relationship between performance tasks representing five cognitive domains (quantitative, categorical, spatial, causal and prepositional reasoning) and self-attribution of ability in regard to them and also in regard to four general cognitive functions (processing speed, working memory, self-monitoring and self-regulation), and the big five factors of personality (extraversion, agreeableness, conscientiousness, neuroticism and openness to experience) on students in the age group of 12-17 years. Structural equations modeling showed that self-attribution of ability are to some extent, dependent on cognitive performance. Cognitive performance is weakly related only to two of the five factors (openness and conscientiousness) of personality Self-attribution of ability is substantially related to all but the neuroticism factor differs. Apart from openness to experience, the dependence of personality dimensions on the dimensions of cognitive self-representation tends to weaken with age. It is concluded that influence of cognitive abilities on personality can be mediated by self-awareness about them.

Garlick (2003) conducted a research on "integrating brain science research with intelligence research" and he says that the possible causes of differences unintelligence are crucial to children who are to achieve their full potential. Such understanding has been hampered until recently, however, because researchers who study intelligence have neglected recent findings in the brain sciences suggesting that the brain develops in response to environmental stimulation. These findings contradict intelligence research, which suggests that intelligence abilities are inherited. However the findings from intelligence research and the brain sciences can be integrated if it is accepted that there are individual differences in the process by which the brain adapts to the environment, such that some peoples' brains are better at adapting than others. The findings obtained from intelligence research are consistent with this integrated model. Such integration has implications for better understanding of the nature of intelligence.

Kinlaw (2003) conducted a research on "The Development of children's beliefs about intelligence." Research was focused on the development of children's beliefs about intelligence and proposed that this development requires simultaneous processes of concept acquisition and theory building. Research in beliefs about the nature of intelligence has focused on children's definitions of intelligence, beliefs about the component structure of intelligence and the criteria, children use to evaluate ability. Children's beliefs about the stability of intelligence have been examined in terms of constancy, controllability, capacity and the origins of intelligence and mechanisms of change. It was found that intelligence and achievement are positively related.

Meullum (2003) conducted a research on comprehensive test of nonverbal intelligence. It discuss the apprehensive test of nonverbal intelligence, which was designed to provide an estimate of the intelligence of individuals who are not proficient in English, or who are deaf, disadvantaged, language disordered, or motor impaired. The test formats and items were selected on the basis of statistical analysis. The results showed that items contained little gender or no ethnic bias

Petrill (2003) conducted a research on, "The development intelligence behavioral genetic approaches". The purpose was to outline the behavioral genetic literature on the development of intelligence in childhood, adolescence and adulthood; to describe the implications of these findings for neuroscience and to search for genetic makers and evil factors influencing intelligence. Behavioral genetic research suggests that genetic influences relating to intelligence becomes the greatest across development stages.

Rushton (2003) conducted a research on African white IQ differences from Zimbabwe on the Weshsler's Intelligence Scale for children revised, mainly in the 'g' factor. It was noted that African white differences on the sub tests of the Wechsler's Intelligence Scale in Zimbabwe were like the black white, differences in the US being positively associated with the sub tests.12-14 years old Zimbabweans in Canada in the ten sub-tests were compared against white Americans.

Junhi (2004) conducted a research on "Low intelligence and levels of lead and cadmium in children. The researcher studied the influence levels of lead and Cadmium in the bodies of children on their intelligence. 112 children with low intelligence and 80 children with high intelligence were selected from 3,700 elementary schools (7-12 years) by using an intelligence test peripheral blood and first urine of both the groups were collected in the morning to measure the levels of lead and Cadmium. The results showed that there was significant difference in the level of lead in the blood between the two groups

INDIAN STUDIES ON INTELLIGENCE

Sinha and Vibha (1998) studied the relationship between level of bed exposure and intelligence and vigilance performance in a sample of 960 school going children of Agra. Biological monitoring of lead through nadir analysis was done to assess the level of lead exposure. The tool used for intelligence and vigilance was Wechsler Intelligence Scale for children. It was found that increased level of lead in the hair caused a decrease in intelligence and vigilance test scores.

Archana (1998), made an investigation on intelligence to find out whether there is any relationship between intelligence, gender, religion and socioeconomic status. The study was done on 480 students. The tools were Mohsin Gender Intelligence test and Socio-economic Status scale by Kuppuswamy. The study revealed the following: General does not exercise any significant influence on the intelligence level. Socio-economic status has significant effect on the subjects. Religion and socio-economic status, independently as well as internationally are significant factors in the determination of IQ. She explored the independent as well as interactions effect of religion on intelligence. Two religious groups-Hindus and Muslims with an incidental sample of 480 college students, were administered using Mohsin General Intelligence Test. A three way ANOVA revealed that religion had significant impact on intelligence level religions interacting with socio- economic status creates significant difference in intelligence scores.

Agarwal (1999) made and attempt to compare the failed and passed students on the basis of their intelligence, family relations, socio-economic status and adjustment. The sample size was 200, who were selected from the higher secondary schools of Uttar Pradesh. The tools used were Jalotai Group Test of General Ability, Bharadwaj, Gupta and Chauhan's Socio-Economic Scale and Sherry and Sinha's Adjustment Inventory for school students. The major findings intelligence, family relations and socio-economic status are permanent factors related to the scholastic achievement of high school students. Intelligence is innate and cannot be increased beyond limit.

Tyagi (1999) made a study to compare the acoustic behavior of boys and girls as a function of intelligence. A Stratified random sample of 480 boys and 480 girls was administered using the Mental Ability Test (Joshi) and Altruism Scale (Tyagi). The results revealed that girls were more intelligent and altruistic than boys. Altruism correlated with intelligence.

Sharma and Kumar (1999) made an attempt to compare the intelligence of the first born child The sample consisted of 120 children and tools used were: For the children of 5-11 years of age, Raven's Colored Progressive Matrices. For the children above 11 years of age, Raven's Advanced Progressive Matrices. The major findings were that there was no significant difference in intelligence of the first –born and the second born child, and no significant difference in intelligence of the first-born and the third born child.

Prabha and Monika (2000) examined the role of sex, intelligence and socio-economic status in the achievement of computer education. The sample size was 223. The tools were the Group Test of Intelligence (Ahuja) and Socio-Economic Status Scale by Bharadwawj. The examination marks scored in computer education were used as an index for computer achievement scores. The study showed that intelligence and computer education are positively and significantly correlated.

Gupta (2000) explored the effect of prolonged deprivation on intelligence and attainment of academic achievement of students. The sample consisted of 1453 students of grade 10. The Bengali version of Prolonged Deprivation Scale (PDS) by Misra and Tripathi and Raven's Progressive Matrices were administered to the subjects. Examination marks were taken as academic achievement score. The main findings were: Boys scored higher on the measures of both the intelligence and academic achievement than girls. There is a positive correlation between intelligence and academic achievement. Prolonged deprivation adversely affects the intelligence of boys and girls.

Deshmukh (2000) designed his study to compare high and low self-concept groups of junior college students with intelligence. The sample consisted of 832 students ranging in the age group of 16-20 years, studying in XII standard. The main finding was that high and low self-concept groups of junior college students differ significantly on intelligence.

Varma and Varma (2000) examined the relationship between academic achievement and intelligence, parental involvement, subject's motivational resources and assessed father and mother's contribution. Samples of 206 secondary school girls were administered using the tests. Analysis of the results control shows the understanding; perceived competence and self-regulation were more powerful than intelligence in academic achievement. Intelligence affect directly and indirectly by influencing motivational variables. Intelligence is not the only factor, which affect academic achievement.

Sangwan (2001) examined the relationship between intelligence and ecological factors in a Sample of 42 slow learn, with an IQ range of 90-110. The Stanford Binet Intelligence Scale was administered to assess the IQ of these children and an Interview Schedule was used to obtain the information on ecological factors like birth order, type of family, school environment, parent's education and occupation. The study revealed that these entire factors except birth order play an unimportant role in children's cognitive development and IQ.

Aswal (2001) made and attempt to examine the relationship between intelligence and achievement in Mathematics across different socio-economic status levels. A Sample of 200 students of grade 11 was administered. Group Test, and the Socio-Economic Status Scale and marks in Mathematics, scored in the high school board examination, were used as indices of Mathematics achievement. The major findings were: there is a significant correlation between intelligence and achievement in Mathematics. The relation between intelligence and achievement is significant across high, average and low socio-economic status. According to this study, intelligence, achievement and socio-economic status are interrelated.

Himain and Asha (2001) examined the relationship of Piaget stages of cognitive development and intelligence and creative thinking potential of female primary school students. The tools used were Culture Fair Test of Intelligence of 'g' and Piaget tasks, Verbal and Figural form of Torrance Test of Creative Thinking. The findings were: There is significant difference in the creative thinking at different stages of Piaget's stages of development and IQ is significant for all the subjects.

Lakxmi Thakur (2001) designed her study to see the effect of the different factors of home (conformity, reward, deprivation, permissiveness) that influence intelligence and educational aspirations. The sample for the study was selected randomly. In the total sample 50% students were males and 50% were females. The findings of the study were: intelligence and educational aspirations positively correlated with each other, which indicate a linear incremental relationship between them. Conformity plays positive role intelligence. Reward is positively correlated with intelligence. Deprivation always has an effect on intelligence. Permissiveness has positive but non-significant correlation with intelligence.

Malini (2003) investigated on the main effect and interactive effect of non-verbal intelligence and mastery learning strategy on achievement in mathematics. Non-equivalent parallel group experimental design was used for the study. Tow variations of mastery learning strategy were tried on two experimental groups. The sample size was 46 drawn from standard IX Students. The major findings were: The main effect t due to non-verbal intelligence is found to be significant. The interaction between non-verbal intelligence on achievement and mastery learning strategy on achievement in mathematics were significant.

Raina (2003) made a study entitled, "Does preference for sons have a differential impact on the intelligence of boys and girls?" The study examined impact of son preference on the intelligence of boys and girls from a developing country. It was hypothesized that preference for sons enhances the intelligence among boys whereas it hampers the intelligence of girls. About 204 boys and 213 girls studying in grade VI to VII in an urban center of the state of Himachal Pradesh was taken as the sample.

FOREIGN STUDIES ON TEACHING COMPETENCE

Gregrersen and Traves (1968) used the projective technique for making a study of the child concept of the teachers. They made use of drawing of children, environment, which have special significance for them. Choeng and Devault at university of Wisconsin also made similar study in 1966.

Richard M. Galger and Tom. D. Freyo (1974) investigated to two research questions (a) would rewarding items on a questionnaire for evaluating faculty teaching effectiveness substantially affect students ratings (b) Would students ratings of professors teaching quality be totally consistent with their ratings of benefits derived from courses? Results shows that students' ratings were affected very little by a major rewarding of items and that a substantial degree of linear independence existed between students perception of the quality benefited from the instructional process.

Garrett and George, W. (1978) Studied the teachers perception of selected factors affecting the success of teaching process. A study sought to determine how various groups of teachers rated selected factors in teaching success. A review of literature of the topic indicated that both teachers and non–teacher was conducted to collect data from teachers of 64 elementary and secondary schools that were part of the test.

Lawrenz, Frances (1987) studied the gender effects for students' perception of the classroom psycho-social environment. This study compared to classroom environments as perceived by fourth grade, seventh grade and high school boys and girls in classes taught by males and females to determine if any perceptual differences existed. The analyses showed no difference for fourth grade students, one for seventh grade students, and three for high school students.

Brosious Janice A. and Smith R. Lyle (1990) studied the impact of Teachers Attractiveness and Gender on Students Perception of the Teacher's Ability. A group of seventh grade maths students (N=28) was chosen for the experiment, the students rated photograph of teachers in the area of organization, classroom management, motivation, communication, sensitivity, imagination, and competence. The results of this analysis revealed a significant main effect of student perceptions due to the attractiveness of the teacher in the area of organization, classroom significant main effect on student's perceptions due to the gender of the teacher. The students rated the female photographs higher than male photographs in the area of organization. Finally, there was a significant interaction between the attractiveness of the teacher and gender of teacher in the areas of organization, sensitivity and imagination. Overall, females rated higher than males and teachers considered attractive were given higher ratings than teachers considered average and unattractive.

Ocepek, Linda Jeanne (1993) tested some "Selected elements of effective teaching: A study of perception of high school teachers in Illinois, Indian and Ohio." This study utilized an export co-relational design. A 42 item Value Rating Scale (VRS) was mailed to a stratified random sample of 384 public high school teachers in Illinois, India and Ohio. The teachers rated 42 indicator behaviors subsumed under the six elements of effective teaching.

Kim Keyng Suk (1999), studied "Teacher's perceptions of competencies needed for working inclusive early childhood education programs". A survey using five-point Likert scales included 7 teacher competency domains, each with a set of competency statements, and 12 teachers roles needed for working in inclusive pre-school program. 23 ECE teachers and 52 ECSE teachers in non-inclusive programs and 39ECE teacher and 25 ECSE teachers inclusive program participated in this study. To determine the early childhood education (ECE) and Early Childhood. Special Education (ECSE) teacher's perceptions of importance teacher competencies, current levels of these competencies and appropriate teacher roles for working in inclusive early childhood programme. They found the ECSE teacher had significantly higher perceptions than the ECE teachers of their self-proficiency of competencies related to child development, curriculum and instruction, assessment procedures, working with other adults, and professionalism.

Kastair, Jamal (1999) carried out a study on "An evaluation of professional teaching competency of the instructors of the institute of Agriculture Sabah, Malaysia." A survey was carried out at the institute involving the instructors, the principal and the first and second year students as respondents. Each instructor and the principal completed a questionnaire containing 40 competency items of 7 categories, while each of the first and the second year students completed a questionnaire containing 33 competency items on 5 categories. The respondents were asked to assess the competence level of the instructors based on a five point Likert type scales. Evaluation by the professional teaching competency of the instructors of the Institute of Agriculture Sabah, Malaysia. They found that instructors' competence level was relatively high with respect to personal characteristics / attribute category, and lower with respect to planning and application of the principles of teaching-learning process.

INDIAN STUDIES ON TEACHING COMPETENCE

Chatter Jee, B.B et al. (1965) studied about the predication of teaching competency as a function of sharing a common frame of reference. The major findings were: The range of the scaled teaching competency scores given by the staff judges increased in the post-presentation assessments as compared to the pre-presentation predication, while the post-presentation scaled scores of teaching competency given by the instructors themselves were found to have low range compared two scores distributions obtained from the staff judges.

Saraswathi, L.S (1973) conducted a study about the jobs held by home scientists and the competencies needed on the jobs held as perceived by the employed home scientists and their employers in the District. The Major Findings were; The high competency perception proportion indicated that majority of the items included in the competency tests were perceived by the two sets of respondents (Teachers and research workers and those on miscellaneous jobs) as required as the job with an exception of those of the jobs of the assistant lecturers in colleges and teachers in secondary schools.

Nair, S.R (1974) reported about and impact of certain sociological factors on teaching ability in the classroom of government training college in Tiruchur. The major finding of this work was that private school teachers in general were found to have better teaching ability than the government school Teachers. Sex was not found to be affecting teaching ability. A positive relationship existed between age and teaching ability. Caste and religion were not found to be affecting teaching ability.

Sharma, S.K (1981) analyzed the various relationship of teaching effectiveness in terms of competency. The study was carried out at three different stages. In the final study 220 classrooms teaching learning situations were observed. The major findings were: There were no significant relationship between the ages of Hindi teachers, their attitude, interest and intelligence and their teaching competency. Male and female Hindi teachers did not differ significantly in their teaching competency. There was significant negative correlation between the self-perception of Hindi teachers teaching at higher secondary level and their teaching competency. There was a significant positive correlation between the teaching competency of teachers at higher secondary level and academic achievement of their pupil of grade XI in Hindi. The teaching competencies identified were: giving assignments, loud reading, asking questions, introducing lessons, pacing, managing the classroom, presenting verbal mode, clarification, using the black board, using appropriate reinforcement, achieving closure, probing question, creation interest and improving pupils reading behavior.

Rajan, S. Sathyagiri (1985) conducted a study about the competency, personality, motivation, perception and profession of college teachers. The major findings were; Teacher competency was related to intelligence, emotional stability, tender mindedness, trusted nature, and placed nature, self-sufficiency, and placed nature, self-sufficiency and relaxedness factors of cattell's 16PF questionnaires. It was significantly related to creativity, dynamism, organized demeanors and warmth and acceptance, self-actualization and professional perception of teachers. The more competent teachers significantly differed from the less competent teachers in all the above variables. Those variables that correlated significantly with teacher competence inter correlated with one another significantly.

Das, B.C (1993) conducted a study about the effectiveness of concept attainment model in terms of teaching competency of pre-service student teachers. It was found that concept attainment model effectively developed the teaching competency of pre-service students teachers.

Naseema, C. (1994) reported about a teaching competence of secondary schools physical science teachers in relation to satisfaction of teaching physical science. The major findings were: It was found that 30.92 percent of physical science teachers differed in perceived teaching competence which can be attributed to work (0.01) rewards (1.73), context of work (o.87), self (0.61), others (0.56); 26.89 percent of physical science teachers differed in observed teaching competence which can be attributed to work (0.86), reward (0.002) context of work (1.5), self (2.32), others (1.91).

Kukreti, B.R. (1994) reported about a correlation study between job motivation and teaching competency. The major findings were: the competent teachers had joined the teaching profession because they regarded teaching 0as a prestigious job. They believed that the teaching profession provided them reasonable salary, security, opportunity of social service, to establish human relation and enhance their knowledge. Incompetent teachers entered the teaching profession because they thought that their profession would get fame, personal freedom, influencing opportunity and enough leisure with little burden of work.

Thigarajan, A. et.al. (1995) conducted a study about the teaching competency and achievement. The major findings were; the teaching competency and achievement of boys had significant relationship. The relationship between teaching competency and achievement of boys and girls differed significantly.

Panda, S.C, (1996), Conducted a study about the effect of competency-based instruction in achieving MLL competencies in grade IV Oriya medium schools. The major findings were: There was remarkable difference in the achievement of both the groups. The competency-based instruction yielded significantly better results than the traditional method of teaching.

Shamala, S.K. (1997) reported about enhancing teaching competency through integration of art education for effective language teaching at the primary stage. The major findings were: Prior the implementation of MLL based curriculum, it was highly essential to orient the primary school teachers to know how to develop local specific competencies based different activities. There was a positive impact of module to empower primary school teachers in developing competency based local specific curriculum. The main Objective are: To determine the value of high school teachers place on these elements: classroom climate, questioning, set induction, stimulus variation, reinforcement and closure. In this study classroom climate, questioning, set induction, stimulus variation, reinforcement and closure are sported as a set of selected elements for improving instruction.

Thamilmani, P. (2000) conducted a study on teacher competency, teacher personality and teacher attitude on student achievement in science in high schools. The study included a sample of 100 teachers (58 male, 42 female teaching science and 300 students X studying under those teachers). The tools used were: Teacher Competency – Student Rating Scale, Teacher personality and teacher attitude of science teachers are related to the academic achievement of X standard students in science. They revealed male and female teachers differed significantly in their personality traits and attitude towards teaching.

Palaniyandi, R (2001) investigated the competency needs of pre-serve teacher trainees. The teacher educators and student teachers from six DIETs constituting 273 pre-service Teacher trainees 106 teacher educators and 462 practicing teachers working in these districts were the samples for the study. To identify the competency needs of pre-service teacher trainees as perceived by the pre-service trainees. They revealed learning process related competencies emerged as a group having the highest number of competencies.

Manjula P. Rao (2002) studied Teacher Competencies and learners' achievement in Tribal areas of Karnataka. Twenty schools belonging to 3 taluks, 261 students of third standard and 31 teachers teaching the same students constituted the sample of this study. The research tool used in this study are: The achievement test developed based on the competencies specified for class III in Language, Mathematics, EVS-I and EVS-II to assess teachers' competence in subject areas. To study the relationship between teachers' competency and students achievement: in language, Mathematics, EVS -I and II. They found that majority of the teachers do not have to knowledge competencies in EVS- I (66.5%) and EVS-II (89.9%).

Amaladoss Xavirer, S and Amalraj, A. (2002), conducted a correlative study on teaching competency and its dimensions in post -graduate chemistry teachers. The study included data from 89 postgraduate chemistry teachers of higher secondary schools in Kanyakumari District in Tamil Nadu. A Teaching Competency Rating Scale was used to assess the teaching competency of chemistry teachers. They revealed that there exists significant relationship between the low-level of post- graduate chemistry teachers with regard to the teaching competency dimensions:content, organization, knowledge, clarity, communication, rapport, audio-visual aids and personality.

Jayakanthan, S.(2003) conducted a study of general teaching competency of secondary school teachers in relation to their attitude in teaching. The study included samples of 3000 teacher from 14 schools. The General Teaching Competency Scale of Passi et al, and Teacher Attitude Scale of Ahulwalia were used to carry out the study found that Government and aided school teachers differed significantly in general teaching competency. Male and female teachers differed significantly in teaching competency.

Krishna Prasad, B. and Mthiah, P.N.(2003). carried out a study on teacher effectiveness and temperament variables of secondary school teacher. The study was carried out to a sample of 300 teachers of various secondary schools in Thirunelveli District in Tamil Nadu. MTA-test of Personality for measuring the variables of Temperament, Checklist on Teacher Effectiveness developed and validated by the investigators, and a Personal Information Schedule were used. They found that there exist significant differences among high, average and low effective teachers in five variables (inferiority, self sufficiency, sociability, stability, objectivity) of temperament.

Laxmidhar Bhara (2004) made an attempt to find out the performance of B.Ed trainees of IASEs and CTEs. Six fifty student-teachers (259 male and 391 female) drew purposively from tow CTEs and one IASE of Orissa in two consecutive sessions 1995-96 and 1996-97. The Major findings were: that women student teachers excel their male counter parts in their aggregate (theory and practical) performance. Jeba A., (2005) studied the teaching competency and mental health of student teachers in DIETs. The size of the sample was 300 student-teachers in a DIET undergoing D.Ed., Elementary Teachers Training course. Tools used in this study are: Mental Health status scale constructed by M. Abraham and K.C.B. Praszanna. Teaching Competency Scale the study was conducted to find out gender and group (Arts, science) difference in teaching competency and mental health status, the relationship between teaching competency and mental health status of student teachers in DIET. Major findings were that there is no significant difference between man and women student teacher.

CONCLUSION

In this chapter, the related literature with regard to the variables, intelligence and teaching competence have been reviewed so as to get proper theoretical orientation of the problem and the design of the study is followed in the next chapter.

❐

3

Methodlogy

This chapter gives an overall view of the design of the study, research tools used in the study, nature and selection of the sample and a brief description of the procedure adopted for collection of data.

METHODOLOGY NEED AND SIGNIFICANCE OF THE STUDY

Teachers play a vital role in the development of future citizens. Teaching is an interactive process, involving four aspects teacher, student, learning process and learning situation. A competent teacher possesses all the necessary qualities to interact with the school and community. Intelligence is the important aspect of an individual, through intelligence tone can know his abilities and capabilities. Intelligence test is used to categories people into different group. Intelligence helps a person to understand the concept and to interpret on it. So, the present study has been conducted to evaluate the level of intelligence and its influence on the teaching competence of the B.Ed teacher trainees.

STATEMENT OF THE PROBLEM

The problem for the present study is titled as, "Intelligence and Teaching competence among the B.Ed teacher trainees".

OPERATIONAL DEFINITION OF KEY TERMS

INTELLIGENCE

In this study, intelligence was assessed by the Standard Progressive Matrices, developed and standardized by Raven. The score obtained by the subject in the test indicate the level of intelligence.

TEACHING COMPETENCE

Teaching competence of the teacher trainees indicates the score obtained by the subjects on the basis of the assessment made by their subject teachers, to know the level of teaching competence of the teacher trainees, the investigator adapted the Teaching Competence Rating Scale (TCRS) developed and standardized by S. Mani (2005).

B.Ed Teacher Trainees

In this investigation the teacher trainees refer to the trainees with minimum qualification of graduation who pursue pre serviced teacher education in course of study to acquire a general B.Ed degree during the academic year 2006-2007 in College of Education.

OBJECTIVES OF THE STUDY

The following objectives are set in the present study;

1. To assess the level of intelligence of B. Ed. teacher trainees.
2. To find out the level of teaching competence of B.Ed teacher trainees.
3. To find out whether there is significant difference between overall scores on intelligence of B. Ed teacher trainees with respect to:
    - Gender
    - Educational Qualification
    - Optional Subject
    - Types of Management of Colleges
    - Medium of Instruction
    - Location of the College
    - Parental Occupation
    - Parental Qualification
4. To find out whether there is any significant difference between the overall score on teaching competence of B. Ed teacher trainees with respect to:
    - Gender
    - Educational Qualification
    - Optional Subject

- Types of Management of Colleges
- Medium of Instruction
- Location of the Colleges
- Parental Occupation
- Parental Educational Qualification:

5. To find out whether there is significant association between intelligence and teaching competence of B.Ed teacher trainees.
6. To find out the relation between intelligence and teaching competence of B.Ed., teacher trainees.

HYPOTHESES

1. The B.Ed., teacher trainees have above average level of intelligence.
2. The B.Ed., teacher trainees are competent in teaching.
3. There is no significant difference between the overall scores on intelligence of the B. Ed teacher trainees with respect to;
    - Gender
    - Educational Qualification
    - Optional Subject
    - Types of Management of Colleges
    - Medium of Instruction
    - Location of the Colleges
    - Parental Occupation
    - Parental Educational Qualification.
4. There is no significant difference between the overall scores on teaching competency of B.Ed teacher trainees with respect to:
    - Gender
    - Educational Qualification
    - Optional Subject
    - Types of Management of Colleges
    - Medium of Instruction
    - Location of the Colleges
    - Parental Occupation
    - Parental Educational Qualification:
5. There is no significant association between intelligence and teaching competence of B.Ed teacher trainees.
6. There is no significant relation between intelligence and teaching competence of B.Ed., teacher trainees.

METHOD OF STUDY

In the present study survey method is employed. This method is used to describe and interpret, what exist at present. It is concerned with the condition of relationships that exist, practices that prevails, beliefs, points of view or attitudes that are held, processes that are going on and effects that are being felt.

VARIABLES OF THE STUDY

Research Variables

1. Intelligence
2. Teaching competence

Personal Variables

1. Gender
2. Educational Qualification
3. Optional subject
4. Parental Occupation
5. Parental Educational Qualification

INSTITUTION RELATED VARIABLES

1. Types of the management of collage.
2. Medium of Instruction
3. Location of the Colleges

TOOLS USED IN THE STUDY

1. Personal Data Sheet developed by the Investigator.
2. Standard Progressive matrices developed and standardized by Raven.
3. Teaching Competence Rating Scale (TCQS) developed and standardized by S.Mani

PERSONAL DATA SHEET

The personal data sheet was prepared to collect information on personal and institutional related details, such as gender, educational qualification, and medium of instruction, types of management, locality, parental annual income, parental educational qualification and parental occupation.

INTELLIGENCE

Description

Raven's Progressive Matrices Test was used to measures the intelligence of the B.Ed teacher trainees, as the purpose of the study is to find out the relationship between intelligence and teaching competence. Intelligence questionnaires consist of 60 questions, which were divided into 5 sets (A, B, C, D and E) of 12 each. In each set, the first problem is as nearly as possible self-evident. The problems, which follow, become progressively more difficult. The order of the tests provides the standard training in the method of working. The five sets provide five opportunities for grasping the method and five progressive assessments of a person's capacity for intellectual activity.

Administration

The investigator with the help of respective school teachers did the administration of the test. The investigator met the students and explained the instructions to them on how to answer the test. The students were asked to answer all the questions without fail and they were given only 30 minutes to answer.

Scoring Procedure

Each item carried one mark. Adding the total marks obtained by the B.Ed. teacher trainees in 5 sets of test was done. By taking the total marks obtained by the students further calculations were done and they were clarified into intelligence average, above average superior.

TEACHING COMPENTENCY - DESCRIPTION

To find the level of teaching competency among the teacher trainees Teaching Competency Rating Scale was used. The tool consists of 3 dimensions and 8 components in classroom teaching.
The Dimensions and the Components are :

1. Planning Preparation and Organization.
    - Planning
    - Preparation
    - Organization
2. Knowledge of the Subject –Matter
    - Mastery in Subject
3. Presentation and Classroom Management
    - Motivation
    - Communication
    - Interaction
    - Evaluation and Closure

The items are rated in 5 point scale as follows

Options	Scores
Very poor	1
Poor	2
Average	3
Good	4
Very good	5

ADMINISTRATION

The Teaching Competence Rating Scale (TCRS) meant to assess teaching competence of teacher trainees were given to the respective optional subject teachers (supervisors/teacher educators). They were requested to rate the teaching competence of their students only after the completion of the intensive teaching practice. The supervisors/teacher educators were asked to encircle only one numerical value for each component of all the three dimensions with the help of the indicators given in the tool. Time limit was not prescribed to finish the rating.

SCORING

The maximum score for all the three dimensions would be 40 and minimum 8. On the basis of the overall score, the teacher-trainees were classified into less competent, competent and more competent by using the m ± 1s procedure.

PILOT STUDY

A Pilot study was carried out to test the suitability of the time required to administer to test, and to establish the validity and reliability of the tool. The test was administered to a group of 50 B. Ed. teacher trainees in the month of September 2006

ESTABLISHING RELIABILITY AND VALIDITY OF THE TOOLS

Reliability of Intelligence Test

In the present study reliability of this tool Standard Progressive Matrices has been established by odd even method on 50 B. Ed. teacher trainees selected for the pilot study. The reliability of this tool has been found as 0.64

Validity of Intelligence Test

The validity is computed as the square root of reliability and this works out to be 0.8.

Reliability of Teaching Competence Rating Scale

Test-retest technique was used to establish the reliability of the tool and it was found to be 0.87

Validity of Teaching Competence Rating Scale

The validity is computed as the square root of reliability and this works out to be 0.93.

MAIN STUDY

The validated tools were used for the main study to collect the necessary data. The study was carried out in the month of November 2006 in six B.Ed colleges in and around Chennai, which are affiliated to University of Madras in the state of Tamil Nadu.

SAMPLE OF THE STUDY

The present study is mainly concerned with 220 B. Ed. teacher trainees of six B.Ed colleges in and around Chennai, which are affiliated to University of Madras, Tamil Nadu.

TABLE. 3.1: Category wise Distribution of the Sample

Variables	Category	Total (220)	Percentage
Gender	Male Female	104 116	47.27 52.73
Educational Qualification	U.G. P.G.	94 122	43.52 56.48
Optional subjects	Language Arts Science	59 47 114	26.82 21.36 51.82
Types of management of colleges	Government Aided Self-financed	81 60 79	36.82 27.27 35.91
Medium of Instruction	Tamil English	81 139	36.82 63.18
Location	Urban Rural	141 79	64.09 35.91
Father's Occupation	Employed Unemployed Self-employed	110 41 69	50 18.64 31.36
Mother's Occupation	Employed Unemployed Self-employed	42 140 38	19.09 63.64 17.27

Father's Education	Illiterate School level College level	18 128 74	8.18 58.18 33.64
Mother's Education	Illiterate School level College level	49 141 30	22.27 64.09 13.64

COLLECTION OF DATA

Necessary permission was obtained from the head of the institutions to administrate the tools. Data are collected from six B.Ed colleges, and five students from each department are selected for the study. In addition to this the optional teachers co-operation was also sought to assess the teaching competency of the B.Ed teacher trainees.

DELIMITATION

The sample for the present study has been restricted to 220 B. Ed. teacher trainees as stratified random sample selecting only 5 samples from each optional subject.

1. The study was restricted to in and around Chennai City only.
2. The age of the sample was restricted to 20-25 years only.
3. The teaching competence assessment was done only by the teacher educator and not by the investigator.

STATISTICAL TECHNIQUES USED

Descriptive and inferential statistical techniques are used in the interpretation of the data to draw out a meaningful picture of results from the obtained data. In the present study the following statistical techniques are used

1. Percentile
2. Differential (Mean, Standard deviation, t-test and ANOVA)
3. Correlation (correlation co-efficient and Chi-square)

CONCLUSION

This chapter outlines the design of the present study. The procedure followed and the nature of the sample. It describes the hypotheses to be tested, the tools used and the methods of administration and scoring. Adopting the methods and procedures discussed earlier in this chapter, tests were administered and information was gathered. The obtained data were then analyzed using appropriate statistical techniques described above and its results are presented in the next chapter.

❐

4

Analysis and Interpretation of the Data Introduction

This chapter presents the results obtained from the analysis of data collected from six different educational colleges based on two variables viz., intelligence and teaching competence. The data has been subjected to various descriptive and inferential statistics correlation among the different variables was computed.

Hypothesis 1

The B.Ed., teacher trainees have above average level of intelligence.

TABLE. 4.1: The level of Intelligence of B.Ed., Teacher Trainees

Groups	Number of Students (N = 220)	Percentage %
Average	63	28.6
Above average	139	63.2
Superior	18	8.2

It is observed from the above table (1) that the intelligence of B.Ed teacher trainees is above average. Hence, hypothesis is accepted.

Hypothesis 2

The B.Ed., teacher trainees are competent in teaching.

TABLE.42: The Level of Teaching Competence of B.Ed., Teacher Trainees

Classification	Score	Number of Students (n = 220)	Percentage %
Low Competent	Below 90	57	25.9
Competent	90 to 160	86	39.1
More Competent	Above 160	77	35.0

It is observed from table (2) that B.Ed teacher trainees are competent in teaching. Hence the hypothesis is accepted.

Hypothesis 3(a)

There is no significant difference between the overall scores of Intelligence of B.Ed teacher trainees with respect to gender

TABLE. 4.3: Significant Difference Between the mean Scores of Intelligence of B.Ed Teacher Traineeswith Respect to Gender

Gender						
Variables	Male		Female		t-Value	LS
	Mean	SD	Mean	SD		
Overall Intelligence Score	45.87	7.41	46.95	6.35	1.17	NS

As the calculated value (1.17) is less than the table value (1.96), it is concluded that there is no significance difference between mean scores of intelligence of B.Ed teacher trainees. Hence, the hypothesis is accepted.

Hypothesis 3(b)

There is no significant difference between the overall scores of Intelligence of B.Ed teacher trainees with respect to their Education qualification.

TABLE. 4.4: Significant Difference Detween the Mean scores of Intelligence of B. Ed Teacher Trainees with Respect to their Education Qualification

Educational Qualification						
Variable	**UG**		**PG**		**t-Value**	**LS**
	Mean	**SD**	**Mean**	**SD**		
Inteligence Score	47.12	6.69	45.84	7.08	1.34	NS

As the calculated value of the above table (1.34) is less than the table value (1.96), it is concluded that there is no significant difference between the Intelligence mean scores of B.Ed teacher trainees with respect to their educational qualification. Hence the hypothesis is accepted.

Hypothesis 3(c)

There is no significant difference between the overall scores of Intelligence of B.Ed teacher trainees with respect to the Medium of Instruction.

TABLE. 4.5: Significant Difference Between the mean Scores of Intelligence of B.Ed Teacher Trainees with Respect to the Medium of Instruction

Medium of Instruction						
Variable	**English**		**Tamil**		**t-Value**	**LS**
	Mean	**SD**	**Mean**	**SD**		
Intelligence Score	45.95	6.29	47.27	7.74	1.38	NS

Since the calculated value (1.38) is less than the table value (1.96), it is concluded that there is no significant difference between the intelligence mean scores of B.Ed teacher trainees with respect to the medium of instruction. Hence, the hypothesis is accepted.

Hypothesis 3(d)

There is no significant difference between the overall mean scores of Intelligence of B.Ed teacher trainees with respect to the location of colleges.

TABLE.4.6: Significant Difference Between the mean Scores of Intelligence of B.Ed Teacher Trainees with Respect to the Location of Colleges

Location						
Variable	**Urban**		**Rural**		**t-Value**	**LS**
	Mean	**SD**	**Mean**	**SD**		
Intelligence Score	46.05	7.92	47.13	4.38	1.12	NS

As the calculated value (1.12) of the above table is less than the table value (1.96), no significant difference between is found the intelligence mean scores of B.Ed teacher trainees with respect to the location of the colleges. Hence, the hypothesis is accepted.

Hypothesis 3(e)

There is no significant difference between the overall mean scores of Intelligence of B.Ed teacher trainees with respect to their Optional subject.

TABLE. 4.7: Significant Difference Between the Mean Scores of Optional Subject on Intelligence

Sources	**df**	**Sum of squares**	**Mean sum of squares**	**F-ratio**	**LS**
Between group	2	106.617	53.39	1.129	NS
Within the group	217	10243.491	47.21		
Total	**219**	**10350.109**			

From the above table, it is noticed that the calculated table value (1.13) is less than the table value (1.96). So it is concluded that there is no significant difference between the mean scores of Intelligence of B.Ed teacher trainees with respect to their optional subject. Hence, the hypothesis is accepted.

Hypothesis 3(f)

There is no significant difference between the overall mean scores of Intelligence of B.Ed teacher trainees with respect to the types of management of college.

TABLE.4.8: Significant Difference between the mean Scores of Types of Management of Colleges.

Sources	df	Sum of squares	Mean sum of squares	F-ratio	LS
Between group	2	342.950	171.475	3.718	0.05
Within the group	217	10007.158	46.116		
Total	**219**	**10350.109**			

As the calculated value (3.72) is grater than the table value (1.96) at 0.05 level in the table 4.08, it is concluded that there is significant difference in the mean scores of Intelligence of B.Ed teacher trainees with respect to the types of management of colleges.

Therefore, further analysis of multiple comparisons of the significant difference of the mean scores of Intelligence among the types of management of colleges have been computed, the details of which are presented in table 9.

TABLE. 4.9: Multiple Comparison of Significant Difference between the mean Scores on Intelligence of B.Ed Teacher Trainees with Respect to the Management of Colleges

Group	Mean	SD	SE of Mean	t-Value	LS
Government vs Aided	47.27	7.74	0.86	2.15	0.05
	44.40	7.93	1.02		
Government vs	47.27	7.74	0.86	0.15	NS
Self-financed	47.12	4.28	0.49		
Aided vs	44.40	7.93	1.02	2.58	0.05
Self-financed	47.12	4.28	0.49		

From the above table, in the first comparison as the calculated table value (2.15) is greater than table value (1.96). Significant difference is found on the mean scores of intelligence of B.Ed. teacher trainees with respect to the types of management of college.

In the second comparison, no significant difference is found between the mean scores of intelligence among the B.Ed teacher trainees with respect to the types of management of college.

In the third comparison, as the calculated table value (2.58) is greater than table value (1.96), significant difference is found between the mean scores on intelligence of B. Ed. teacher trainees with respect to the types of management of colleges. Hence, the hypothesis is partially accepted.

Hypothesis 3 (g)

There is no significant difference between the overall mean scores of intelligence of B.Ed teacher trainees with respect to their parental occupation.

TABLE. 4.10: Significant Difference between the mean Scores of Fathers' Occupation on Intelligence of B.Ed Teacher Trainees

Sources	df	Sum of squares	Mean sum of squares	F-ratio	LS
Between group	2	173.283	86.641		
Within the group	217	10176.826	46.987	1.848	NS
Total	**219**	**10350.109**			

TABLE. 4.11: Significant Difference Between the mean Scores of Mothers' Occupation on Intelligence of B.Ed Teacher Trainees

Sources	df	Sum of squares	Mean sum of squares	F-ratio	LS
Between group	2	39.722	19.861	0.418	NS
Within the group	217	10310.388	47.513		
Total	**219**	**10350.109**			

As the calculated values are less than (1.848,0.418) table value(1.96), no significant difference is found between the means scores on intelligence of B.Ed teacher trainees with respect to their parental (Father & Mother) occupation, Hence, the hypothesis in accepted.

Hypothesis 3 (h)

There is no significant difference between the overall mean scores of Intelligence of B.Ed teacher trainees with respect to parental educational qualification.

TABLE. 4.12: Significant Difference Between the mean Scores of Intelligence of B.Ed Teacher Trainees with Respect to their Fathers' Educational Qualification

Sources	df	Sum of squares	Mean sum of squares	F-ratio	LS
Between group	2	12.617	6.308		
Within the group	217	2571.069	11.848	0.532	NS
Total	**219**	**2583.686**			

TABLE. 4.13: Significant Difference Between the mean Scores of Intelligence of B.Ed Teacher Trainees with Respect to Mothers' Educational Qualification

Sources	df	Sum of squares	Mean sum of squares	F-ratio	LS
Between group	2	61.175	30.587	0.645	NS
Within the group	217	10288.934	47.414		
Total	**219**	**10350.109**			

As the calculated table values (0.532, 0.645) is less than table value (1.96) it is concluded that there is no significant difference between the means scores of intelligence of B.Ed teacher trainees with respect to their Parental education qualification. Hence, the hypothesis in accepted.

Hypothesis 4 (a)

There is no significant difference between the overall mean scores of teaching competence of B.Ed teacher trainees with respect to gender.

TABLE. 4.14: Showing the Significant Difference Between the Mean scores of Teaching Competence of B.Ed Teacher Trainees with Respect to Gender

Variable	Gender				F-ratio	LS
	Male		Female		0.71	NS
	Mean	SD	Mean	SD		
Teaching Competency	29.50	3.96	29.58	2.89		

From the above table (14) no significant difference is found between the mean scores on the teaching competence of B.Ed teacher trainees. Hence, the hypothesis is accepted.

Hypothesis 4(b)

There is no significant difference between the overall mean scores of teaching competence of B.Ed teacher trainees with respect to their education qualification.

TABLE. 4.15: Significant Difference Between the mean Scores of Teaching Competence of B.Ed Teacher Trainees with Respect to their Education Qualification

Variables	Educational Qualification				t-value	L S
Teaching Competency	UG		PG		0.45	NS
	Mean	SD	Mean	SD		
	29.54	3.36	29.33	3.55		

As the calculated table value (0.45) is less than the table value (1.96), no significant difference is found between the mean scores of teaching competence of B.Ed teacher trainees with respect to their educational qualification. Hence the hypothesis is accepted.

Hypothesis 4 (c)

There is no significant difference between the overall man scores of teaching competence of B.Ed teacher trainees with respect to their Medium of Instruction.

TABLE. 4.16: Significant Difference Between the mean Scores of Teaching Competence of B.Ed Teacher Trainees with Respect to their Medium of Instruction

Medium of Instruction						
Variable	English		Tamil		t-Value	LS
	Mean	SD	Mean	SD		
Teaching Competency	29.04	3.79	30.07	2.61	2.17	0.05

In the above table the calculated value (2.17) is greater than the table value (1.96) at 0.05 level, significant difference is found between the mean scores on teaching competence of B.Ed teacher trainees with respect to the medium of instruction. Hence, the hypothesis is rejected.

Hypothesis 4 (d)

There is no significant difference between the overall mean scores of teaching competence of B.Ed teacher trainees with respect to the location of college

TABLE. 4.17: Significant Difference Between the mean Scores of Teaching Competence with Respect to the Location of Colleges

Location						
Variable	Urban		Rural		t-Value	LS
	Mean	SD	Mean	SD		
Teaching Competency	29.26	3.66	29.71	2.99	0.92	NS

In the above table, the calculated value (0.92) is less than the table value (1.96), no significant difference is found between teaching competences of B.Ed teacher trainees with respect to the location of colleges. Hence, the hypothesis is accepted.

Hypothesis 4 (e)

There is no significant difference between the overall mean scores of teaching competence of B.Ed teacher trainees with respect to their optional subject.

TABLE. 4.18: Significant Difference Between the mean Scores of Optional Subject on Teaching Competence

Sources	df	Sum of squares	Mean sum of squares	F-ratio	LS
Between group	2	44.498	22.249	1.90	NS
Within the group	217	2539.188	11.701		
Total	**219**	**2583.686**			

From the above table (4.07), the calculated table value (1.90) is less than table value (1.96), no significant difference is found between the mean scores of teaching competence of teacher trainees with respect to their optional subject. Hence, the hypothesis is accepted.

Hypothesis 4 (f)

There is no significant difference between the overall mean scores of teaching competence of B.Ed teacher trainees with respect to the types of management of colleges

TABLE. 419: Significant Difference Between the mean Scores of Teaching Competence of B.Ed Teacher Trainees the Types of Management of College

Sources	df	Sum of squares	Mean sum of squares	F-ratio	LS
Between group	2	135.493	67.746	6.005	0.01
Within the group	217	2448.193	11.282		
Total	**219**	**2583.686**			

In the above table(4.19) as the calculated value (6.005) is greater than the table value (2.58) at 0.01 level, significant different is observed between the mean scores of teaching competence of B.Ed teacher trainees with respect to the types of management of colleges

Therefore further analysis of multiple comparison of the significant difference of the mean scores of teaching competence among the three types of management of colleges have been computed, the details of which are presented in table (20).

TABLE. 4.20: Multiple Comparison of Significant Difference Between the mean Scores of Teaching Competence of B.Ed Teacher Trainees with Respect to the Types of Management of Colleges

Variables	Mean	SD	SE of Mean	t- value	LS
Government Vs Aided	30.07 28.17	2.61 4.52	0.290 0.583	3.16	0.01
Government Vs Self-financed	30.07 29.71	2.61 2.99	0.290 0.337	0.82	NS
Aided Vs Self-financed	28.17 29.71	4.52 2.99	0.583 0.337	2.42	0.05

From the above table, in the first comparison the calculated table value (3.16) is greater than table value (2.56), which shows the significant difference is found at 0.01 level, between the men scores of teaching competence of B. Ed. teacher trainees. It is also noted that the teacher trainees of government colleges got higher mean value (30.07) than the teacher trainees of aided colleges.

In the second comparison, no significant difference is observed between the mean scores of B. Ed teacher trainees teaching competence with respect the types of management of college.

In the third comparison, the calculated table value (2.42) is greater than table value (1.96) at 0.05 level, which indicates the significant difference between the mean scores of teaching competence of B.Ed teacher trainees with respect to Aided and Self-finance colleges.

Therefore, the hypothesis is partially accepted.

Hypothesis 4 (g)

There is no significant difference between the overall mean scores of teaching competence of B.Ed teacher trainees with respect to their parental occupation.

TABLE. 4.21: Significant Difference Between the Teaching Competences Mean Scores of B.Ed Teacher Trainees of with Respect to their Fathers' Occupation.

Sources	df	Sum of squares	Mean sum of squares	F-ratio	LS
Between group	2	8.595	4.297	0.362	NS
Within the group	217	2575.091	11.867		
Total	**219**	**2583.686**			

TABLE. 4.22: Significant Difference Between the Teaching Competences Means Scores of B.Ed Teacher Trainees with Respect to their Mothers' Occupation.

Sources	df	Sum of squares	Mean sum of squares	F-ratio	LS
Between group	2	13.969	6.985	0.589	NS
Within the group	217	2528.716	11.842		
Total	**219**	**2583.687**			

From the above tables (4.21,4.22) it is observed that the calculated table (0.362,0.589) value is less than the table value no significant difference are observed between the means scores of teaching competence of B. Ed teacher trainees with respect to their parental occupation, Hence, the hypothesis is accepted.

Hypothesis 4 (h)

There is no significant difference between the overall mean scores of teaching competence of B.Ed teacher trainees with respect to their parents educational qualification

TABLE. 4.23: Significant Difference Between the Teaching Competences Means Scores of B.Ed Teacher Trainees with Respect to their Fathers' Educational qualification

Sources	df	Sum of squares	Mean sum of squares	F-ratio	LS
Between group	2	9.574	4.787	0.815	NS
Within the group	217	1274.808	5.875		
Total	**219**	**1284.382**			

From table (23) it is noticed that the calculated value (0.815) is less than the table value (1.96), no significant difference is found between the mean scores of teaching competence of B.Ed teacher trainees with respect to their fathers' educational qualification.

TABLE. 4.24: Significant Difference Between the Teaching Competences Means Scores of B.Ed Teacher Trainees with Respect to their Mothers' Educational Qualification

Sources	df	Sum of squares	Mean sum of squares	F-ratio	LS
Between group	2	90.238	45.119	3.926	0.05
Within the group	217	2493.448	11.490		
Total	**219**	**2583.686**			

From table (24) it is noticed that the calculated value (3.926) is greater than the table value (1.96) at 0.05 level, significant difference is found between mean scores of teaching competence of B.Ed teacher trainees with respect to their mothers' educational qualification.

Hence, further analysis of multiple comparisons of the significant difference of the scores of teaching competence among the parental education qualification have been computed, the details of which are presented below.

TABLE. 4.25: Multiple Comparison of Significant Difference Between the Mean Scores of Teaching Competence of B.Ed Teacher Trainees with Respect to Parental Education Qualification

Source Variation	Mean	SD	SE of Mean	t-Vlaue	LS
Illiterate Vs School level	29.59	3.47	0.496	0.98	NS
	29.04	3.37	0.284		
Illiterate Vs College level	29.59	3.47	0.946	1.69	NS
	30.92	3.36	0.614		
School level Vs College level	29.04	3.37	0.284	2.79	0.01
	30.92	3.36	0.614		

From the above table, in the first and second comparison, there no significant difference is found between the mean scores of teaching competence of B.Ed teacher trainees with respect to their parental educational qualification.

But in the third comparison, the calculated value (2.79) is grater than table value (2.56) at 0.01 level, significant difference is observed between the mean scores of teaching competence of B.Ed teacher trainees with respect to their mothers' educational qualification Hence, the hypothesis is partially accepted.

Hypothesis 5

There is no significant association between intelligence and teaching competence of B.Ed teacher trainees.

TABLE. 4.26: Significant Association Between Intelligence and Teaching Competence of B. Ed Teacher Trainees.

Intelligence	Less Competent	Competent	More Competent	Total
Average	25 (16.3)	25 (24.6)	13 (22.1)	63 (28.6)
Above Average	32 (36)	51 (54.3)	56 (48.7)	139 (63.2)
Superior	0 (4.7)	10 (7)	8 (6.3)	18 (8.2)
Total (%)	**57 (25.9)**	**86 (39.1)**	**77 (35)**	**220 (100)**

Chi-square value 16.466 df-4 LS - 0.01

From the above table, the Chi-square value (16.466) is greater than the table value (13.28) for df 4 it is concluded that there exit significant association between intelligence and teaching competence of B. Ed. teacher trainees. Hence, the hypothesis is rejected.

Hypothesis 6

There is no significant relation between intelligence and teaching competence of B. Ed teacher trainee.

TABLE. 4.27: Significant Relation between the Overall Scores of and Intelligence and Teaching Competence of B. Ed. Teacher Trainees

Variables	Intelligence	LS
Teaching Competency	0.2878	0.01

df=219

In the above table as the correlation co-efficient value (0.2878) is greater than the table value (0.273). it is concluded that there exist significance positive correlation between intelligence and teaching competence of B. Ed. teacher trainees. Hence, the hypothesis is rejected.

MAJOR FINDINGS

1. The B.Ed., teacher trainees have above average level of intelligence.
2. The B.Ed., teacher trainees are competent in teaching.
3. No significant difference is found between male and female B.Ed., teacher trainees in intelligence.
4. No significant difference is found in intelligence between the U.G. and P.G. qualified B.Ed., teacher trainees.
5. No significant difference is found in intelligence between the English and Tamil medium B.Ed., teacher trainees.

6. No significant difference is found in intelligence between the Urban and Rural B.Ed., college teacher trainees.
7. No significant difference is found in intelligence of different optional subject B.Ed., teacher trainees.
8. Significant difference is found in intelligence among the B.Ed., teacher trainees studying in different types of management of colleges (Government vs aided, Aided vs Self-Finance).
9. Parents' Occupation do not influence the intelligence of B.Ed., teacher trainees.
10. Parental Educational Qualification do not influence the intelligence of B.Ed., teacher trainees.
11. Gender does not influence the teaching competence of B.Ed., teacher trainees.
12. Educational qualifications of B.Ed., teacher trainees do not have bearing on the teaching competence.
13. Medium of instructions in B.Ed., colleges influences the teaching competence of B.Ed., teacher trainees.
14. No significant difference is found between urban and rural colleges B.Ed., teacher trainees teaching competence.
15. No significant difference is found between the different optional subjects B.Ed., teacher trainees teaching competence.
16. Significant difference is found in teaching competence of B.Ed., teacher trainees studying in different types of management of colleges (Government vs aided, aided vs self-finance).
17. Parental Occupations do not influence the teaching competence of B.Ed., teacher trainees.
18. Parental Educational Qualifications (Mothers') significantly influence the teaching competence of B.Ed., teacher trainees (Mothers' school level vs college level education).
19. Significant positive correlation is found between intelligence and teaching competence of B.Ed., teacher trainees.
20. Significant association is found between intelligence and teaching competence of B.Ed., teacher trainees.

CONCLUSION

This chapter analyses the hypotheses of the study. The finding and conclusions thus obtained from the analyses of this chapter have been summarized and presented along with a brief report of the research study and implications of the study in the following chapter.

❒

5

Summary and Conclusion

The present chapter provides a brief summary of the entire study and it also gives the statistical analysis of data presented in the previous chapter. The implications along with suggestions for replicating the study or for investigation at other closely related problems in other settings and with different samples and tools are also presented.

REVIEW OF THE RELATED LITERATURE

Review of related literature gives a broad idea to the investigator to carry out his research work in a successful manner. It also helps him get thorough knowledge in his research work reviews tells the researcher what has been done and what needs to be done particular topic.

METHODOLOGY

NEED AND SIGNIFICANCE OF THE STUDY

Teachers play a vital role in the development of future citizens. Teaching is an interactive process, involving four aspects teacher, student, learning process and learning situation. A competent teacher possesses all the necessary qualities to interact with the school and community. Intelligence is the important aspect of an individual, through intelligence tone can know his abilities and capabilities. Intelligence test is used to categories people into different group. Intelligence helps a person to understand the concept and to interpret on it. So, the present study has been conducted to evaluate the level of intelligence and its influence on the teaching competence of the B.Ed teacher trainees.

STATEMENT OF THE PROBLEM

The problem for the present study is titled as, "Intelligence and Teaching competence among the B.Ed teacher trainees".

OPERATIONAL DEFINITAIONS OF KEY TERMS:

Intelligence

In this study, the intelligence was assessed by the Standard Progressive Matrices, which was developed and standardized by Raven. The score obtained by the subject in the test indicate the level of intelligence.

Teaching Competence

Teaching competence of the teacher trainees indicates the score obtained by the subjects on the basis of the assessment made by their subject teachers, for the purpose the investigator adapted the Teaching Competence Rating Scale developed and standardized by Dr.S. Mani (2005).

B.Ed Teacher trainers

In this investigation the teacher trainees refer to the trainees with minimum qualification of graduation who pursue pre serviced teacher education in course of study to acquire a general B.Ed degree during the academic year 2006-2007.

OBJECTIVES OF THE STUDY

The following objectives are set in the present study;

1. To assess the level of intelligence of B. Ed. teacher trainees.
2. To assess the level of teaching competence of B.Ed teacher trainees.
3. To find out whether there is significant difference between overall scores on intelligence of B. Ed teacher trainees with respect to:
    - Gender
    - Educational Qualification
    - Optional Subject
    - Types of Management of Colleges
    - Medium of Instruction
    - Location of the College
    - Parental Occupation
    - Parental Educational Qualification
4. To find out whether there is any significant difference between the overall score on teaching competence of B. Ed teacher trainees with respect to:

- Gender
- Educational Qualification
- Optional Subject
- Types of Management of Colleges
- Medium of Instruction
- Location of the Colleges
- Parental Occupation
- Parental Educational Qualification:

5. To find out whether there is significant association between intelligence and teaching competence of B.Ed teacher trainees.

HYPOTHESES

1. The B.Ed., teacher trainees have above average level of intelligence.
2. The B.Ed., teacher trainees are competent in teaching.
3. There is no significant difference between the overall mean scores on intelligence of the B. Ed teacher trainees with respect to;
    - Gender
    - Educational Qualification
    - Optional Subject
    - Types of Management of Colleges
    - Medium of Instruction
    - Location of the Colleges
    - Parental Occupation
    - Parental Educational Qualification.
4. There is no significant difference between the overall mean scores on teaching competency of B. Ed teacher trainees with respect to:
    - Gender
    - Educational Qualification
    - Optional Subject
    - Types of Management of Colleges
    - Medium of Instruction
    - Location of the Colleges
    - Parental Occupation
    - Parental Educational Qualification:

5 To find out the relation between intelligence and teaching competence of B.Ed., teacher trainees.

6. There is no significant association between intelligence and teaching competence of B. Ed teacher trainees.

METHOD OF STUDY

In the present study survey method is employed. This method is used to describe and interpret, what exist at present. It is concerned with the condition of relationships that exist, practices that prevails, beliefs, points of view or attitudes that are held, processes that are going on and effects that are being felt.

VARIABLES OF THE STUDY

RESEARCH VARIABLES

1. Intelligence
2. Teaching competence

PERSONAL VARIABLES

1. Gender
2. Educational Qualification
3. Optional subject
4. Parental Occupation
5. Parental Qualification

INSTITUTIONAL RELATED VARIABLES

1. Types of the management of collage.
2. Medium of Instruction
3. Location of the Colleges

TOOLS USED IN THE STUDY

1. Personal data sheet developed by the investigator. (Appendix I)
2. Standard Progressive matrices developed and standardized by Raven. (Appendix II)
3. Teaching Competence Rating Scale developed and standardized by S. Mani (Appendix III)

PERSONAL DATA SHEET

The personal data sheet was prepared to collect information on personal and institutional related details, such as gender, educational qualification, and medium of instruction, types of management, locality, parental annual income, parental educational qualification and parental occupation.

SAMPLE OF THE STUDY

The present study is mainly concerned with 220 B. Ed. teacher trainees of six B.Ed colleges in and around Chennai, which are affiliated to University of Madras, Tamil Nadu.

COLLECTION OF DATA

Necessary permission was obtained from the head of the institutions to administrate the tools. Data are collected from six B.Ed colleges, and five students form each department are selected for the study. In addition to this the optional teachers co-operation was also sought to assess the teaching competency of the B.Ed teacher trainees.

DELIMITATION

1. The sample for the present study has been restricted to 220 B. Ed. teacher trainees as stratified random sample selecting only 5 samples from each optional subject.
2. The study was restricted to in and around Chennai City only.
3. The age of the sample was restricted to 20-25 years only.
4. The teaching competence assessment was done only by the teacher educator and not by the investigator.

STATISTICAL TECHNIQUES USED

Descriptive and inferential statistical techniques are used in the interpretation of the data to draw out a meaningful picture of results from the obtained data. In the present study the following statistical techniques are used

- Percentile
- Differential (Mean, Standard deviation, t-test and ANOVA)
- Correlation (correlation co-efficient and Chi-square)

MAJOR FINDINGS

- The B.Ed., teacher trainees have above average level of intelligence.
- The B.Ed., teacher trainees are competent in teaching.
- No significant difference is found between male and female B.Ed., teacher trainees in intelligence.
- No significant difference is found in intelligence between the U.G. and P.G. qualified B.Ed., teacher trainees.
- No significant difference is found in intelligence between the English and Tamil medium B.Ed., teacher trainees.
- No significant difference is found in intelligence between the Urban and Rural B.Ed., college teacher trainees.
- No significant difference is found in intelligence of different optional subject B.Ed., teacher trainees.
- Significant difference is found in intelligence among the B.Ed., teacher trainees studying in different types of management of colleges (Government vs aided, Aided vs Self-Finance).

- Parents' Occupation does not influence the intelligence of B.Ed., teacher trainees.
- Parental Educational Qualification does not influence the intelligence of B.Ed., teacher trainees.
- Gender does not influence the teaching competence of B.Ed., teacher trainees.
- Educational qualifications of B.Ed., teacher trainees do not have bearing on the teaching competence.
- Medium of instructions in B.Ed., colleges influences the teaching competence of B.Ed., teacher trainees.
- No significant difference is found between urban and rural colleges B.Ed., teacher trainees teaching competence.
- No significant difference is found between the different optional subjects B.Ed., teacher trainees teaching competence.
- Significant difference is found in teaching competence of B.Ed., teacher trainees studying in different types of management of colleges (Government vs aided, aided vs self-finance).
- Parental Occupations do not influence the teaching competence of B.Ed., teacher trainees.
- Parental Educational Qualifications (Mothers') significantly influence the teaching competence of B.Ed., teacher trainees (Mothers' school level vs college level education).
- Significant positive correlation is found between intelligence and teaching competence of B.Ed., teacher trainees.
- Significant association is found between intelligence and teaching competence of B.Ed., teacher trainees.
- The B.Ed., teacher trainees have above average level of intelligence.
- The B.Ed., teacher trainees are competent in teaching.
- No significant difference is found between male and female B.Ed., teacher trainees in intelligence.
- No significant difference is found in intelligence between the U.G. and P.G. qualified B.Ed., teacher trainees.
- No significant difference is found in intelligence between the English and Tamil medium B.Ed., teacher trainees.
- No significant difference is found in intelligence between the Urban and Rural B.Ed., college teacher trainees.
- No significant difference is found in intelligence of different optional subject B.Ed., teacher trainees.
- Significant difference is found in intelligence among the B.Ed., teacher trainees studying in different types of management of colleges (Government vs aided, Aided vs Self-Finance).

- Parents' Occupation does not influence the intelligence of B.Ed., teacher trainees.
- Parental Educational Qualification does not influence the intelligence of B.Ed., teacher trainees.
- Gender does not influence the teaching competence of B.Ed., teacher trainees.
- Educational qualifications of B.Ed., teacher trainees do not have bearing on the teaching competence.
- Medium of instructions in B.Ed., colleges influences the teaching competence of B.Ed., teacher trainees.
- No significant difference is found between urban and rural colleges B.Ed., teacher trainees teaching competence.
- No significant difference is found between the different optional subjects B.Ed., teacher trainees teaching competence.
- Significant difference is found in teaching competence of B.Ed., teacher trainees studying in different types of management of colleges (Government vs aided, aided vs self-finance).
- Parental Occupations do not influence the teaching competence of B.Ed., teacher trainees.
- Parental Educational Qualifications (Mothers') significantly influence the teaching competence of B.Ed., teacher trainees (Mothers' school level vs college level education).
- Significant positive correlation is found between intelligence and teaching competence of B.Ed., teacher trainees.
- Significant association is found between intelligence and teaching competence of B.Ed., teacher trainees.

EDUCATIONAL IMPLICATION

1. Necessary facilities and opportunities need to be provided to teacher trainees to acquire and develop the essential competences that are required in teaching profession.
2. Selection of teacher trainees should be made on certain criteria like testing their oral expressions and presence of mind, testing the depth knowledge of the subject and interpersonal relationships.
3. Entry behaviour of teacher trainees needs to assess and necessary supportive programme need to be organized to develop competences required for the teaching profession.

SUGGESSTION FOR FURTHER STUDY

1. The study also may be extended to school teachers and college teachers.
2. This study can also be done to the DIET teacher trainees.
3. This inquiry can also be carried out to teacher trainees and teachers in other districts of Tamil Nadu.
4. A comparative study of gender difference among the teachers with respect to teaching competence and intelligence can also be done.
5. A study on the teaching competence and psychological factors of the different subject teachers can be taken up.

CONCLUSION

The quality of the teacher is determined by many factors and intelligence is the most vital factor among them. The present study indicates the close relationship between intelligence and teaching competence. Further it is also ensured in this present study that there is positive correlation between intelligence and teaching competence. The significant aspect, the types of management of college greatly influences not only the intelligence of the teacher trainees but also their teaching competence. However quality in education is possible only by preparing competent teacher.

❐

6

The Problem and its Perspectives

Teachers occupy a place of paramount importance in any system of Education. Dr.Radhakrishnan says. The teacher's place in society is of vital importance. He acts on the point of transmission of intelluctual tradition and technical skills from generation to generation and helps to keep the lamp of civilization burning.

The Secondary Education Commission (1952-53) has remarked that the secret of good education consists in enabling the student to realize what are his talents and aptitudes, and in what manner and what extent he can best develop those so as to achieve proper social adjustment and seek right types of employment.

Today `humanity' is perhaps sitting on the top of volcano and is facing many challenges in bringing about a healthy society. Every one today appears to be tenser than the past either due to lack of understanding and confidence among themselves or because of psychopathic morbidities like parent child relationship, loveless domestic life, broken families, global terrorism and narrow considerations. Values have sunken to gain their selfish motives. People can be both humanly pro-social and destructively anti-social as they are not necessarily aware of their values, some may even conflict with conscious values. The necessity of making a choice commonly leads to a specific `cognitive strain' and it appears to be difficult to make up one's mind especially, when each alternative offers values that the other does not and the choice is an important one (Coleman, 1976). It is at times minimal or immense, at times ridden or open and at times constructive or destructive, any time in making a choice at the cost of another, conflict is a perceived incompatibility of actions and goals that prevents, obstructs interfere, injuries or in some way makes another activity less likely or less effective (Myers, 1993).

Conflicts as a state of being torn between competing forces (Davidson and Neale, 1998), strive simultaneously for expression, where satisfaction of one drive is accompanied by frustration of another. Drive occurs at all the levels of social structure, whenever two or more incompatible principles, ideologies, religion, socio - politico aspirations and cultural identities are active at the same time they can be said as value conflicts. Since value conflicts lie at the very root of persons identity, they are extremely difficult to resolve and de-escalation of these conflicts shall be a prime concern for the well being of the man. The opposition of basic impulses by a rigid conscience appears to be associated with wide spread effect on the growth of personality that may also serve positive as well as negative functions in making adjustments to the environment.

Mental health of the learner is very important for efficient learning and proper development of personality. A child is born in a home where he remains in the constant company of his mother in the formative years of his infancy. The impressions and experiences which a child has in these formative years leave permanent and indelible impressions on his mind. From the point of view of psychoanalysis, the early childhood experiences are very important for the future development of personality.

A healthy individual is not only physically healthy, but also mentally healthy. The modern concept of health extends beyond proper functioning of the body. It includes a sound, efficient mind and controlled emotions. Health is a state of being hale, sound or whole in body and mind. It means that both body and mind are working efficiently and harmoniously. Man is an integrated psychomatic unit, whose behaviour is determined by both physical and mental factors.

Social Maturity is an indication of good social adjustment. Social maturity has been defined as an indication of willingness and ability to orient oneself in the various activities and customs of the group to make a proportionate contribution to the work to be done to take a suitable part in the social exchange to assume a reasonable amount of the responsibility and to adjust himself to the inevitable limitations and restrictions of community life without waste of energy or loss of satisfaction.

CONCEPT OF CONFLICTS

The term `conflict' is used in so many ways in our day to day set up. There may be conflicts between the ideologies of two sects, cultures, religions and organisations. Conflict may be aroused between husband and wife, father and his son, the teacher and the taught. They may also show their presence among brothers and sisters, members of an organisation or community, states of a country and countries of the world at large. Apart from these external or outer conflicts, there are inner or internal conflicts which are called psychological conflicts.

Conflicts means a painful emotional state which results from a tension between opposed and contradictory wishes- Dougals and Holland

Psychological conflict is a state of tension brought by the presence in the individual of two or more opposing desires- Barney and Lehnar

Conflict may be defined as a state of affairs in which two or more incompatible behaviour tends are evoked that cannot be satisfied fully at the same time.

These definitions conclude that:

i. Conflict is a painful state or condition of an individual.
ii. He feels intense emotional tension during this state.
iii. The tension is the result of the presence of two or more desires or wishes in the individual. These desires are contradictory in nature and therefore cannot be satisfied at the same time.
iv. The individual being at the cross roads and not able to choose between the two opposing desires becomes tense and restless.
v. Thus becoming a victim of the two opposing desires, he suffers from an inner conflict, do not or not to satisfy one or the other desire.

CONFLICT OF MOTIVES

The individual is complex with many different activities that can be aroused.The environment is complex, affording stimuli for various activities. Conflict then, is sure to rise, and a selection must be made between inconsistent activities.

When a conflict arises, the first result is a state of indecision, this "state" being really a complex activity, often very intense and very confused. It works itself out, somehow, into the state of being committed to one of the alternative lines of action.

The state of indecision may amount simply to hesitancy, when the conflict is between doing something on the positive side and fear, shyness or inertia on the negative side.

THE NATURE OF CONFLICTS

1. Awareness of the existence of a conflict is the first step to know what the problem is, who is involved and how they can be solved.
2. Conflicts encourage change for the better.
3. Conflicts increase physical energy and motivation to solve problems and put one's plan into action.
4. Conflicts increase curiosity and stimulate interest to find a solution.
5. A healthy opposition leads one to make better decisions.
6. Conflicts reduce the day-to-day invitations of relating to someone.
7. Dealing with a conflict, the person has a better understanding of himself / herself, the cause of anger and fear.
8. The humorous side of a conflict often balances a tendency to behave too emotional and unbalanced in our decision - making.
9. Conflicts deepen and enrich a relationship. It also strengthens each person's conviction that positive feelings should be nurtured.

TYPES OF CONFLICTS

Approach - Approach Conflict

An approach - approach conflict is a conflict between two positive goals, goals that are equally attractive at the same time. For instance a physiological conflict arises, when a person is hungry and sleepy at the same time. These types of conflicts are usually resolved either by satisfying first one goal and then the other. Approach - approach conflicts are usually easy to resolve and generate little emotional behaviour.

Avoidance - Avoidance Conflict

A second type of conflict, avoidance - avoidance involves two negative goals and is a fairly common experience. For example a boy must do his arithmetic home work or get a spanking. A student must spend the next 2 days studying for an examination or face the possibility of failure. Such conflicts are capsuled in the saying "caught between the devil and the deep blue sea". We can think of all things we do not want to, but must do or face even less desirable elements.

Two kinds of behaviour are likely to be conspicuous in avoidance - avoidance conflicts. One is vacillation of behaviour and thought, meaning that people are inconsistent in what they do and think. A second important behavioural feature of this kind of conflict is an attempt to leave the conflict situation. Theoretically a person can escape from avoidance - avoidance conflict by running away and people do.

Many intense emotions are generated by avoidance - avoidance conflicts. If the two negative goals are fear - producing and threatening, a person caught between them will experience fear or the individual may be angry and resentful at being trapped in a situation where the goals are negative.

Approach - Avoidance Conflict

The third type of conflict, approach - avoidance, is often the most difficult to resolve because, in this type of conflict, a person is both attracted and repelled by the same goal object. Because of the positive valence of the goal, the person approaches it; but as it is approached, the negative valence becomes stronger. If, at some point during the approach to the goal, its repellent aspects become stronger than its positive aspects; the person will stop before reaching the goal. Because the goal is not reached, the individual is frustrated.

Multiple Approaches - Avoidance Conflict

Many of life's major decisions involve multiple approaches - avoidance conflicts, meaning that several goals with positive and negative valences are involved. A multiple approach - avoidance conflict depends on the relative strengths of all the positive and negative valences involved. These valences, which are obstacles to reaching a goal are generally, internalized, such internalised obstacles, or inner negative valences, usually result from the training in social values which a person has received. The emotional reactions generated by approach - avoidance conflict in which internal obstacles play a part are at the root of many behavioural problems. On the more positive side, if we have insight into our own conflicts and the internalized obstacles which create them, we will probably be happier and experience less distress in our lives.

DIFFERENT FORMS OF CONFLICTS

Conflicts are the creation of the dissatisfaction felt by an individual due to the non - fulfillment of his two contradictory desires. The forces of the environment are infact responsible for these conflicts, as they provide necessary ground for their occurrence, but at the same time we teachers, parents and society are also responsible for giving birth to so many conflicts in our youngsters.

The following are different forms of conflict.

i. Self conflict
ii. Mental conflict
iii. Role conflict
iv. Sex conflict and
v. Family conflict

VALUE CONFLICTS

A value conflict arises, when one value can only be realised at the expense of another value. For example an artist might believe that commercial art provides security; but little creativity. By contrast, independent artists lack security, yet enjoy opportunities for creativity. Across the artist's range of options, realizing one value seems to acquire forgoing another value. In stronger cases of conflict, a person's whole set of values can be divided into groups that clash with one another. In weaker cases, conflict might be limited to a few values.

Conflict within decision making is common. Conflict prompts a decision whatever option is examined. There are apt to be gains and losses, and it is this struggle between what to realise and what to neglect that calls for a decision

SOURCES OF VALUE CONFLICTS

Home Environment

The facility upbringing at home, unhealthy or impleasant relationship among the family members is the potential source of conflicts in children. Over protection, dominance, part of parents does not cope with experiences during social contracts with other children at school and thus, he may become a victim of the opposing desires in future.

School Environment

Uncongenial school environment, dominant or submission role of the teachers, faulty methods of teaching, denial of opportunities for self expression. Contradictory demands of the teachers and class mates are some of the bases which may give birth to conflicts.

Social and Cultural Environment

The social environment and cultural value may also prove a potential source of conflicts. Chief among them are the sex conflicts for the reason that the demands of our culture have not been well adjusted to the sexual need of the individual. The taboos, inhibitions and the negative attitude towards the sex is the cause of so many sex conflicts in the minds of our youths. The pattern of conflicting values is responsible for a number of conflicts. For example, on the one hand we give incentive to competitive gains and on the other advocate, co-operation and submission. Frustration suffered due to lack of opportunities in the developing countries like India; also give birth to so many conflicts. Similarly, non fulfillment of the need for status, many financial worries and dissatisfaction with the working conditions and career fulfillment do also prove the sources of many conflicts.

CONFLICT AS A TYPE OF SOCIAL INTERACTIONS

Conflict is probably the most complex form of social interaction. Here, it is found that goals, behaviour, and the motivation of the members are all contradictory. There is no process which is shared. The movements of the different members are in opposite directions. Each individual perceives the other as a threat and each is opposed to the other. Conflicting behaviour involves two basic elements, defense and offence. In competition, the goal is to do better than the others. That is why it is seen that sometimes competition can produce better results and performance than conflict. For example, in an athletic contest, very often we find the contestants improving their earlier records. This scarcely happens in a conflicting situation. This is why conflict is maladjustive, non - productive, and sometimes even positively injurious. Co-operation, on the other hand, seems to produce the best results and the maximum utilisation of human resources, energy, ideas etc. It is ironical that co-operation can be used for good purposes or otherwise.

While considering the above mechanisms of interaction, a few points is important. Firstly, these interactions can take place at three levels, between one individual and another, between one individual and a group and between one group and another group. For example, in the family, the adolescent son can conform comply with co-operate, compete or conflict with his father, when he suggests something. Secondly, in a group of boys, a member can react in any of the above ways in response to the suggestions or demands of the others. At the third level, a minority group of boys of a student union can respond in any of the above ways to the majority.

Thus, smaller groups such as families, play - groups, work groups, organisations etc. tend to project and nurture one or more of the styles of interaction as the general mode among the members. Thus, autocratic organisations tend to generate conformity and compliance as common types of interaction. Democratic and liberal organisations tend to promote compliance, co-operation and competition as the most characteristic types of interaction.

THE CONCEPT OF MENTAL HEALTH

Ivey and Simek Dowing (1980) defined a Mentally Healthy Person as follows:

The person, who acts intentionally, has a sense of capability. He can generate alternative behaviours in a given situation and approach a problem from different vantage points. The intentional and fully functioning individual is not bound to one course of action; but responds in a moment of changing life situations and look forward to longer term goal.

DEFINITIONS OF MENTAL HEALTH

According to **Norma E. Cutts and Nicholas Mosely,**

Mental Health is the various strains of the environment we meet in life and mental hygiene as the means we take to assure the adjustment.

According to **Hadfield,**

Mental health is the full and harmonies functioning of whole personality.

Jahoda (1950) defined,

The mentally healthy person as one who actively masters his or her environment, demonstrates a considerable unity or consistency of personality and is able to perceive self and world realistically.

Bernard (1970) defines mental health as,

The adjustment of individual of themselves and the world at large, with maximum of effectiveness, satisfaction, cheerfulness and socially considerate behaviour and the ability of facing and accepting the realities of life.

Mosby's Medical dictionary defined,

Mental health as a relative state of mind in which a person is healthy to cope with and adjust to the recurring stress of everyday living in an acceptable way.

IMPORTANCE OF MENTAL HEALTH

Man is basically a mind body unit and these two aspects vitally influence each other. For efficient functioning of the individual, he should, not only possess sound bodily health, but also sound mental health. The terrific advances in the field of preventive and curative medicine coupled with continual attempts in all countries, to improve the standard of living of its people have a large extent enabled us to eradicate most of the diseases of the body and helped to provide for longevity of human life with sufficient physical health. A sound body has now become an easy possibility within the reach of everyone and a sound body is basic to a sound mind and bodily handicaps, diseases do affect mental ability and outlook. But in contemporary society, mental health has become a major problem affecting almost every person. Mental health hazards significantly increased in number and complexity, but these have also affected the physical efficiency of individuals, causing a variety of psychomatic disorders. So mental health is now recognised as an important aspect of an individual's total development and mental hygiene is accepted as an integral part of the school programme.

FACTORS RESPONSIBLE FOR POOR MENTAL HEALTH

One can divide the factors responsible for poor mental health, mental illness and disorders into three main categories.

Hereditory Factors

Sometimes the roots of mental ailments and diseases are found in the effective genes inherited from the parents. Moreover the inherited potentialities in terms of intelluctual abilities, psychological structure and appearance etc. put limits on one's mental health and the deficicncy and appropriates of any sort in these potentialities.

Psychological factors

Psychological constitution, appearance and physical health of an individual affect his mental health. A sound body is said to possess a sound mind and is capable of making adjustment in life. On the other hand, poor health, physical defects, ailments and diseases bring deterioration to one's strength and stamina for performing one's duties. It arouses inferiority feelings and mental complexes that create serious adjustment problems. In this way, improper physical and psychological conditions furnish the soil for the growth of poor and ill mental health.

Environmental or Social Factors

It has now been established on account of various researches in the field of mental hygiene that environmental forces like family, school, and society are more responsible for bringing mental illness than the hereditory or constitutional forces. Social and emotional maladjustment has been found to be the root cause of all mental illness and disorder.

CHARACTERISTICS OF A MENTALLY HEALTHY PERSON

Mental health is a way of life. It enables one to accept unchangeable realities in life and to seek to life's problems in a constructive way consistent with one's abilities, instead of trying to turn away from them.

A mentally healthy person is one who:

i. is able to live joyfully and peacefully.
ii. is not disturbed by mental conflicts.
iii. has a true self - appraisal of his strength and weakness.
iv. tries to cooperate with others and wins friends and thus naturally gives him feeling of security.
v. has diverse and varied interests and lives, according to a philosophy dominated by constructive and realistic goals.

vi. understands the intricacies of practical life and is very pragmatic in his approach.
vii. is emotionally stable and socially mature.
viii. has high degree of frustration tolerance such an individual has necessarily good physical health as bodily health and mentally health are interrelated.

CONCEPT OF SOCIAL MATURITY

Social maturity refers to the values that are found in the society. For the advancement in Education, proper social maturity, values and adjustment pattern should be there.

Maturity implies the following five criteria:

1. A satisfactory fulfillment of one's capacity.
2. An adequate balanced self concept based upon self insight.
3. An ability to meet reality without developing crippling emotional and mental conflicts.
4. The ability to love beyond oneself and to turn personal experience into human experience.
5. Adjustment to and creative participation in one's environment.

DEFINITIONS OF SOCIAL MATURITY

Nazareth RJM, N.Pia and **Marie. E. Waples** (1978) defines that

Maturity is the blossoming of man's character into a unified totality. It discerns the process that contributes to the psychological and physical growth and well being of man.

Abraham Sperling (1967) defines that,

An adolescent who gets along with and work well with others, he ought to develop self relience in matters of taste and he ought to develop tolerance of human differences.

Henry .E. Garrett (1968) defines that

Social maturity is the degree of social participation as measured by child's activities, attitudes and play interests. It is related to physical growth, maturity and mental health.

IMPORTANCE OF SOCIAL MATURITY

Maturity assures accountability, constantly assets, judges and take appropriate decisions. Maturity develops a balanced emotional outlook, helping the individual to accept himself his talents and limitations and to accept others as they are. It helps towards progressive advancement in spiritual growth, impelling the individual to adapt himself to change life without emotional crisis.

SOME STAGES OF SOCIAL MATURITY

An individual takes time in his social development. So, we may think of some stages of social maturity, accordingly to the physical, mental, emotional and language development of the individual.

The child reaches another stage of social maturity, when he / she begins to understand the relationship between the various members of the society.

A stage in his social maturity reaches, when he / she begins to understand and relationship between the man and the women, the servant and master, the husband and the wife, the teacher and the taught, the shopkeeper and the customer, the ruler and the ruled, the government and its organisation. Understanding all the things refers to his stage of social maturity.

SOCIAL MATURITY AND ITS CHARACTERISTICS

Social maturity is the final expected outcome of a socially developed individual. They are :

1. A socially matured person has a sense of his proper place and role as a member of the social group. He is willing and able to orient himself in the various activities and customs to the group.
2. He is able to assume a reasonable amount of responsibility, to adjust himself to the inevitable limitations and restrictions of the community life.
3. He can be original and yet conform to the broad pattern of his social environment.
4. He evaluates social problems not from a purely selfish point of view; but has regard to the right and opinion of others.
5. He accepts responsibility for his actions, does not indulge in self pitying.
6. It is relatively free from devastating emotions and is able to release his emotions in socially acceptable behaviour problems.
7. He has a realistic level of aspiration and has a sound moral and social code that saves him from conflicts and feelings of guilt.
8. He has many friends and contributes to social welfare.
9. He has a realistic self concept, being conscious of his assets and limitations.
10. He is relatively secure and so open to new experiences which contribute to his continuous development.

In short, co-operation, pleasing manner, consideration for others, positive and optimistic outlook on life and emotional maturity are signs of socially matured individual.

By considering the conceptual frame work of the above variables, an investigation has been made by the researcher to study the relationship between the selected variables namely value conflict, mental health and social maturity of the higher secondary school students.

STATEMENT OF THE PROBLEM

The problems for the study are titled as follows:

A study on value conflicts and mental health of students at the Higher Secondary level in relation to their social maturity

OPERATIONAL DEFINITIONS

Value Conflicts

Whenever two or more incompatible principles, ideologies, religion, socio - politic aspirations and cultural identifies are active at the same time, they are said as value conflicts. In this study, it is assessed by Value Conflict Scale prepared by R.L. Bharadwaj.

Mental Health

Mental health refers to a condition and a level of social functioning which is socially and personally satisfying in all aspects of life. In this present study Mental Health Inventory constructed by Droved Augustine is used to measure it.

Social Maturity

Social maturity is the final expected outcome of social development and socialization. The social mature person knows his role as a member of the social group. In this present investigation, it is assessed by Social Maturity Scale prepared by Rao.

Higher Secondary Level

It refers to students studying in XI standard under Tamil Nadu State Board Syllabus.

OBJECTIVES FOR THE STUDY

The following objectives are set in the present study.

i. To find out the dimension of value conflict of higher-secondary students.
ii. To identify the level of mental health of higher secondary students
iii. To find out the level of social maturity of higher secondary students
iv. To investigate whether the different dimensions of value conflict viz. Fortitude, Self - Reliance, Probity, Affection, Assertion and Idealism exhibit different levels of (ie) low, average and high social maturity among students studying in higher secondary level.

v. To find whether categories of mental health exhibit different levels (ie) low, average and high social maturity.

vi. To find whether there is significant association between value conflict and mental health of students studying at higher secondary level.

vii. To find whether there is significant difference between scores of value conflict of students studying at higher secondary level with respect to

- Sex
- Type of management of schools (Government / Government aided / Private).
- Type of family (Nuclear / Joint)
- Birth order of the child (1st / 2nd / 3rd / and above)
- Father's educational qualification (Illiterate / School level / College level)
- Mother's educational qualification (Illiterate/School level/ College level)
- Father's monthly income (less than Rs.3000 / above Rs.3000)
- Mother's monthly income (less than Rs.3000/ above Rs.3000).

viii. To find whether there is any significant difference between scores of fortitude of students studying at higher secondary level with respect to

- Sex
- Type of management of Schools
- Type of family
- Birth order of the child
- Father's educational qualification
- Mother's educational qualification
- Father's monthly income
- Mother's monthly income

ix. To find whether there is any significant difference between scores of self-reliance of students studying at higher secondary level with respect to

- Sex
- Management of schools
- Type of family
- Birth order of the child
- Father's educational qualification
- Mother's educational Qualification
- Father's monthly income
- Mother's monthly income

x. To find whether there is any significant difference between scores of probity of students studying at higher secondary level with respect to

- Sex
- Type management of schools
- Type of family
- Birth order of the child
- Father's educational qualification
- Mother's educational qualification
- Father's monthly income
- Mother's monthly income

xi. To find whether there is any significant difference between scores of love of students studying at higher secondary level with respect to

- Sex
- Type of management of schools
- Type of family
- Birth order of the child
- Father's educational qualification
- Mother's educational qualification
- Father's monthly income
- Mother's monthly income

xii. To find whether there is any significant difference between scores of assertion of students studying at higher secondary level with respect to

- Sex
- Type of management of schools
- Type of family
- Birth order of the child
- Father's educational qualification
- Mother's educational qualification
- Father's monthly income
- Mother's monthly income

xiii. To find whether there is any significant difference between scores of Idealism of students studying at higher secondary level with respect to

- Sex
- Type of management of schools
- Type of family
- Birth order of the child
- Father's educational qualification
- Mother's educational qualification

- Father's monthly income
- Mother's monthly income

xiv. To find whether there is any significant difference between mental health of students studying at higher secondary level with respect to

- Sex
- Type of management of schools
- Type of family
- Birth order of the child
- Father's educational qualification
- Mother's educational qualification
- Father's monthly income
- Mother's monthly income

xv. To find whether there is any significant difference between social maturity of students studying at higher secondary level with respect to

- Sex
- Type of management of schools
- Type of family
- Birth order of the child
- Father's educational qualification
- Mother's educational Qualification
- Father's monthly income
- Mother's monthly income

SIGNIFICANCE OF THE STUDY

Values are the important factor which influences the behaviour. Every individual have a well defined set of personal values such as cleanliness, dignity of labour, deligence, punctuality, regularity, honesty, courage, ambition, hope etc. which give him a sense of direction in life and a purpose of life, when he / she differs from these values, conflict arises. Mental health implies good adjustment and such a good adjustment yields pleasure and achievement in personal as well as inter personal activities.

A person having good social maturity will know his responsibilities and will be able to adjust himself in the society as he would have good self concept.

So, the present study is conducted to know the effect of the value conflict and mental health over social maturity of higher, secondary students.

LIMITATIONS OF THE STUDY

The present study has the following limitations.

1. The study is done only in Chennai City.
2. The XI - Standard Students are taken as the sample.
3. The study is done with 302 samples.

CONCLUSION

In the first chapter, a brief outline of the three variables such as value conflicts, mental health and social maturity is given. The meaning, definition types and characteristics of the variables are stated and the review of literature of the variables is followed in the second chapter.

❒

7

Review of Related Literature

For any worthwhile study in any field of knowledge, the research worker needs an adequate familiarity with work which has already been done in some area. In review of related studies, the researcher attempts to determine what others have learned about similar research problems and to gather informations relevant to the research problem at hand. The review of related literature serves multiple purposes and it is essential to a well designed research study.

IMPORTANCE OF REVIEW

The importance of review is well explained by Borg et al., (1983) in the following words. The review of the literature is an important part of the scientific approach and is carried out in all areas of scientific research whether in the physical, natural or social sciences. It gives the scholar, of previous work that has been done. It provides the means of getting to the frontiers in the particular field of knowledge.

The related literature available on the proposed study is presented in this chapter under the following heads.

1. Studies related to value conflicts.
2. Studies related to mental health.
3. Studies related to social maturity.

STUDIES RELATED TO VALUE CONFLICTS

Studies in India

Bharadwaj and Mithas (2003) attempted a study to find out the existing value assumption of evasion and fortitude in relation to gender and socio-economic status in various caste groups a sample of 300 adults of age 25-45 years are administered. The tool used was revised scale of socio-economic status (Bharadwaj, 2001) and the value conflict scale (Bharadwaj 1998). Results revealed a significant effect of socio-economic status indicating that high socio-economic adults manifested fortitude value.

Magadalin, Sujaritha et al., (2002) attempted a study on the development of adolescent's moral value. The sample consisted of 60 boys and 60 girls of age 14-26 years. The tool was prepared by the investigators and it included Likert type items covering different conflicting situations in five enquiry areas-honesty, responsibility, moral courage, friendliness and kindness. The results showed that the calculated internal consistency was found to be significant.

Chakabarthy, Subhra et al., (2002) attempted a study to measure the customer conflict handling styles. The sample consisted of 108 sales persons of age ranging from 27 - 30 years. The tools used were the Rahin organisational conflict inventory II. The author concluded that sales researches would use his measure to examine the conflict handling styles of sales persons.

Commons, Mandy et al., (2000) attempted a study to examine the effect of parental divorce, parental remarriage and familial conflict on the ability of young adult off spring to achieve intimacy in other non - familial relationships. A sample of 200 male and female university students were administered. The tools used was the conflict subscale of the family environemnt scale by Moos et al., Miller Social intimacy by Miller let court and the fear of intimacy scale by Deswitner and Thelen.The results revealed a significant association between familial conflict and intimacy achievement; but there was no significant relationship between parental marital status and intimacy achievement. Moreover, high familial conflict experienced during childhood was found to be the most significant contributor to maladjustment in young adult offspring as measured by fear of intimacy.

Srivastava and Ashok (1999) attempted a study to find out the value preferences of parents belonging to two generations. A sample of 120 mothers, 120 fathers and 120 grandmothers of children below 10 years of age from 3 types of residential back grounds (rural / urban / metropolitan) and two levels of economic status (low / high) were interviewed. The results showed that honesty and hard work were the obedience and benevolence which parents irrespective of their residential background and economic status, wanted their children to develop. Disobedience, laziness, quarrelsomeness, greed, fear and stealing were cited as undesirable characteristics.

Bharadwaj (1998) attempted a study to examine the perceived parenting to rejection - acceptance and adolescent's values conflicts. The sample of the present study consists of 500 adolescents of both the sexes studying in 11th and 12th standard of intermediate colleges of Aligarh. The tools used were the parenting scale and value conflict scale constructed and standardised by R.L.Bharadwaj. The major finding was that the existence of value conflicts in the Indian adolescents is almost negligible despite their desirable and non-desirable value orientedness. The effects of parental acceptance and rejection emerge as an important dynamics associated with the development of different value patterns in Indian adolescents.

Sudha and Lakkamma (1994) attempted a study to find out the levels of assertive communication between rural and urban community students of standard X. The sample of the study comprised 200 students of standard X of rural and urban schools of Bangalore District. The tools used were Assertive Communication Scale developed by Sudha and Sathyanarayana and Self-Esteem Inventory developed by copper smith. The major finding was that the effect of sex on the assertive communication of standard X students was significant in favour of girls. The urban and rural community on the assertive communication did not differ.

Studies in Abroad

Dhand et al., (1993) attempted a study to find out the value clarification of undergraduate students. The present study compared the effects of the implementation of the value discussion model, in terms of value clarification and its dimensions on Canadian and Indian undergraduate students. The sample consisted of 295 undergraduate students from Indian and 201 from Canada. The experimental group was treated through the value discussion model and the other two control groups followed their routine activities. The value clarification scale (VCS) was used to collect the data. The major finding was that the value discussion model group was found to be superior to the control groups.

Timofeev and Mikhael (1993) attempted a study to determine the association between irrational belief and conflict handling orientations. The sample was selected from among 61 women managers and engineers in the age ranging from 22 - 51 years and 71 men managers and engineers in the age ranging from 26 - 66 years. The results showed that the different conflict handling orientations are associated with different irrational beliefs. Sharing orientation was negatively correlated with the irrational beliefs related to upsetness for women and negatively correlated with the irrational beliefs related to disgust, frustration, guilt and shame for men. The more rational women and men were more likely to endorse a compromising strategy for conflict - resolution.

Roy and Ramashray (1991) attempted a study to find out the conflict, conflict resolution and human needs theories. The need theories inherently conceive conflict and growth of individuals in terms of fulfillment of material needs. The concept of self in these theories is a problematic one and can only be realized at an intellectual level. Highlighting these limitations, the author argues in favour of the concept of spiritual self which alone can liberate human beings from conflicts.

Young, Robert et al., (1991) attempted a study to measure the essential values of student affairs work. The sample was selected from 68 teaching and non teaching professionals in student affairs about the relevance of 7 essential values identified by the American Association of Colleges of Nursing. They included altruism, equality aesthetics, freedom, human dignity, justice and both. The major findings were 97% of the respondents agreed that every value was essential value of the field. Additional insights were derived concerning the values of equality, community and aesthetics.

STUDIES RELATED TO MENTAL HEALTH

Studies in India

Anand, S.P. (1988) made an attempt to develop a mental health scale. The objective of the study was to study the mental health of high school students belonging to class X. A sample of 120 teachers was used. Also, reliability and validity were determined using separate samples, using 78 and 75 teachers respectively. A neuroticim scale was used for validity. Chi-square, "t" test and correlation were used for data analysis. The major findings of the study were (1). The retest reliability of the scale has been estimated at 0.88, and split - half reliability at 0.79 (2). It has a fairly acceptable degree of construct - validity (3) A score of 150 was found to be the minimum for a healthy person.

Mohapatra.C (1992) studied the relationships between coping and mental health among different professional groups, and studied the experience of job stress among coping strategies in different professional groups. An incidental random sample of 1,020 respondents from lawyers, doctors and police officers was undertaken. Their age - range was 30 to 50 years. The tools used included Job Stress Questionnaire of Singh and Sinha and Subjective Mental Health Questionnaire by Brynt and Verott. The major findings are the three professional groups differed significantly on job stress dimensions. The lawyers and the doctors differed on mental health dimensions.

An investigation was made by Kamau and Catherine (1992) to study the level of burn - out, laws of control and mental health of teachers a sample of 385 teachers of both sexes participated in the study. Teacher's Mental Health Scale developed by the Kamu and Catherine was used. The major finding was male teachers were emotionally over extended, exhausted, internally controlled, anxious, callous towards students and personally accomplished, but less capable of establishing constructive relationship; however, they were more capable of coping with stresses than female teachers.

A comparative study had been done by Mohanty. S (1992) to investigate occupational stress, coping style, mental health states and social support in a group of executives from public and private sectors. The study was conducted on 240 executives with 60 subjects in each of the designs. The major findings are private sector executives in general, experienced greater job stress, mental health problems and perceived greater organised support than public sector executives. They also used problem - focussed coping more than public sector executives.

The study was conducted by Muralidharan. R. et al., (1993) to help young primary school children to develop an interest in learning and acquiring the required competence, and improve their learning and social skills. The sample consisted of 200 low achievers from Class II of four Municipal Corporation of Delhi schools and 163 children from four public school of Delhi. The major findings are the results of the mathematics tests revealed that the maximum problem existed in the following areas concept of place value, concept of shape, concept of ascending and descending order, and number of days in a week.

Studies in Abroad

A study undertaken by Constantine et al., (2004) presented an extensive literature review and discusses the cultural relevance of indigenous healing practices in promoting psychological, physical and spiritual well being in people of colour. Suggestions are also presented for the ways counsellors might work with indigenous healing resources to promote the well - being of people of color.

Ruffolo, Mary G, Sarri, Rosemary; Goodkind, Saral; (2004). This study examined risk and protective factors for delinquent, diverted and high risk adolescent girls to inform the development of effective mental health prevention and intervention programs. Deliquent, diverted and high risk adolescent girls (N=159) involved or at risk of involvement with the juvenile justice system, who were receiving home - based or community based open or closed residential services, completed a written, self - administered, structural questionnaire. A majority of the girls reported moderate to severe depression, but only about one third had received mental health speciality services. Girls in the community based closed residential settings had significantly higher levels of depression, experienced more negative life events, reported more sexual abuse, more often had special education status, were more likely to come from families who received welfare, had more disruption in living situations, exhibited more delinquent behaviour, and used more negative coping behaviours than did girls in the other programs.

The study examined whether the general stress - care giver strain - mental health outcome model may be as appropriate for caregivers of minor - age children as it has been for caregivers of adults with chronic illness. Sales, Esther; Greeno, Catherine; Shear, M. Katherine et al., (2004) examined whether children's behavioural problems are related to mothers' care giving strains, which then in relation to greater maternal mental health symptomatology, Mothers of 222 children referred for mental health services completed the child behaviour checklist, caregiver strain questionnaire and three dependent variable measures. Beak Depression Inventory (BDI), Beak Anxiety Inventory (BAI), and the SF-36 Mental Health Scale. Path analyses and sobel tests supported the tested model that maternal caregiving strain mediates between children mental health problems, and three indicators of maternal mental health problems with significant indirect pathway through maternal caregiving strain replacing the formerly significant direct contribution of child's problem severity to each maternal mental health measure.

According to the Journal of American College Health (2005). Over the past decade, college and university counseling centers have seen an increase in severe psychological problems. In two studies, more than 80 percent of counseling centers reported an increase in the number of severe psychological problems and reported that such problems have become a greater concern. In another study, student affairs administrators reported marked increases in eating disorders, drug abuse, alcohol abuse, classroom disruption, gambling, and suicide attempts. The increasing level and seriousness of psychopathology among college students is attributed to a variety of social and cultural, including divorce, family dysfunction, instability, violence, early experimentation with drugs and alcohol and poor interpersonal attachments. On the individual level, mental health problems affect the student's physical, emotional, cognitive and social functioning. On the institutional level, mental health problems are the cause of poor retention and graduation rates, as well as adversely affecting classmates, roommates, faculty, and staff, and posing legal challenges. In response, counseling center directors and student affairs officers must educate higher level administrators about the importance and value of counseling services, particularly in terms of the institutional mission. In addition, counseling center directors report that the brief therapy model allows for the more effective management of caseloads.

Decades of research have generally shown that being more rigid is associated with poorer mental health. Ciarrochi, Joseph; Said, Terri; Deane, Frank P. (2006) investigated whether all aspects of what has been termed "rigidity" are harmful. In particular, they are hypothesized that the desire for simple structure (DSS) will not be associated with poor mental health and in some cases might be associated with better mental health. In contrast, the intolerance of uncertainty (IU) was hypothesized to be associated with a wide range of indices of poor mental health. They are also hypothesized that people high in IU would be less resilient in the face of stressful life events. Results across two cross - sectional surveys (N = 240; N=331) supported our hypotheses. DSS was associated with less hopelessness, whereas IU was associated with more depression, anxiety, stress, suicidal ideation, and hopelessness. In addition, mode rational analysis supported the hypothesis that IU magnifies the advertise effect of stressful life events on depression, anxiety and hopelessness. IU was more strongly related to the negative indices of well-being than to the positive index of life satisfaction. The implications of these findings for cognitive behavioural therapy practice are discussed.

A study was done by Thinklin. T; Riddells, (2005) on a massive expansion in students number in higher education, coupled with an overall reduction in funding, has led to higher staff - student ratios and a reduction in the amount of staff time available to support students. This had been linked to rising demands being placed on student support services. This article drew on care for students experiencing mental health difficulties, to provide insight into those issues from the students perspective. The students confirmed that aspects of the higher education environment had exacerbated their difficulties. An innovative model of support was described. Traditionally interventions for students with mental health difficulties had focused at the individual level. It is aruged that attention also needs to be paid to changing aspects of the environment and that this would improve the learning experience for all students.

An investigation was made by Watson Anmy C, (2005). The use of legal coercion to compel individuals to participate in mental health treatment is expanding despite a lack of empirical support for many of its forms. Policies supporting mandated treatment are made by legislators and judges often based on perceptions of public concern. Using data from the Mac Artheol Mental Health module contained in 1996 general social survey (N=1,444). The authors examined the impact of political ideology, attribution about the cause of mental illness, and perceptions of dangerousness in determining public support for legally mandated mental health treatment perceived dangerousness and attributions about the cause of the mental disorder were significant predictors of support for legally mandated treatment. Conservative political ideology was related to attributing the vignette problem to bad character, indirectly affecting support for legal coercion.

STUDIES RELATED TO SOCIAL MATURITY

Studies in India

Kathuria, M. (1974) has investigated some personality determinants of vocational maturity and carrier inductiveness and the sample consists of 1000 female undergraduates in arts and science course at two women colleges and two women colleges at Ajmer in Rajasthan State, the sample was in the age range of 16 to 21 years. Vocational maturity was measured by a scale analogus to the vocational development inventory by critics. This inventory was prepared by the investigator and it had a reliability index of 0.73. This scale was termed as vocational maturity scale. The major findings were informal experience related to higher scores on the vocational maturity scale and lower scores on the vocational indecision scale.

Rao, N.A. (1978) Reports Social Maturity of Children to be positively in correlation with such parental behaviour as protecting, loving, casual symbolic love, rewarding, direct object, rewarding, symbolic love punishing.

Malin A.J. (1990) conducted a study on the relationship of social maturity with classroom climate and academic achievement. The sample consisted of 1200 students of classes VIII and IX. The tools used were Edward's Social Maturity Scale and achievement test. It is found that students studying in classes IX have higher maturity as compared to students of class VIII.

Studies in Abroad

Saovaluk Thongamkham (1983) made a study of social maturity as a function of some psycho - social adjustment factors of higher secondary students of North - Central Region of Thailand. The major findings were that the college students with high SES background were found more socially matured than those of coming from SES strata. The students having dominant personality trait were more socially matured than those of having submissive personality trait. The two groups of students having high suggestibility and low suggestibility trait did not differ on social maturity. The students having good social adjustment were more socially matured than those having poor personal social adjustment. The students having good family adjustment were found to be more socially matured than those with poor family adjustment.

Pattraman Junpangren (1986), studied social maturity of higher secondary students of western region of Thailand, in the context of some psycho - social factors "Ph.D., Education SPU, 1986. The higher secondary students coming from urban areas were found to be more matured than those coming from rural areas. The male higher secondary students were found superior to the female students. The higher secondary students having emotional stability were more matured than those having low emotional stability. The higher secondary students having good personal adjustment were more socially matured than those having poor personal social adjustment.

Sarojamma, Y.H. (1990) has conducted a comparative study on reading ability and social maturity of over normal and under achievers of standard VIII, the final sample comprised of 476 boys and 524 girls. The social maturity scale by Sathya Narayana and Sudha were used. The major findings were, there was significant difference in the reading ability of over normal and under achievers of standard VIII and also in the other variables like gender; type of school etc.

Mulia R.D. (1991) conducted a study on the social maturity of the higher secondary students in the context of their stream, sex and I.Q. The tools used included non verbal intelligence maturity. No interaction effect of streams and sex, I.Q was found significant on social maturity.

Bhusan A. (1994) conducted a study on social maturity across sex and family vocations. The sample comprised 200 student teachers from two colleges equally divided between two sexes. Major variables used were sex, values and family vocations. It is found that social maturity differs between family vocations in the case of male group were logic, independence and ambition as subdivision from the female group.

CONCLUSION

This chapter gives clear related studies on the variables of the present study. It involves the systematic identification, location and analysis of documents containing information related to the research problem.

❒

8

Design of the Study and Method of Investigation

This chapter gives an overall picture of the design of the study, research tool used for the study, nature and selection of the sample and a brief description of the procedure, adopted for collection of data.

HYPOTHESES

The following hypotheses are set in the present study.

i. The dimension of value conflict of higher secondary students is idealism in nature.
ii. The level of mental health of higher secondary students is average in nature.
iii. The level of social maturity of higher secondary students is average in nature.
iv. The different dimensions of value conflict viz fortitude, self-reliance, porbity, affection, assertion and idealism will exhibit different levels of social maturity (i.e) low, average and high social maturity among students studying at the higher secondary level.
v. The different categories of mental health (i.e) low, average and high will exhibit different levels of social maturity.

vi. There is significant association between value conflict and mental health of students studying at the higher secondary level.

vii. There is no significant difference between the mean scores of "value conflict" of students studying at higher secondary level with respect to:

- Sex
- Type of management of schools (Government / Government aided / Private).
- Type of family (Nuclear / Joint).
- Birth order of the child (1st / 2nd / 3rd and above).
- Father's educational qualification (Illiterate / school level / college level).
- Mother's educational qualification (Illiterate / school level / college level).
- Father's monthly income (less than Rs.3000/- above Rs.3000).
- Mother's monthly income (less than Rs.3000 / above Rs.3000).

viii. There is no significant difference between the mean scores of "fortitude" of students studying at the higher secondary level with respect to

- Sex
- Type of management of schools
- Type of family
- Birth order of the child
- Father's educational qualification
- Mother's educational qualification
- Father's monthly income
- Mother's monthly income

ix. There is no significant difference between the mean scores of "self - reliance" of students studying at the higher secondary level with respect to

- Sex
- Type of management of schools
- Type of family
- Birth order of the child
- Father's educational qualification
- Mother's education qualification
- Father's monthly income
- Mother's monthly income

x. There is no significant difference between the mean scores of "probity" of students studying at the higher secondary level with respect to

- Sex
- Type of management of schools
- Type of family
- Birth order of the child
- Father's educational qualification
- Mother's educational qualification
- Father's monthly income
- Mother's monthly income

xi. There is no significant difference between the mean scores of "Affection" of students studying at the higher secondary level with respect to

- Sex
- Type of management of schools
- Type of family
- Birth order of the child
- Father's educational qualification
- Mother's educational qualification
- Father's monthly income
- Mother's monthly income

xii. There is no significant difference between the mean scores of "assertion" of students studying at the higher secondary level with respect to

- Sex
- Type of management of schools
- Type of family
- Birth order of the child
- Father's educational qualification
- Mother's educational qualification
- Father's monthly income
- Mother's monthly income

xiii. There is no significant difference between the mean scores of "Idealism" of students studying at the higher secondary level with respect to

- Sex
- Type of management of schools
- Type of family
- Birth order of the child
- Father's educational qualification
- Mother's educational qualification
- Father's monthly income
- Mother's monthly income

xiv. There is no significant difference between "mental health" of students studying at the higher secondary level with respect to

- Sex
- Type of management of schools
- Type of family
- Birth order of the child
- Father's educational qualification
- Mother's educational qualification
- Father's monthly income
- Mother's monthly income

xv. There is no significant difference between "social maturity" of students studying at the higher secondary level with respect to

- Sex
- Type of management of schools
- Type of family
- Birth order of the child
- Father's educational qualification
- Mother's educational qualification
- Father's monthly income
- Mother's monthly income

TOOLS AND TECHNIQUES USED

The following tools have been used

a. Value Conflict Scale
b. Mental Health Inventory and
c. Social Maturity Scale

VALUE CONFLICT SCALE

Description

The standardised value conflict scale prepared by R.L. Bharadwaj (1998) was used for finding the value conflict score. The present scale is intended to measure six types of value conflicts. Fortitude, Self-reliance, Probity, Affection, Assertion and Idealism.

The scale contains 24 items to measure six value conflict probabilities. Each dimension contains four items. Each item or question is provided with five alternatives. Responses are obtained on the test booklet itself. There is no time limit; but generally 15 minutes have been found sufficient for responding all the items.

TABLE. 8.1: Showing the Items Pertaining to Different Dimensions of Value Conflicts

	Description	Item Numbers			
A.	Fortitude	1	7	13	19
B.	Self reliance	2	8	14	20
C.	Probity	3	9	15	21
D.	Affection	4	10	16	22
E.	Assertion	5	11	17	23
F.	Idealism	6	12	18	24

Administration

This scale was administered individually to a large group at a time. After establishing a good rapport, the subjects were asked to respond to any one alternative of each question by making a tick mark. There was no time limit to the scale for recording the responses and the average time needed to give responses was around 15 minutes.

Scoring

The scoring of value conflict scale is based on the line of Likerts five point scale. Scoring of item number 1, 2, 3, 5, 7, 8, 9, 11, 13, 14, 15, 17, 19, 20, 21 and 23 are to be scored from upper to lower in the form of 1, 2, 3, 4 and 5. The scoring of item number 4, 6, 10, 12, 16, 18, 22 and 24 will be in reverse order from upper to lower in the form of 5, 4, 3, 2 and 1. The obtained scores are to be added horizontally to determine the value conflict score.

MENTAL HEALTH INVENTORY

Description

Mental Health Inventory Standardized by Droved and Augustine used in this present study. The inventory consists of 60 statements, out of which 20 items are positive statements and the rest

TABLE. 8.2: Showing the Nature of items of Mental Health Inventory

Nature of Statements	Item Number
Positive	1,2,5,8,9,10,14,16, 17, 27, 31, 34, 35, 38, 44, 45, 46, 54, 58 & 60.
Negative	3, 4, 6, 7, 11, 12, 13, 15, 18, 19, 20, 21, 22, 23, 24, 25, 26, 28, 29, 30, 32, 33, 36, 37, 39, 40, 41, 42, 43, 47, 48, 49, 50, 51, 52, 53, 55, 56, 57 & 59

Administration

This questionnaire consists of single statements, which expresses the different way in which students think, feel and behave in their life situation. The students were required to select any one of the two responses to indicate their ability to adjust to one's own social, vocational and environmental demands. The investigator requested the students to give their responses frank and said that it would be confidential.

Scoring

Since the questionnaire consists of both positive and negative statements two different patterns of scoring have to be adopted for the types of items. The following table provided guidelines to score the responses given to the two categories of items.

TABLE. 8.3: Showing the Guidelines to Score the Responses given to the two Categories of Items.

Nature of Statements	Scoring	
	Positive statement	Negative statement
Yes	1	0
No	0	1

SOCIAL MATURITY SCALE

Description

1. The social maturity scale was developed by "Dr.Nalini Rao".
2. The final form of the questionnaire consists of 90 items known as Rao's social maturity scale.

Administration

The social maturity scale was administered to the respondents in group in the regular class room situation. The instruction provided on the first page of the scale booklet was self expanatory. Reading of the instructions by the examiner to the group, however ensured better conditions for responding to the items of the scale. The answers were recorded by the respondent on the scale protocol. The time required to complete the scale items was about 45 minutes.

Scoring

The final form of the questionnaire consists of 90 items. Each item was accorded a four point response speed the intervals of which are labelled as.

a. Strongly Agree
b. Agree
c. Disagree

d. Strongly Disagree

The successive response intervals were subsequently scored as 4, 3, 2 and 1 with the high score represents matured response. There was no right (or) wrong answers. The answers were checked against the key and point was given for each item ticked as per key. The total points obtained give a measure of social maturity.

TABLE. 8.4: Scoring key of the Questionnaire According to the Nature of Items.

Nature of the Items	Strongly Agree	Agree	Disagree	Strongly disagree
Positive 17, 21, 24, 26, 36, 39, 41, 42, 50, 51, 52, 54, 56, 57, 59, 63, 74, 77, 89, 90	4	3	2	1
Negative 1, 2, 3, 4, 5, 6, 7, 8, 9, 10, 11, 12, 13, 14, 15, 16, 18, 19, 20, 22, 23, 25, 27, 28, 29, 30, 31, 32, 33, 34, 35, 37, 38, 40, 43, 44, 45, 46, 47, 48, 49, 53, 55, 58, 60, 61, 62, 64, 65, 66, 67, 68, 69, 60, 71, 72, 73, 75, 76, 78, 79, 80, 81, 82, 83, 84, 85, 86, 87, 88	1	2	3	4

SAMPLE FOR THE STUDY

The present study is mainly concerned with XI - standard students studying in schools following the syllabus of Tamil Nadu State Board of Secondary Education.

For the present study, a sample of 302 students of standard XI studying in Chennai City during the academic year 2006 - 2007 were taken.

TABLE. 8.5: Showing the Details of the Composition of Students in the Sample

Type of Management	Name of the School	Number of Students	
		Boys	Girls
Government	Government Higher Secondary School for Boys, Saidapet, Chennai - 15.	53	-
	Lady Willingdon Higher Secondary School for Girls, Triplicane, Chennai - 5.	-	67
Government Aided	St. Joseph Higher Secondary School, Bharathi Nagar, Chennai - 39.	52	-
	K.K.Nirmala Girls' Higher Secondary School, Ashok Nagar, Chennai - 83.	-	48
Private	Madras Christian College Matric. Higher Secondary School, Chetpet, Chennai - 31.	41	-
	Fathima Matriculation Higher Secondary School, Kodambakkam, Chennai - 24	-	41

PILOT STUDY

Before finalizing the final from the tools and collecting data for main study, a pilot study was attempted. It was conducted in the month of September, 2006 on 30 XI Standard students drawn from each school selected randomly from the whole sample to establish reliability and validity of the various tools used in the study.

ESTABLISHING RELIABILITY AND VALIDITY OF TOOLS USED

Value Conflict Scale

Reliability

The reliability of this scale was determined by test and re-test method with an interval of fifteen days. The obtained reliability co-efficients for six value conflict areas may be given as under

TABLE. 8.6: Showing the Coefficient of Reliability for of Value Conflict Scale

Value conflict	A	B	C	D	E	F
Co-efficient of reliability	0.67	0.72	0.76	0.70	0.69	0.65

Validity

The content validity of this value conflict scale is high as the areas and then the selection of items in the scale are based on research proven techniques.

The validity of value conflict scale was also determined with the parallel form, which may be enumerated as under

TABLE. 8.7: Showing the Co-Efficient of Validity for each Demension of Value Conflict Scale

Value conflict	A	B	C	D	E	F
Co-efficient of validity	0.82	0.85	0.87	0.84	0.83	0.80

Mental Health Inventory

Reliability

In order to establish the reliability of the mental health inventory, odd - even method is used. The correlation between the items was calculated by using Karl Pearson's product moment formula and the coefficient of reliability is obtained to be 0.63.

Validity

The index of validity has been computed by finding the square root of reliability. It has been found to be 0.79 and hence the scale (i.e) considered to have high validity.

3:09:03 Social Maturity scale

Reliability

In order to establish the reliability of social maturity scale, the odd - even method was used. The reliability of social maturity scale was found to be 0.84. Hence, social maturity scale was considered as reliable.

Validity

The index of validity which is the square root of the reliability was found to be 0.92. Hence, social maturity scale selected for the study was considered to be highly valid.

MAIN STUDY

The tools described below:

1. Value Conflict Scale
2. Mental Health Inventory
3. Social Maturity Scale

were used to collect the data for the main study following the procedures mentioned for the administration of the tests. The tests were administered on the sample of XI standard students in the month of November 2006.

TABLE. 8.8: Showing the time Schedule of Administered Tools

S.No.	Name of the tool	Time taken (in minutes)
1.	Value conflict scale	15 minutes
2.	Mental health inventory	15 minutes
3.	Social maturity scale	45 minutes

STATISTICAL TECHNIQUES USED

Suitable descriptive and inferential statistical techniques were used in the interpretation of the data to draw out a meaningful picture of results from collected Data. In the present study, the following statistical means were used.

I. MEAN

$$X = A + \frac{\sum fd}{\sum f} xi$$

Where, A = Assumed mean

f = Frequency

d = Deviation from the assumed mean

i = Class interval

II. STANDARD DEVIATION

$$SD, \sigma = \sqrt{\frac{\sum fd^2}{N} - \left(\frac{\sum fd^2}{N}\right)} xi$$

Where, f = Frequency

d = Deviation from arithmetic mean

i = Class interval

N = total frequency

III. STANDARD ERROR DEVIATION

$$SED = \sqrt{\frac{\sigma_1^2}{N_1} + \frac{\sigma_2^2}{N_2}}$$

Where,

σ_1, σ_2 = Standard deviations

N_1, N_2 = Total number of sample

IV. 't' TEST

To complete the significance of difference between means of various measures, `t' test is used `t' ratio is calculated from the relation.

$$t\ ratio = \frac{M_1 \sim M_2}{\sqrt{\frac{\sigma_1^2}{N_1} + \frac{\sigma_2^2}{N_2}}} = \frac{M_1 \sim M_2}{SEC}$$

where,

M_1, M_2 = Means of groups

SED = Standard Error Deviation

V. CHI - SQUARE DISTRIBUTION

$$X^2 = \frac{\sum (f_o - f_e)^2}{f_e}$$

Where,

f_o = Observed frequency

f_e = Expected frequency

VI. 'F' - TEST

$$C = \frac{\left(\sum x_1 + \sum x_2 + \sum x_3\right)^2}{N}$$

$$TSS = \sum x_1^2 + \sum x_2^2 + \sum x_3^2 + C$$

$$BSS = \frac{\left(\sum x_1\right)^2}{n_1} + \frac{\left(\sum x_2\right)^2}{n_2} + \frac{\left(\sum x_3\right)^2}{n_3} - C$$

$$WSS = TSS\text{-}BSS$$

$$t_1 = \frac{BSS}{dfB}$$

$$t_2 = \frac{WSS}{dfw}$$

$$f = \frac{t_1}{t_2}$$

Where, C = Correction term

$\sum x_1, \sum x_2, \sum x_3$ = Sum of the scores of each group

N = Total number of the samples

n_1, n_2, n_3 = Number of sample of each group

TSS = Total number of squares

BSS = Sum of squares between the group means.

WSS = Sum of squares within the group

dfB = Degrees of freedom for the between group means

dfw = Degrees of freedom for the within group means

t_1 = Mean sum of squares between the group

t_2 = Mean sum of squares within the group

CONCLUSION

This chapter outlines the design of the present study, the procedures followed and nature of the sample. It describes the hypotheses to be tested, the tools used and the methods of administration and scoring. The collected data were analysed, using appropriate statistical techniques described above to study the value conflict and mental health of students at higher secondary level in relation to their social maturity.

❐

9

Analysis and Interpretation of the Data

Analysis of data involves verification of the hypothesis through testing. The problem raised by the analysis of data are directly related to the complexity of the hypothesis- Good and Hatt.

Research data becomes meaningful in the process of being analysed and interpreted – Mouly.

This chapter presents the results obtained from the analysis of data collected from six different schools based on the variables viz. Value conflict, mental health and social maturity. The data has been subjected to various descriptive and inferential statistics. Association among the different variables was computed. The criterion for the purpose is quartiles. Descriptive analysis for examining mean, median and mode were computed to study the nature of distribution and their support for the use of critical ratio.

CLASSIFICATION OF STUDENTS BASED ON THE VARIABLES OF THE STUDY

Categories of Value Conflicts

Value conflicts have been categorised into six dimensions, viz., fortitude, self - reliance, probity, affection, assertion and idealism. The percentage of these categories is shown below.

TABLE. 9.1: Showing the Criteria of Classifying the Sample based on Categories of Value Conflicts

Dimensions of value conflicts	Percentage
Fortitude	51.7
Self - reliance	62.9
Probity	49.3
Affection	48.7
Assertion	59.3
Idealism	64.6

From the above table, it is clear that the dimension of value conflicts of the higher secondary student is idealism.

Hence, Hypothesis I which states that "The dimension of value conflict is idealism in nature" is accepted.

Categories of Mental Health

The quartile points for the distribution of the mental health score have been computed and those fall above `$Q_3$' are taken as the high group, those below `Q_1' are termed as low mental health group. The moderate group lies in between these two group scores. The details are computed below.

TABLE. 9.2: Showing the Criteria of Classifying the Sample into three Groups of Mental Health

Groups	Mental Health Score range	Number of students	Percentage
Low	0 - 28	44	14.6
Moderate	29 - 39	205	67.9
High	40 - 49	53	17.5
Total		**302**	**100**

It is observed that the mental health of XI standard students is average in nature.

Hence, Hypothesis II which states that "The level of mental health of higher secondary students is average in nature" is accepted.

Categories of Social Maturity

The quartile points for the distribution of social maturity score have been computed and those full above `$Q_3$' are taken in the high group, those below `Q_1' are in the low group. The moderate group lies in between these two group scores. These details of the categories are stated as follows.

Table. 9.3: Showing the criteria of classifying the sample into three groups of social maturity

Groups	Social Maturity Score range	Number of students	Percentage
Low	0 - 28	69	22.8
Moderate	219 - 257	226	74.8
High	258 - 297	7	2.3
Total		**302**	**100**

It is observed that the social maturity of XI Standard students is average in nature.

Hence, Hypothesis III which states that "The level of social maturity of higher secondary students is average in nature" is accepted.

ASSOCIATION BETWEEN VALUE CONFLICTS AND SOCIAL MATURITY

The association between the variables, value conflicts and social maturity has been assessed through chi - square test, the details of which are found in the following table.

Table. 9.4: Showing the Chi - Square Distribution to find out the Association between Value Conflicts and Social Maturity

Value conflicts	Social Maturity			Total
	Low	Moderate	High	
Low	28 (10.5)	17 (34.4)	1 (1.1)	46
Moderate	38 (4.57)	159 (149.7)	3 (4.6)	200
High	3 (12.8)	50 (41.9)	3 (1.3)	56
Total	**69**	**226**	**7**	**302**

$$\chi 2 = \frac{\sum(f_o \quad f_e)}{}$$

$$= 51.67680$$

At df = 4; table value = 13.28 at .01 level

It is observed that the calculated value (51.68) is greater than the standard table value (13.28). So it is clear that there is significant association between the value conflicts and social maturity of students.

Hence, Hypothesis IV which states that "The different dimensions of value conflict viz. fortitude, self - reliance, porbity, affection, assertion and idealism will exhibit different levels of social maturity (ie) low, average and high social maturity among students studying at the higher secondary level" is accepted.

ASSOCIATION BETWEEN MENTAL HEALTH AND SOCIAL MATURITY

The association between the variables, mental health and social maturity has been assessed through chi-square test, the details are computed as follows.

TABLE. 9.5: Showing the Chi - Square Distribution to find out the Association between Mental Health and Social Maturity

Mental Health	Social Maturity			Total
	Low	Moderate	High	
Low	24 (10.05)	19 (32.93)	1 (1.02)	44
Moderate	39 (46.84)	162 (153.41)	4 (4.75)	205
High	6 (12.11)	45 (37.43)	2 (1.23)	53
Total	69	226	7	302

$$\chi 2 = \frac{\sum(f_o - f_e)^2}{f_e}$$

$$= 31.43703$$

At df = 4; table value = 13.28 at .01 level

It is observed that the calculated value (31.44) is greater than the table value (13.28). So it is clear that there is significant association between the mental health and social maturity of students.

Hence, Hypothesis V which states that "The different categories of mental health (ie) low, average and high will exhibit different levels of social maturity" is accepted.

ASSOCIATION BETWEEN VALUE CONFLICTS AND MENTAL HEALTH

The significant association between the variables value conflicts and mental health has been assessed through chi - square test, the details of which are found in the following table.

TABLE. 9.6: Showing the Chi - Square Distribution to find out the Association between Value Conflicts and Mental Health

Value Conflicts	Mental Health			Total
	Low	Moderate	High	
Low	19 (7.46)	24 (30.46)	3 (8.07)	46
Moderate	21 (32.45)	150 (132.45)	29 (35.09)	200
High	4 (9.08)	31 (37.09)	21 (9.83)	56
Total	49	200	53	302

$$\chi 2 = \frac{\sum (f_o - f_e)^2}{f_e}$$

$$= 48.36707$$

At df = 4; table value = 13.28 at .01 level

It is observed that the calculated value (48.37) is greater than the table value (13.28). So it is clear that there is significant association between value conflicts and mental health of students.

Hence, Hypothesis VI which states that "There is significant association between value conflicts and mental health of students studying at the higher secondary level" is accepted.

INFLUENCE OF SEX ON VALUE CONFLICTS

The mean scores of value conflicts of boys and girls have been computed and the difference is tested for significance as shown below.

TABLE. 9.7: Showing the Ssignificant Difference between the mean Scores of value Conflicts of Male and Female XI Standard Students

Group	Number of Students	Mean	Standard Deviation	Standard Error	Critical ratio	Level of Significance
Male	145	75.0000	9.387	.780	1.28	N.S.
Female	157	73.5606	10.167	.811		

The calculated table value (1.28) is less than the standard table value (1.96) at .05 level. So, it is clear that there is no significant difference between themean scores of value conflicts of male and female students.

Hence, Hypothesis VII (a) which states that "There is no significant difference between the mean scores of "value conflicts" of students studying at the higher secondary level with respect to sex" is accepted.

INFLUENCE OF TYPE OF MANAGEMENT OF SCHOOLS ON VALUE CONFLICTS

The mean scores of value conflicts on management of schools have been computed and the difference is tested for significance as shown below.

TABLE. 9.8: ANOVA Showing the Significant Difference between the mean Scores of Value Conflicts with Respect to type of Management of Schools

Source	Degrees of Freedom	Sum of Squares	Mean Squares	F ratio	Level of Significance
Between group	2	3164.3280	1582.1640	18.3327	.01
Within groups	299	25804.5462	86.3028		
Total	**301**	**28968.8742**			

From the above table, the calculated value (18.3327) is greater than the standard table value (4.66) at 0.01 level, it is clear that there is significant difference between the mean scores of value conflicts, with respect to type of management of schools.

On probing further, multiple comparisons of the significant difference of the scores of value conflict among the three type of management of schools have been computed, the details of which are presented below.

TABLE. 9.9: Showing Multiple Comparisons of the Significant Difference of the mean Scores of value Conflicts of Students Studying in Different type of Management of Schools

Groups compared	Number of Students	Mean	Standard Deviation	Standard Error	Critical Ratio	Level of Significance
Government Vs Government Aided	119	71.5630	8.649	.793	1.29	N.S.
	101	73.2178	10.095	1.005		
Government Vs Private	119	71.5630	8.649	.793	6.12	0.01
	82	79.4268	9.153	1.011		
Government Aided Vs Private	101	73.2178	10.095	1.005	4.36	0.01
	82	79.4268	9.153	1.011		

The above table reveals that in the first comparisons, since the calculated `t' value (1.29) is less than the standard table value (1.96), there is no significant difference between the mean scores of value conflicts with respect to type of management of schools.

In the second comparisons, there is significant difference between the mean scores of value conflicts with respect to type of management of schools.

In the third comparisons, there is significant difference between the mean scores of value conflicts with respect to type of management of schools.

Hence, Hypothesis VII (b) which states that "There is no significant difference between the mean scores of "value conflict" of students studying at the higher secondary level with respect to type of management of schools" is partially accepted.

INFLUENCE OF TYPE OF FAMILY ON VALUE CONFLICTS

The mean scores of value conflicts on type of family have been computed and the difference is tested for significance as shown below.

Table. 10.10: Showing the Significant Difference between the mean Scores of value Conflicts with Respect to type of Family

Groups	Number of Students	Mean	Standard Deviation	Standard Error	Critical Ratio	Level of Significance
Nuclear Family	212	74.3491	9.928	.682	0.27	N.S.
Joint family	90	74.0222	9.578	1.010		

The calculated table value (0.27) is less than the standard table value (1.96) so, it is clear that there is no significant difference between the mean scores of value conflicts with respect to type of family.

Hence, Hypothesis VII(c) which states that "There is no significant difference between the mean scores of "value conflicts" of students studying at the higher secondary level with respect to type of family" is accepted.

INFLUENCE OF BIRTH ORDER OF THE CHILD ON VALUE CONFLICTS

The obtained scores of value conflicts on birth order of the child have been computed and the difference is tested for significance as shown below.

TABLE. 9.11: ANOVA showing the Significant Difference between the mean Scores of value Conflicts with Respect to Birth Order of the Child

Source	Degrees of Freedom	Sum of Squares	Mean Squares	F ratio	Level of Significance
Between groups	2	.5590	.2795	0.8265	N.S.
Within groups	299	101.1099	.3382		
Total	**301**	**101.6689**			

The calculated table value (0.8265) is less than the standard table value (3.02) so, it is clear that there is no significant difference between the mean scores of value conflicts with respect to birth order of the child.

Hence, Hypothesis VII (d) which states that "There is no significant difference between the mean scores o f "value conflicts" of student studying at the higher secondary level with respect to birth order of the child" is accepted.

INFLUENCE OF FATHER'S EDUCATIONAL QUALIFICATION ON VALUE CONFLICTS

The mean scores of value conflicts on father's educational qualification have been computed and the difference is tested for significance as shown below.

TABLE. 9.12: ANOVA Showing the Significant Difference between the mean Scores of Value Conflicts with Respect to Father's Educational Qualification

Source	Degrees of Freedom	Sum of Squares	Mean Squares	F ratio	Level of Significance
Between groups	2	135.1930	67.5965	.7010	N.S.
Within groups	299	28833. 6812	96.4337		
Total	301	28968. 8742			

The calculated table value (0.7010) is less than the standard table value (3.02) so, it is clear that there is no significant difference between the mean scores of value conflicts with respect to father's educational qualification.

Hence, Hypothesis VII (e) which states that "There is no significant difference between the mean scores of "value conflicts" of student studying at higher secondary level with respect to father's educational qualification" is accepted.

INFLUENCE OF MOTHER'S EDUCATIONAL QUALIFICATION ON VALUE CONFLICTS

The obtained scores of value conflicts on Mother's educational qualification have been computed and the difference is tested for significant as shown below.

TABLE. 9.13: ANOVA showing the Significant Difference between the mean Scores of value Conflicts with Respect to Mother's Educational Qualification

Source	Degrees of Freedom	Sum of Squares	Mean Squares	F ratio	Level of Significance
Between goups	2	2115.5335	1057.7717	11.7778	.01
Within groups	299	26853.3307	89.8105		
Total	**301**	**28968. 8742**			

From the above the calculated table value (11.778) is greater than the standard table value (4.66) at .01 level it is clear that there is significant difference between the mean scores of value conflicts with respect to mother's educational qualification.

On probing further, multiple comparisons of the significant difference between the mean scores of value conflicts among the three groups of mother's educational qualification have been computed, the details of which are presented below.

TABLE. 9.14: Showing Multiple Comparisons of the Significant Difference of the mean Scores of value Conflicts of Students with Respect to Mothers Educational Qualification

Groups compared	Number of Students	Mean	Standard Deviation	Standard Error	Critical Ratio	Level of Significance
Illiterate Vs School Level	24	71.3750	8.899	1.817	1.11	N.S.
	242	73.4917	9.457	.608		
Illiterate Vs College Level	24	71.3750	8.899	1.817	4.48	.01
	36	81.2778	9.967	1.661		
School Level Vs College Level	242	73.4917	9.457	.608	4.40	.01
	36	81.2778	9.967	1.661		

The above table reveals that in the first comparisons, since the calculated \`t' value (1.11) less than the standard table value (1.96) at .05 levels, so it is clear that there is no significant difference between the mean scores of value conflict with respect to mother's educational qualification.

In the second comparisons, the calculated table value is (4.48) greater than the standard table value (2.58) at .01 level, so it is clear that there is significant difference between the mean scores of value conflict with respect to mother's educational qualification.

In the third comparison, the calculated table value is (4.40) greater than the standard table value (2.58) at .01 level, so it is clear that there is significant difference between the mean scores of value conflict with respect to mother's educational qualification.

Hence, Hypothesis VII (f) which states that "There is no significant difference between the mean scores of "value conflicts" of students studying at higher secondary level with respect to mother's educational qualification" is partially accepted.

INFLUENCE OF FATHER'S MONTHLY INCOME ON VALUE CONFLICTS

The obtained scores of value conflict with respect to father's monthly income have been computed as the difference is tested for significance as shown below.

TABLE. 9.15: Showing the Significant Difference between the mean Scores of value Conflicts with Respect to Father's Monthly Income

Group	Number of Students	Mean	Standard Deviation	Standard Error	Critical ratio	Level of Significance
Less than Rs.3,000	87	73.4713	9.417	1.010	0.90	N.S
Above Rs.3,000	215	74.5674	9.969	.680		

The calculated table value (0.90) is less than the standard table value (1.96) at .05 level, so it is clear that there is no significant difference between the mean scores of value conflicts with respect to father's monthly income.

Hence, Hypothesis VII (g) which states that "There is no significant difference between the mean scores of "value conflicts" of students studying at higher secondary level with respect to father's monthly income" is accepted.

INFLUENCE OF MOTHER'S MONTHLY INCOME ON VALUE CONFLICTS

The obtained scores of value conflict with respect to mother's monthly income have been computed as the difference is tested for significance as shown below.

TABLE. 9.16: Showing the Significant Difference between the mean Scores of Value Conflicts with Respect to Mother's Monthly Income

Group	Number of Students	Mean	Standard Deviation	Standard Error	Critical ratio	Level of Significance
Less than Rs.3,000	275	73.5745	9.623	.580	4.08	N.S.
Above Rs.3,000	27	81.1481	9.164	1.764		

The calculated table value (4.08) is less than the standard table value (1.96) so it is clear that there is no significant difference between the mean scores of value conflicts with respect to mother's monthly income.

Hence, Hypothesis VII (h) which states that "There is no significant difference between the mean scores of "value conflicts" of students studying at higher secondary level with respect to mother's monthly income" is accepted.

INFLUENCE OF SEX ON FORTITUDE

The mean scores of fortitude of boys and girls have been computed and the difference is tested for significance as shown below.

TABLE. 9.17: Showing the Significant Difference between the mean Scores of Fortitude of Male and Female XI Standard Students

Group	Number of Students	Mean	Standard Deviation	Standard Error	Critical ratio	Level of Significance
Male	145	12.7862	2.366	.197	2.19	0.05
Female	157	12.1911	2.351	.188		

The calculated table value (2.19) is greater than the standard table value (1.96), so it is clear that there is significant difference between the mean scores of fortitude of male and female students.

Hence, Hypothesis VIII (a) which states that "There is no significant difference between the mean scores of "fortitude" of students studying at the higher secondary level with respect to sex" is rejected.

INFLUENCE OF TYPE OF MANAGEMENT OF SCHOOLS ON FORTITUDE

The mean scores of fortitude on management of schools have been computed and the difference is tested for significance as shown below.

TABLE. 9.18: ANOVA Showing the Significant Difference between the Mean Scores of Fortitude with Respect to Type of Management of Schools

Source	Degrees of freedom	Sum of Squares	Mean Squares	F ratio	Level of Significance
Between groups	2	98.3451	49.1725	9.2064	.01
With in groups	299	1596.9927	5.3411		
Total	**301**	**1695.3377**			

From the above, the calculated table value (9.0264) is greater than the standard table value (4.66) at .01 level, it is clear that there is significant difference between the mean scores of fortitude with respect to type of management of schools.

On probing further, multiple comparisons of the significant difference of the scores of fortitude among the three types of management of schools have been computed, the details of which are presented below.

TABLE. 9.19: Showing Multiple Comparisons of the Significant Difference of the Mean Scores of Fortitude of Students Studying in Different type of Management of Schools

Groups compared	Number of Students	Mean	Standard Deviation	Standard Error	Critical Ratio	Level of Significance
Government Vs Government Aided	119	12.4118	2.039	.187	1.89	N.S.
	101	11.8614	2.245	.223		
Government Vs Private	119	12.4118	2.039	.187	2.59	0.01
	82	13.3293	2.726	.301		
Government Aided Vs Private	101	11.8614	2.245	.223	3.92	0.01
	82	13.3283	2.726	.301		

The above table reveals that in the first comparison, since the calculated `t' value (1.89) is less than standard table value (1.96) at .05 level, there is no significant difference between the mean scores of fortitude with respect to type of management of schools.

In the second comparison there is significant difference between the mean scores of fortitude with respect to type of management of school. In the third comparison, there is significant difference between the mean scores of fortitude with respect to type of management of schools.

Hence, Hypothesis VIII (b) which states that "There is no significant difference between the mean scores of "fortitude" of students studying at the higher secondary level with respect to type of management of schools" is partially accepted.

INFLUENCE OF TYPE OF FAMILY ON FORTITUDE

The mean scores of fortitude on type of family have been computed and the difference is tested for significance as shown below.

TABLE. 9.20: Showing the Significant Difference Between the mean Scores of Fortitude with Respect to Type of Family

Group	Number of Students	Mean	Standard Deviation	Standard Error	Critical ratio	Level of Significance
Nuclear Family	212	12.4434	2.444	.168	.39	N.S.
Joint Family	90	12.5556	2.209	.233		

The calculated table value (0.39) is less than the standard table value (1.96) at .05 level so it is clear that there is no significant difference between the mean scores of fortitude with respect to type of family.

Hence, Hypothesis VIII(c) which states that "There is no significant difference between the mean scores of "fortitude" of students studying at the higher secondary level with respect to type of family" as accepted.

INFLUENCE OF BIRTH ORDER OF THE CHILD ON FORTITUDE

The mean scores of fortitude on birth order of the child have been computed and the difference is tested for significance as shown below.

TABLE. 9.21: ANOVA Showing the Significant Difference Between the mean Scores of Fortitude with Respect to Birth Order of the Child

Source	Degrees of freedom	Sum of Squares	Mean Squares	F ratio	Level of Significance
Between groups	2	13.1030	6.5515	1.2450	N.S.
With in groups	299	1682.2341	5.2620		
Total	**301**	**1695.3377**			

The calculated table value (1.2450) is less than the standard table value (3.02) at .05 level so it is clear that there is no significant difference between the mean scores of fortitude with respect to birth order of the child.

Hence, Hypothesis VIII(d) which states that "There is no significant difference between the mean scores of "fortitude" of students studying at the higher secondary level with respect to birth order of the child" as accepted.

INFLUENCE OF FATHER'S EDUCATIONAL QUALIFICATION ON FORTITUDE

The mean scores of fortitude with respect to father's educational qualification have been computed and the difference is tested for significance as shown below.

TABLE. 9.22: ANOVA Showing the Significant Difference Between the mean Scores of Fortitude with Respect to Father's Educational Qualification

Source	Degrees of freedom	Sum of Squares	Mean Squares	F ratio	Level of Significance
Between groups	2	12.4182	6.2091	1.1032	N.S.
Within groups	299	1682.9196	5.6285		
Total	301	1695.3377			

The calculated table value (1.1032) is less than the standard table value (3.02) at .05 level so it is clear that there is no significant difference between the mean scores of fortitude with respect to father's educational qualification.

Hence, Hypothesis VIII(e) which states that "There is no significant difference between the mean scores of "fortitude" of students studying at the higher secondary level with respect to father's educational qualification" as accepted.

INFLUENCE OF MOTHER'S EDUCATIONAL QUALIFICATION ON FORTITUDE

The mean scores of fortitude with respect to mother's educational qualification have been computed and the difference is tested for significance as shown below.

Table. 9.23: ANOVA Showing the Significant Difference between the mean Scores of Fortitude with Respect to Mother's Educational Qualification

Source	Degrees of freedom	Sum of Squares	Mean Squares	F ratio	Level of Significance
Between groups	2	20.9454	10.4727		
Within groups	299	1674.3923	5.6000	1.8701	N.S.
Total	**301**	**1695.3377**			

The calculated table value (1.8701) is less than the standard table value (1.96) at .05 level so it is clear that there is no significant difference between the mean scores of fortitude with respect the mother's educational qualification.

Hence, Hypothesis VIII (f) which states that "There is no significant difference between the mean scores of "fortitude" of students studying at the higher secondary level with respect to mother's educational qualification" as accepted.

INFLUENCE OF FATHER'S MONTHLY INCOME ON FORTITUDE

The mean scores of fortitude with respect to father's monthly income have been computed and the difference is tested for significance as shown below.

TABLE. 9.24: Showing the Significant Difference between the mean Scores of Fortitude with Respect to Father's Monthly Income

Group	Number of Students	Mean	Standard Deviation	Standard Error	Critical ratio	Level of Significance
Less than Rs.3000	87	12.1839	2.143	.230	1.45	N.S.
Above Rs.3000	215	12.5953	2.455	.167		

The calculated table value (1.45) is less than the standard table value (1.96) at .05 level so it is clear that there is no significant difference between the mean scores of fortitude with respect the father's monthly income.

Hence, Hypothesis VIII (g) which states that "There is no significant difference between the mean scores of "fortitude" of students studying at the higher secondary level with respect to father's monthly income" as accepted.

INFLUENCE OF MOTHER'S MONTHLY INCOME ON FORTITUDE

The mean scores of fortitude with respect to mother's monthly income have been computed and the difference is tested for significance as shown below.

TABLE. 9.25: Showing the Significant Difference Between the mean Scores of Fortitude with Respect to Mother's Monthly Income

Source	Number of Students	Mean	Standard Deviation	Standard Error	Critical ratio	Level of Significance
Less than Rs.3000	275	12.3818	2.362	.142	2.28	0.05
Above Rs.3000	27	13.4444	2.309	.444		

The calculated table value (2.28) is greater than the standard table value (1.96). So it is clear that there is significant difference between the mean scores of fortitude with respect to mother's monthly income.

Hence, Hypothesis VIII (h) which states that "There is no significant difference between the mean scores of "fortitude" of students studying at higher secondary level with respect to mother's monthly income" as accepted.

INFLUENCE OF SEX ON SELF-RELIANCE

The mean scores of self-reliance of boys and girls have been computed and the difference is tested for significance as shown below.

TABLE. 9.26: Showing the Significant Difference Between the mean Scores of Self-Reliance of Male and Female XI Standard Students

Group	Number of Students	Mean	Standard Deviation	Standard Error	Critical ratio	Level of Significance
Male	145	12.2276	2.463	.205	1.80	NS
Female	157	11.7389	2.231	.178		

The calculated table value (1.80) is less than the standard table value (1.96) at .05 level. So it is clear that there is significant difference between the mean scores of self-reliance of male and female students.

Hence, Hypothesis VIII (h) which states that "There is no significant difference between the mean scores of "self-reliance" of students studying at the higher secondary level with respect to sex" is accepted.

INFLUENCE OF TYPE OF MANAGEMENT OF SCHOOLS ON SELF-RELIANCE

The mean scores of self - reliance of students on management of schools have been computed and the difference is tested for significance as shown below.

TABLE. 9.27: ANOVA Showing the Significant Difference Between the mean Scores of Self - Reliance with Respect to Type of Management

Source	Degrees of freedom	Sum of Squares	Mean Squares	F ratio	Level of Signifi-cance
Between groups	2	52.9329	26.4664	4.9004	0.01
With in groups	299	1614.8552	5.4009		
Total	**301**	**1667.7881**			

From the above, the calculated table value (4.9004) is greater than the standard table value (4.66), so it is clear that there is significant difference between the mean scores of self - reliance.

On probing further, multiple comparison of the significant difference of the scores of self - reliance among the three types of management of schools have been computed, the details of which are presented below.

TABLE. 9.28: Showing Multiple Comparisons of the Significant Difference of the mean Scores of Self - Reliance of Students Studying in Different Type of Management of Schools

Groups compared	Number of Students	Mean	Standard Deviation	Standard Error	Critical Ratio	Level of Significance
Government Vs Government Aided	119	11.6975	1.968	.180	0.15	N.S.
	101	11.7426	2.390	.238		
Government Vs Private	119	11.6975	1.968	.180	2.76	0.01
	82	12.6585	2.691	.297		
Government Aided Vs Private	101	11.7426	2.390	.238	2.42	0.05
	82	12.6585	2.691	.297		

The above table reveals that in the first comparison, since the calculated `t' value (0.15) is less than standard table value (1.96) at .05 level, there is no significant difference between the mean scores of self - reliance with respect to management of schools.

In the second comparison, there is significant difference between the mean scores of self - reliance with respect to type of management.

In the third comparison, there is significant difference between the mean scores of self - reliance with respect to type of management.

Hence, Hypothesis IX (b) which states that "There is no significant difference between the mean scores of "self - reliance" of students studying at the higher secondary level with respect to type of management of schools" is partially accepted.

INFLUENCE OF TYPE OF FAMILY ON SELF - RELIANCE

The mean scores of self - reliance of students on type of family have been computed and the difference is tested for significance as shown below.

TABLE.9.29: Showing the Significant Difference between the mean Scores of Self - Reliance with Respect to Type of Family

Group	Number of Students	Mean	Standard Deviation	Standard Error	Critical ratio	Level of Significance
Nuclear family	212	12.0377	2.322	.159	0.71	N.S.
Joint family	90	11.8222	2.434	.257		

The calculated table value (0.71) is less than the standard table value (1.96) so it is clear that there is no significant difference between the mean scores of self - reliance with respect to type of family.

Hence, Hypothesis IX(c) which states that "There is no significant difference between the mean scores of "self-reliance" of students studying at the higher secondary level with respect to type of family" is accepted.

INFLUENCE OF BIRTH ORDER OF THE CHILD ON SELF - RELIANCE

The mean scores of self - reliance of students with respect to birth order of the child have been computed and the difference is tested for significance as shown below.

TABLE. 9.30: ANOVA Showing the Significant Difference Between the mean Scores of Self - Reliance with Respect to Birth Order of the Child

Source	Degrees of freedom	Sum of Squares	Mean Squares	F ratio	Level of Significance
Between groups	2	6.1971	3.0985	.5575	N.S.
Within groups	299	1661.5910	5.5571		
Total	**301**	**1667.7881**			

The calculated table value (.5575) is less than the standard table value (3.02), so it is clear that there is no significant difference between the mean scores of self - reliance with respect to birth order of the child.

Hence, Hypothesis IX (d) which states that "There is no significant difference between the mean scores of "self-reliance" of students studying at the higher secondary level with respect to birth order of the child" is accepted.

INFLUENCE OF FATHER'S EDUCATIONAL QUALIFICATION ON SELF - RELIANCE

The mean scores of self - reliance of students with respect to father's educational qualification have been computed and difference is tested for significance as shown below.

TABLE. 9.31: ANOVA Showing the Significant Difference Between the mean Scores of Self-Reliance with Respect to Father's Educational qualification

Source	Degrees of freedom	Sum of Squares	Mean Squares	F ratio	Level of Significance
Between groups	2	2.5643	1.2821		
Within groups	299	1665.2238	5.5693	.2302	N.S.
Total	**301**	**1667.7881**			

The calculated table value (.2302) is less than the standard table value (1.96), so it is clear that there is no significant difference between the mean scores of self - reliance with respect to father's educational qualification.

Hence, Hypothesis IX (e) which states that "There is no significant difference between the mean scores of "self-reliance" of students studying at the higher secondary level with respect to father's educational qualification" is accepted.

INFLUENCE OF MOTHER'S EDUCATIONAL QUALIFICATION ON SELF - RELIANCE

The mean scores of self - reliance of students with respect to mother's educational qualification have been computed and the difference is tested for significance as shown below.

TABLE. 9.32: ANOVA Showing the Significant Difference Between the Mean Scores of Self - Reliance with Respect to Mother's Educational Qualification

Source	Degrees of freedom	Sum of Squares	Mean Squares	F ratio	Level of Significance
Between groups	2	27.2645	13.6323	2.4846	N.S.
Within groups	299	1640.5235	5.4867		
Total	301	1667.7881			

The calculated table value (2.4846) is less than the standard table value (3.02) at .05 level, so it is clear that there is no significant difference between the mean scores of self reliance with respect to mother's educational qualification.

Hence, Hypothesis IX(f) which states that "There is no significant difference between the mean scores of "self-reliance" of students studying at the higher secondary level with respect to mother's educational qualification" is accepted.

INFLUENCE OF FATHER'S MONTHLY INCOME ON SELF- RELIANCE

The mean scores of self - reliance of students with respect to father's monthly income have been computed and the difference is tested for significance as shown below.

TABLE. 9.33: Showing the Significant Difference between the mean Scores of Self - Reliance with Respect to Father's Monthly Income

Group	Number of Students	Mean	Standard Deviation	Standard Error	Critical ratio	Level of Significance
Less than Rs.3000	87	12.2759	2.182	.234	1.48	N.S.
Above Rs.3000	215	11.8512	2.414	.165		

The calculated table value (1.48) is less than the standard table value (1.96), so it is clear that there is no significant difference between the mean scores of self - reliance of students with respect to father's monthly income.

Hence, Hypothesis IX(g) which states that "There is no significant difference between the mean scores of "self-reliance" of students studying at the higher secondary level with respect to father's monthly income" is accepted.

INFLUENCE OF MOTHER'S MONTHLY INCOME ON SELF- RELIANCE

The mean scores of self - reliance of students with respect to mother's monthly income have been computed and the difference is tested for significance as shown below.

TABLE. 9.34: Showing the Significant Difference Between the mean Scores of Self - Reliance with Respect to Mother's Monthly Income

Group	Number of Students	Mean	Standard Deviation	Standard Error	Critical ratio	Level of Significance
Less than Rs.3000	275	11.8873	2.300	.139	1.77	N.S.
Above Rs.3000	27	12.8519	2.741	.528		

The calculated table value (1.77) is less than the standard table value (1.96), so it is clear that there is no significant difference between the mean scores of self - reliance of students with respect to mother's monthly income.

Hence, Hypothesis IX (h) which states that "There is no significant difference between the mean scores of "self-reliance" of students studying at the higher secondary level with respect to mother's monthly income" is accepted.

INFLUENCE OF SEX ON PROBITY

The mean scores of probity of boy's and girl's have been computed and the difference is tested for significance as shown below.

TABLE. 9.35: Showing the Significant Difference Between the mean Scores of Probity of Male and Female XI Standard Students

Group	Number of Students	Mean	Standard Deviation	Standard Error	Critical ratio	Level of Significance
Male	145	13.0069	2.747	.228	0.55	N.S.
Female	157	13.1847	2.826	.226		

The calculated table value (0.55) is less than the standard table value (1.96) at .05 level, so it is clear that there is no significant difference between the mean scores of probity of male and female students.

Hence, Hypothesis X (a) which states that "There is no significant difference between the mean scores of "probity" of students studying at the higher secondary level with respect to sex" is accepted.

INFLUENCE OF TYPE OF MANAGEMENT OF SCHOOLS ON PROBITY

The mean scores of probity of students on type of management of schools have been computed and the difference is tested for significance as shown below.

TABLE .9.36: ANOVA Showing the Significant Differencc between the mean Scores of Probity with Respect to Type of Management of Schools

Source	Degrees of freedom	Sum of Squares	Mean Squares	F ratio	Level of Significance
Between groups	2	116.5562	58.2781	7.8546	.01
Within groups	299	2218.4637	7.4196		
Total	**301**	**2335.0199**			

From the above table, the calculated table value (7.8546) is greater than the standard table value (4.66) at .01 level, so it is clear that there is significant difference on the mean scores of probity.

On probing further, multiple comparison of the significant difference of the scores of probity among the three types of management of schools have been computed, the details of which are presented below.

TABLE. 9.37: Showing Multiple Comparisons of the Significant Difference of the mean Scores of Probity of Students Studying in Different type of Management of Schools

Groups compared	Number of Students	Mean	Standard Deviation	Standard Error	Critical Ratio	Level of Significance
Government Vs Government Aided	119	12.5042	2.494	.229	1.42	N.S.
	101	13.0297	2.920	.291		
Government Vs Private	119	12.5042	2.494	.229	4.02	0.01
	82	14.0488	2.793	.308		
Government Aided Vs Private	101	13.0297	2.920	.291	2.41	0.05
	82	14.0488	2.793	.308		

The above table reveals that in the first comparison, the calculated table value (1.42) is less than the standard table value (1.96) at .05 level, so there is no significant difference of the mean scores of probity with respect to type of management of schools.

In the second comparison, there is significant difference of the mean scores of probity with respect to type of management.

In the third comparison, there is significant difference of the mean scores of probity with respect to type of management.

Hence, Hypothesis X (b) which states that "There is no significant difference between the mean scores of "probity" of students studying at the higher secondary level with respect to type of management of schools" is partially accepted.

INFLUENCE OF TYPE OF FAMILY ON PROBITY

The mean scores of probity of students on type of family have been computed and the difference is tested for significance as shown below.

TABLE. 9.38: Showing the Significant Difference between the mean Scores of Probity with Respect to Type of Family

Group	Number of Students	Mean	Standard Deviation	Standard Error	Critical ratio	Level of Significance
Nuclear family	212	13.1557	2.891	.199	0.57	N.S.
Joint family	90	12.9667	2.528	.267		

The calculated table value (0.57) is less than the standard table value (1.96), so it is clear that there is no significant difference between mean scores of probity with respect to type of family.

Hence, Hypothesis X(c) which states that "There is no significant difference between the mean scores of "probity" of students studying at the higher secondary level with respect to type of family" is accepted.

INFLUENCE OF BIRTH ORDER OF THE CHILD ON PROBITY

The mean scores of probity of students with respect to birth order of the child have been computed and the difference is tested for significance as shown below.

TABLE. 9.39: ANOVA Showing the Significant Difference Between mean Scores of Probity with Respect to Birth Order of the Child

Source	Degrees of freedom	Sum of Squares	Mean Squares	F ratio	Level of Significance
Between groups	2	50.8926	25.4463	2.9454	N.S.
Within groups	299	2284.1273	8.6392		
Total	**301**	**2335.0199**			

The calculated table value (2.9454) is less than the standard table value (3.02) at .05 level, so it is clear that there is no significant difference between the mean scores of probity with respect to birth order of the child.

Hence, Hypothesis X (d) which states that "There is no significant difference between the mean scores of "probity" of students studying at the higher secondary level with respect to birth order of the child" is accepted.

INFLUENCE OF FATHER'S EDUCATIONAL QUALIFICATION ON PROBITY

The mean scores of probity of students with respect to father's educational qualification have been computed and difference is tested for significance as shown below.

TABLE. 9.40: ANOVA Showing the Significant Difference Between the mean scores of Probity with Respect to Father's Educational Qualification

Source	Degrees of freedom	Sum of Squares	Mean Squares	F ratio	Level of Significance
Between groups	2	6.2197	3.1099	.3993	N.S.
Within groups	299	2328.8002	7.7886		
Total	**301**	**2335.0199**			

The calculated table value (.3993) is less than the standard table value (3.02) at .05 level, so it is clear that there is no significant difference between the mean scores of probity with respect to father's educational qualification.

Hence, Hypothesis X (e) which states that "There is no significant difference between the mean scores of "probity" of students studying at the higher secondary level with respect to father's educational qualification" is accepted.

INFLUENCE OF MOTHER'S EDUCATIONAL QUALIFICATION ON PROBITY

The mean scores of probity of students with respect to mother's educational qualification have been computed and the difference is tested for significance as shown below.

TABLE. 9.41: ANOVA Showing the Significant Difference between mean Scores of Probity with Respect to Mother's Educational Qualification

Source	Degrees of freedom	Sum of Squares	Mean Squares	F ratio	Level of Significance
Between groups	2	90.0250	45.0125	5.9950	.01
Within groups	299	2244.9948	7.5083		
Total	**301**	**2335.0199**			

From the above, the calculated table value (5.9950) is greater than the standard table value (4.66) at .01 level, so it is clear that there is significant difference between on the mean scores of probity with respect to mother's educational qualification.

On probing further, multiple comparison of the significant difference of the scores of probity among the three levels of mother's educational qualification have been computed, the details of which are presented below.

Table. 9.42: Showing Multiple Comparisons of the Significant Difference of the mean Scores of Probity of Students with Respect to Mother's Educational Qualification

Groups compared	Number of Students	Mean	Standard Deviation	Standard Error	Critical Ratio	Level of Significance
Illiterate Vs School Level	24	12.8750	2.755	.562	0.04	N.S.
	242	12.9008	2.653	.171		
Illiterate Vs College Level	24	12.8750	2.755	.562	2.18	0.05
	36	14.5833	3.272	.545		
School Level Vs College Level	242	12.9008	2.653	.171	2.94	0.01
	36	14.5833	3.272	.545		

The above table reveals that in the first comparison, since the calculated `t' value (0.04) less than the standard table value (1.96) there is no significant difference between the mean scores of probity with respect to mother's educational qualification.

In the second comparison, there is significant difference of the mean scores of probity with respect to mother's educational qualification.

In the third comparison, there is significant difference of the mean scores of probity with respect to mother's educational qualification.

Hence, Hypothesis X (f) which states that "There is no significant difference between the mean scores of "probity" of students studying at higher secondary level with respect to mother's educational qualification" is partially accepted.

INFLUENCE OF FATHER'S MONTHLY INCOME ON PROBITY

The mean scores of probity of students with respect to father's monthly income have been computed and the difference is tested for significance as shown below.

TABLE. 9.43: Showing the Significant Difference Between the mean Scores of Probity with Respect to Father's Monthly Income

Group	Number of Students	Mean	Standard Deviation	Standard Error	Critical ratio	Level of Significance
Less than Rs.3000	87	12.8506	2.855	.306	0.97	N.S.
Above Rs.3000	215	13.2000	2.757	.188		

The calculated table value (0.97) is less than the standard table value (1.96) at .05 level, so it is clear that there is no significant difference between the mean scores of probity of students with respect to father's monthly income.

Hence, Hypothesis X (g) which states that "There is no significant difference between the mean scores of "probity" of students studying at higher secondary level with respect to father's monthly income" is accepted.

INFLUENCE OF MOTHER'S MONTHLY INCOME ON PROBITY

The mean scores of probity of students with respect to mother's monthly income have been computed and the difference is tested for significance as shown below.

TABLE. 9.44: Showing the Significant Difference Between the mean Scores of Probity with Respect to Mother's Monthly Income

Group	Number of Students	Mean	Standard Deviation	Standard Error	Critical ratio	Level of Significance
Less than Rs.3000	275	12.9455	2.738	.165	3.03	0.01
Above Rs.3000	27	14.6667	2.828	.544		

The calculated table value (3.03) is less than the standard table value (2.58) at .01 level, so it is clear that there is no significant difference between the mean scores of probity of students with respect to mother's monthly income.

Hence, Hypothesis X (h) which states that "There is no significant difference between the mean scores of "probity" of students studying at higher secondary level with respect to mother's monthly income" is rejected.

INFLUENCE OF SEX ON AFFECTION

The mean scores of affection of boys and girls have been computed and the difference is tested for significance as shown below.

TABLE. 9.45: Showing the Significant Difference Between the mean Scores of Affection of Male and Female XI Standard Students

Group	Number of Students	Mean	Standard Deviation	Standard Error	Critical ratio	Level of Significance
Male	145	12.9379	2.644	.220	0.20	N.S.
Female	157	12.8726	3.012	.240		

The calculated table value (0.20) is less than the standard table value (1.96), so it is clear that there is no significant difference between the mean scores of affection of male and female students.

Hence, Hypothesis XI (a) which states that "There is no significant difference between the mean scores of "affection" of students studying at higher secondary level with respect to sex" is accepted.

INFLUENCE OF TYPE OF MANAGEMENT OF SCHOOLS ON AFFECTION

The mean scores of affection of students on type of management of schools have been computed and the difference is tested for significance as shown below.

TABLE. 9.46: ANOVA Showing the Significant Difference between the Mean Scores of Affection with Respect to Type of Management of Schools

Source	Degrees of freedom	Sum of Squares	Mean Squares	F ratio	Level of Significance
Between groups	2	342.9841	171.4921	24.6611	.01
With in groups	299	2079.2311	6.9540		
Total	**301**	**2422.2152**			

From the above table, the calculated value (24.6611) is greater than the standard table value (4.66) at .01 level, so it is clear that there is significant difference on the mean scores of affection with respect to type of management.

On probing further, multiple comparison of the significant difference of the scores of affection among the three types of management of schools have been computed, the details of which are presented below.

TABLE. 9.47: Showing Multiple Comparisons of the Significant Difference of the mean Scores of Affection of Students Studying in Different Types of Management of Schools

Groups compared	Number of Students	Mean	Standard Deviation	Standard Error	Critical Ratio	Level of Significance
Government Vs Government Aided	119	12.1849	2.610	.239	0.43	N.S.
	101	12.3366	2.551	.254		
Government Vs Private	119	12.1849	2.610	.239	6.33	0.01
	82	14.6463	2.777	.307		
Government Aided Vs Private	101	12.3366	2.551	.254	5.80	0.01
	82	14.6463	2.777	.307		

The above table reveals that in the first comparison, the calculated table value (0.43) is less than the standard table value (1.96) at .05 level, so there is no significant difference of the mean scores of affection with respect to management of schools.

In the second comparison, there is significant difference of the mean scores of affection with respect to type of management.

In the third comparison, there is significant difference of the mean scores of affection with respect to type of management.

Hence, Hypothesis XI (b) which states that "There is no significant difference between the mean scores of "affection" of students studying at the higher secondary level with respect to type of management of schools" is partially accepted.

INFLUENCE OF TYPE OF FAMILY ON AFFECTION

The mean scores of affection of students on type of family have been computed and the difference is tested for significance as shown below.

TABLE. 9.48: Showing the Significant Difference Between mean Scores of Affection with Respect to Type of Family

Group	Number of Students	Mean	Standard Deviation	Standard Error	Critical ratio	Level of Significance
Nuclear family	212	12.9198	2.901	.199	0.15	N.S.
Joint family	90	12.8667	2.695	.284		

The calculated table value (0.15) is less than the standard table value (1.96) at .05 level, so it is clear that there is no significant difference between the mean scores of affection with respect to type of family.

Hence, Hypothesis XI(c) which states that, "There is no significant difference between the mean scores of "affection" of students studying at the higher secondary level with respect to type of family" is accepted.

INFLUENCE OF BIRTH ORDER OF THE CHILD ON AFFECTION

The mean scores of affection of students with respect to birth order of the child have been computed and the difference is tested for significance as shown below.

TABLE-49: ANOVA Showing the Significant Difference Between the mean Scores of Affection with Respect to Type of Birth Order of the Child

Source	Degrees of freedom	Sum of Squares	Mean Squares	F ratio	Level of Significance
Between groups	2	17.1544	8.5772	1.0663	N.S.
With in groups	299	2405.0608	8.0436		
Total	**301**	**2422.2152**			

The calculated table value (1.0663) is less than the standard table value (3.02) of .05 level so it is clear that the mean scores of affection with respect to birth order of the child.

Hence, Hypothesis XI (d) which states that "There is no significant difference between the mean scores of "affection" of students studying at the higher secondary level with respect to birth order of the child" is accepted.

INFLUENCE OF FATHER'S EDUCATIONAL QUALIFICATION ON AFFECTION

The mean scores of affection of students with respect to father's educational qualification have been computed and the difference is tested for significance as shown below.

TABLE. 9.50: ANOVA Showing the Significant Difference Between mean Scores of Affection with Respect to Father's Educational Qualification

Source	Degrees of freedom	Sum of Squares	Mean Squares	F ratio	Level of Significance
Between groups	2	9.9356	4.9678	.6158	N.S.
Within groups	299	2412.2797	8.0678		
Total	**301**	**2422.2152**			

The calculated table value (.6158) is less than the standard table value (3.02) of .05 level, so it is clear that there is no significant difference between the mean scores of affection with respect to father's educational qualification.

Hence, Hypothesis XI (e) which states that "There is no significant difference between scores of "affection" of students studying at higher secondary level with respect to father's educational qualification" is accepted.

INFLUENCE OF MOTHER'S EDUCATIONAL QUALIFICATION ON AFFECTION

The mean scores of affection of students on mother's educational qualification have been computed and the difference is tested for significance as shown below.

TABLE. 9.51: ANOVA Showing the Significant Difference Between the Mean Scores of Affection with Respect to Mother's Educational Qualification

Source	Degrees of freedom	Sum of Squares	Mean Squares	F ratio	Level of Significance
Between groups	2	128.6022	64.3011		
Within groups	299	2293.6131	7.6709	8.3824	.01
Total	301	2422.2153			

From the above, the calculated table value (5.9950) is greater than the standard table value (2.58) at .01 level, so it is clear that there is significant difference on the mean scores of affection with respect to mother's educational qualification.

On probing further, multiple comparison of the significant difference of the scores of affection among the three levels of educational qualification have been computed, the details of which are presented below.

TABLE. 9.52: Showing Multiple Comparisons of the Significant Difference of the mean Scores of Affection of Students with Respect to Mother's Educational Qualification

Groups compared	Number of Students	Mean	Standard Deviation	Standard Error	Critical Ratio	Level of Significance
Illiterate Vs School Level	24	11.8750	2.328	.475	1.74	N.S.
	242	12.7603	2.808	.180		
Illiterate Vs College Level	24	11.8750	2.328	.475	4.04	0.01
	36	14.5556	2.772	.462		
School Level Vs College Level	242	12.7603	2.808	.180	3.62	0.01
	36	14.556	2.772	.462		

The above table reveals that in the first comparison, since the calculated `t' value (1.74) is less than the standard table value (1.96) there is no significant difference between the mean scores of affection with respect to mother's educational qualification.

In the second comparison, there is significant difference of the mean scores of affection with respect to mother's educational qualification.

In the third comparison, there is significant difference of the mean scores of affection with respect to mother's educational qualification.

Hence, Hypothesis XI (f) which states that "There is no significant difference between the mean scores of "affection" of students studying at higher secondary level with respect to mother's educational qualification" is partially accepted.

INFLUENCE OF FATHER'S MONTHLY INCOME ON AFFECTION

The mean scores of affection of students with respect to father's monthly income have been computed and the difference is tested for significance as shown below.

TABLE .9.53: Showing the Significant Difference Between the mean Scores of Affection with Respect to Father's Monthly Income

Group	Number of Students	Mean	Standard Deviation	Standard Error	Critical ratio	Level of Significance
Less than Rs.3000	87	12.4828	2.610	.280	1.72	N.S.
Above Rs.3000	215	13.0744	2.912	.199		

The calculated table value (1.72) is less than the standard table value (1.96) at .05 level, so it is clear that there is no significant difference between mean scores of affection of students with respect to father's monthly income.

Hence, Hypothesis XI(g) which states that "There is no significant difference between the mean scores of "affection" of students studying at higher secondary level with respect to father's monthly income" is accepted.

INFLUENCE OF MOTHER'S MONTHLY INCOME ON AFFECTION

The mean scores of affection of students with respect to mother's monthly income have been computed and the difference is tested for significance as shown below.

TABLE. 9.54: Showing the Significant Difference between the mean Scores of Affection with Respect to Mother's Monthly Income

Group	Number of Students	Mean	Standard Deviation	Standard Error	Critical ratio	Level of Significance
Less than Rs.3000	275	12.8218	2.822	.170	1.57	0.01
Above Rs.3000	27	13.7407	2.903	.559		

The calculated table value (1.57) is less than the standard table value (1.96) at .05 level, so it is clear that there is no significant difference between the mean scores of love of students with respect to mother's monthly income.

Hence, Hypothesis XI(h) which states that "There is no significant difference between the mean scores of "affection" of students studying at higher secondary level with respect to mother's monthly income" is rejected.

INFLUENCE OF SEX ON ASSERTION

The mean scores of assertion of boys and girls have been computed and the difference is tested for significance as shown below.

TABLE. 9.55: Showing the Significant Difference Between the mean Scores of Assertion of Male and Female XI Standard Students

Group	Number of Students	Mean	Standard Deviation	Standard Error	Critical ratio	Level of Significance
Male	145	11.8897	2.667	.221	0.59	N.S
Female	147	11.7006	2.919	.233		

The calculated table value (0.59) is less than the standard table value (1.96) at 0.5 level it is clear that there is no significant difference between the mean scores of assertion of male and female students.

Hence, Hypothesis XII (a) which states that "There is no significant difference between the mean score of "assertion" of students studying at the higher secondary level with respect to sex" is accepted.

INFLUENCE OF TYPE OF MANAGEMENT OF SCHOOLS ON ASSERTION

The mean scores of assertion of students on type of management of schools have been computed and the difference is tested for significance as shown below.

TABLE. 9.56: ANOVA Showing the Significant Different Between the mean Scores of Assertion with Respect to type of Management of Schools

Source	Degrees of Freedom	Sum of Squares	Mean Squares	F Ratio	Level of significant
Between groups	2	20.4041	10.2021	1.3061	N.S
Within groups	299	2335.4535	7.8109		
Total	**301**	**2355.8576**			

The calculated table value is (1.3061) is less than the standard table value (3.02) at .05 level so it is clear that there is no significant difference between the mean scores of assertion on students with respect to type of management.

Hence, Hypothesis XII (b) which states that "There is no significant difference between the mean scores of "assertion" of students studying at higher secondary level with respect to type of management of schools" is accepted.

INFLUENCE OF TYPE OF FAMILY ON ASSERTION

The mean scores of assertion on type of family have been computed and the difference is tested for significance as shown below.

TABLE. 9.57: Showing the Significant Difference Between the Mean Scores of Assertion with Respect to Type of Family

Groups compared	Number of Students	Mean	Standard Deviation	Standard Error	Critical Ratio	Level of Significance
Nuclear Family	212	11.7123	2.889	.198	0.79	N.S
Joint Family	90	11.9778	2.575	.271		

The calculated table value (0.79) is less than the standard table value (1.96) at .05 level so it is clear that there is no significant difference between the mean scores of assertion with respect to type of family.

Hence, Hypothesis XII(c) which states that "There is no significant difference between the scores of "assertion" of students studying at the higher secondary level with respect to type of family" is accepted.

INFLUENCE OF BIRTH ORDER OF THE CHILD ON ASSERTION

The mean scores of assertion of students with respect to birth order of the child have been computed and the difference is tested for significance as shown below.

TABLE. 9.58: ANOVA showing the significant difference between the mean scores of assertion with respect to birth order of the child

Source	Degrees of Freedom	Sum of squares	Mean Squares	F ratio	Level of significance
Between groups	2	12.4944	6.2472	.7971	N.S
Within groups	299	2343.3632	7.8373		
Total	**301**	**2355.8576**			

The calculated table value (.7971) is less than the standard table value (3.02) at .05 level, so it is clear that there is no significant difference between the mean scores of assertion with respect to birth order of the child.

Hence, Hypothesis XII (d) which states that "There is no significant difference between the mean scores of "assertion" of students studying at the higher secondary level with respect to birth order of the child" is accepted.

INFLUENCE OF FATHER'S EDUCATIONAL QUALIFICATION OF ASSERTION

The mean scores of assertion of students with respect to father's educational qualification have been computed and the significance as shown below.

TABLE. 9.59: ANOVA Showing the Significant Difference Between the mean Scores of Assertion with Respect to Father's Educational Qualification

Source	Degrees of Freedom	Sum of squares	Mean Squares	F ratio	Level of significance
Between groups	2	.8536	.4268	0.542	N.S
Within groups	299	2355.0040	7.8763		
Total	**301**	**2355.8576**			

The calculated table value (.0542) is less than the standard table value (3.02) at .05 level, so it is clear that there is no significant difference between the mean scores of assertion with respect to father's educational qualification.

Hence, Hypothesis XII (e) which states that "There is no significant difference between the mean scores of "assertion" of students studying at higher secondary level with respect to father's educational qualification" is accepted.

INFLUENCE OF MOTHER'S EDUCATIONAL QUALIFICATION OF ASSERTION

The mean scores of assertion of students with respect to mother's educational qualification have been computed and the significance as shown below.

TABLE. 9.60: ANOVA Showing the Significant Difference Between the mean Scores of Assertion with Respect to Mother's Educational Qualification

Source	Degrees of Freedom	Sum of squares	Mean Squares	F ratio	Level of significance
Between groups	2	85.4912	42.2456	5.5612	0.01
Within groups	299	2271.3664	7.5965		
Total	**301**	**2355.8576**			

From the above the calculated table value (5.5612) is greater than the standard table value (4.66) at .05 level, so it is clear that there is significant difference of the mean scores of assertion.

On probing further, multiple comparison of the significant difference of the scores of assertion among the levels of educational qualification have been computed, the details of which are presented below.

TABLE. 9.61: Showing Multiple Comparisons of the Significant Difference of the Mean Scores of Assertion of Students with Respect to Mother's Educational Qualification

Groups compared	Number of Students	Mean	Standard Deviation	Standard Error	Critical Ratio	Level of Significance
Illiterate Vs School Level	24	11.0833	2.205	.450	1.19	N.S.
	242	11.6570	2.714	.174		
Illiterate Vs College Level	24	11.0833	2.205	.450	2.92	0.01
	36	13.1667	3.317	.553		
School Level Vs College Level	242	11.6570	2.714	.174	2.60	0.01
	36	13.1667	3.317	.553		

The above table reveals that in the first comparison, since the calculated `t' value (1.74) is less than the standard table value (1.96), it is clear that there is significant difference between the mean scores of assertion with respect to mother's educational qualification.

In the second comparison, there is significant difference between the mean scores of assertion of students with respect to mother's educational qualification.

In the third comparison, there is significant difference between the mean scores of assertion of students with respect to mother's educational qualification.

Hence, Hypothesis XII (f) which states that "There is no significant difference between the mean scores of "assertion" of students studying at higher secondary level with respect to mother's educational qualification" is partially accepted.

INFLUENCE OF FATHER'S MONTHLY INCOME ON ASSERTION

The mean scores of assertion of students with respect to father's monthly income have been computed and the difference is tested for significance as shown below.

TABLE.9.62: Showing the Significant Difference Between the mean Scores of Assertion with Respect to Father's Monthly Income

Group	Number of Students	Mean	Standard Deviation	Standard Error	Critical ratio	Level of Significance
Less than Rs.3000	87	11.8966	2.492	.267	0.44	N.S.
Above Rs.3000	215	11.7488	2.917	.199		

The calculated table value (0.44) is less than the standard table value (1.96) at .05 level, so it is clear that there is no significant difference between the mean scores of assertion of students with respect to father's monthly income.

Hence, Hypothesis XII(g) which states that, "There is no significant difference between the mean scores of "assertion" of students studying at higher secondary level with respect to father's monthly income" is accepted.

INFLUENCE OF MOTHER'S MONTHLY INCOME ON ASSERTION

The mean scores of assertion of students with respect to mother's monthly income have been computed and the difference is tested for significance as shown below.

TABLE. 9.63: Showing the Significant Difference Between the mean Scores of Assertion with Respect to Mother's Monthly Income

Group	Number of Students	Mean	Standard Deviation	Standard Error	Critical ratio	Level of Significance
Less than Rs.3000	275	11.6727	2.752	.166	2.19	0.05
Above Rs.3000	27	13.0000	3.026	.582		

The calculated table value (2.19) is greater than the standard table value (1.96) at .05 level, so it is clear that there is no significant difference between the mean scores of assertion of students with respect to mother's monthly income.

Hence, Hypothesis XII(h) which states that "There is no significant difference between the mean scores of "assertion" of students studying at higher secondary level with respect to mother's monthly income" is rejected.

INFLUENCE OF SEX ON IDEALISM

The mean scores of idealism of boys and girls have been computed and the difference is tested for significance as shown below.

TABLE. 9.64: Showing the Significant Difference between the mean Scores of Idealism of Male and Female XI Standard Students

Group	Number of Students	Mean	Standard Deviation	Standard Error	Critical ratio	Level of Significant
Male	145	12.1517	2.755	.229	0.90	N.S
Female	157	11.8726	2.631	.210		

The Calculated table value (0.90) is less than the standard table value (1.96) at 0.5 level, so it is clear that there is no significant difference between the mean scores of idealism of male and female students.

Hence, Hypothesis XIII(a) which states that, "There is no significant difference between the mean score of "idealism" of students studying at the higher secondary level with respect to sex" is accepted.

INFLUENCE OF TYPE OF MANAGEMENT OF SCHOOLS ON IDEALISM

The mean scores of idealism of students on type of management of schools have been computed and the difference is tested for significance as shown below.

TABLE. 9.65: ANOVA Showing the Significant Difference between the mean Scores of Idealism with Respect to Type of Management of Schools

Source	Degrees of Freedom	Sum of squares	Mean Squares	F ratio	Level of significance
Between groups	2	127.8922	63.9461	9.3263	.01
Within groups	299	2050.0946	6.8566		
Total	**301**	**2177.9868**			

The calculated table value is (9.3263) is greater than the standard table value (4.66) at .01 level, so it is clear that there is significant difference on the mean scores of idealism of students with respect to type of management.

On probing further, multiple comparison of the significant difference of the scores of idealism among the type of management have been computed, the details of which are presented below.

TABLE. 9.66: Showing Multiple Comparison of the Significant Difference of the mean Scores of Idealism of Students with Respect to Type of Management of Schools

Groups compared	Number of Students	Mean	Standard Deviation	Standard Error	Critical Ratio	Level of Significance
Government Vs Government Aided	119	11.2773	2.652	.243	2.52	0.05
	101	12.1584	2.529	.252		
Government Vs Private	119	11.2773	2.652	.243	4.18	0.01
	82	12.8780	2.678	.296		
Government Aided Vs Private	101	12.1584	2.529	.252	1.85	N.S.
	82	12.8780	2.678	.296		

The above table reveals that in the first comparison, the calculated table value (2.58) greater than the standard table value (1.96) at .05 level it is clear that there is significant difference between the mean scores of idealism with respect to type of management of schools.

In the second comparison there is significant difference between the mean scores of idealism with respect to type of management.

In the third comparison there is no significant difference between the mean scores of idealism with respect to type of management.

Hence, Hypothesis XIII (b) which states that "There is no significant difference between the mean scores of "idealism" of students studying at the higher secondary level with respect to type of management of schools" is partially accepted.

INFLUENCE OF TYPE OF FAMILY ON IDEALISM

The mean scores of idealism on type of family have been computed and the difference is tested for significance as shown below.

TABLE .9.67: Showing the Significant Difference Between the mean Scores of Idealism with Respect to Type of Family

Groups compared	Number of Students	Mean	Standard Deviation	Standard Error	Critical Ratio	Level of Significance
Nuclear Family	212	12.0802	2.752	.189	0.75	N.S
Joint Family	90	11.8333	2.545	.268		

The calculated table value is (0.75) is less than the standard table value (1.96) at .05 level, so it is clear that there is no significant difference on the mean scores of idealism of students with respect to type of family.

Hence, Hypothesis XIII(c) which states that, "There is no significant difference between the mean scores of "idealism" of students studying at higher secondary level with respect to type of family" is accepted.

INFLUENCE OF BIRTH ORDER OF THE CHILD ON IDEALISM

The mean scores of idealism of students on birth order of the child have been computed and the difference is tested for significance as shown below.

TABLE. 9.68: ANOVA Showing the Significant Difference Between the mean Scores of Idealism with Respect to Birth Order of the Child

Source	Degrees of Freedom	Sum of squares	Mean Squares	F ratio	Level of significance
Between groups	2	39.9311	19.9655	2.7921	N.S.
Within groups	299	2138.0557	7.1506		
Total	**301**	**2177.9868**			

The calculated table value (2.7921) is less than the standard table value (3.02), so it is clear that there is no significant difference between the mean scores of idealism with respect to birth order of the child.

Hence Hypothesis XIII (d), which states that, "There is no significant difference between the mean scores of "idealism" of students studying at the higher secondary level with respect to birth order of the child" is accepted.

INFLUENCE OF FATHER'S EDUCATIONAL QUALIFICATION ON IDEALISM

The mean scores of idealism of students with respect to father's educational qualification have been computed and the significance as shown below.

TABLE. 9.69: ANOVA Showing the Significant Difference between the mean Scores of Idealism with Respect to Father's Educational Qualification

Source	Degrees of Freedom	Sum of squares	Mean Squares	F ratio	Level of significance
Between groups	2	50.1600	25.0800		
Within groups	299	2127.8267	7.1165	3.5242	.05
Total	**301**	**2177.9868**			

The calculated table value (3.5242) is greater than the standard table value (3.02) so it is clear that there is significant difference between the mean scores of idealism with respect to father's educational qualification.

On probing further, multiple comparison of the significant difference of scores of idealism among the levels of educational qualification have been computed, the details of which are presented below.

TABLE. 9.70: Showing Multiple Comparisons of the Significant Difference of the mean Scores of Idealism of Students with Respect to Father's Educational Qualification

Groups compared	Number of Students	Mean	Standard Deviation	Standard Error	Critical Ratio	Level of Significance
Illiterate Vs School Level	3	10.0000	1.000	.577	2.75	.01
	157	11.6879	2.710	.216		
Illiterate Vs College Level	3	10.0000	1.000	.577	3.88	.01
	142	12.4014	2.637	.221		
School Level Vs College Level	157	11.6879	2.710	.216	2.31	0.01
	142	12.4014	2.637	.221		

The above table reveals that in the first comparison, since the calculated table value (2.74) is greater than the standard table value (2.58) at .01 level, so it is clear that there is significant difference between the mean scores of idealism with respect to father's educational qualification.

In the second comparison, there is significant difference between the mean scores of idealism of students with respect to father's educational qualification.

In the third comparison, there is significant difference between the mean scores of idealism of students with respect to father's educational qualification.

Hence Hypothesis XIII (e) which states that "There is no significant difference between the mean scores of "idealism" of students studying at higher secondary level with respect to father's educational qualification" is rejected.

INFLUENCE OF MOTHER'S EDUCATIONAL QUALIFICATION ON IDEALISM

The mean scores of idealism of students with respect to mother's educational qualification have been computed and the significance as shown below.

TABLE. 9.71: ANOVA Showing the Significant Difference Between the mean Scores of Idealism with Respect to Mother's Educational Qualification

Source	Degrees of Freedom	Sum of squares	Mean Squares	F ratio	Level of significance
Between groups	2	55.8848	27.9424	3.9370	.05
Within groups	299	2122.1019	7.0973		
Total	**301**	**2177.9868**			

From the above the calculated table value (3.5370) is greater than the standard table value (3.02), so it is clear that there is significant difference between the mean scores of idealism.

On probing further, multiple comparison of the significant difference of scores of idealism among the levels of educational qualification have been computed, the details of which are presented below.

TABLE. 9.72: Showing Multiple Comparisons of the Significant Difference of the mean Scores of Idealism of Students with Respect to Mother's Educational Qualification

Groups compared	Number of Students	Mean	Standard Deviation	Standard Error	Critical Ratio	Level of Significance
Illiterate Vs School Level	24	11.6667	2.200	.449	0.42	N.S.
	242	11.8678	2.687	.173		
Illiterate Vs College Level	24	11.6667	2.200	.449	2.32	0.05
	36	13.1667	2.783	.464		
School Level Vs College Level	242	11.8678	2.687	.173	2.62	0.01
	36	13.1667	2.783	.464		

The above table reveals that in the first comparison, since the calculated table value (0.42) is less than the standard table value (1.96), it is clear that there is no significant difference between the scores of idealism with respect to mother's educational qualification.

In the second comparison, there is significant difference between the mean scores of idealism of students with respect to mother's educational qualification.

In the third comparison, there is significant difference between the mean scores of idealism of students with respect to mother's educational qualification.

Hence Hypothesis XIII (f) which states that "There is no significant difference between the mean scores of "idealism" of students studying at higher secondary level with respect to mother's educational qualification" is partially accepted.

INFLUENCE OF FATHER'S MONTHLY INCOME ON IDEALISM

The mean scores of idealism of students with respect to father's monthly income have been computed and the difference is tested for significance as shown below.

TABLE. 9.73: Showing the Significant Difference Between the mean Scores of Idealism with Respect to Father's Monthly Income

Group	Number of Students	Mean	Standard Deviation	Standard Error	Critical ratio	Level of Significance
Less than Rs.3000	87	11.7816	2.549	.273	0.95	N.S.
Above Rs.3000	215	12.0977	2.745	.187		

The calculated table value (0.95) is less than the standard table value (1.96) at .05 level, so it is clear that there is no significant difference between the mean scores of idealism with respect to father's monthly income.

Hence, Hypothesis XIII (g) which states that "There is no significant difference between the mean scores of "idealism" of students studying at higher secondary level with respect to father's monthly income" is accepted.

INFLUENCE OF MOTHER'S MONTHLY INCOME ON IDEALISM

The mean scores of idealism of students with respect to mother's monthly income have been computed and the difference is tested for significance as shown below.

TABLE. 9.74: Showing the Significant Difference Between the mean Scores of Idealism with Respect to Mother's Monthly Income

Group	Number of Students	Mean	Standard Deviation	Standard Error	Critical ratio	Level of Significance
Less than Rs.3000	275	11.8655	2.611	.157	2.56	0.05
Above Rs.3000	27	13.4444	3.093	.595		

The calculated table value (2.56) is greater than the standard table value (1.96) at .05 level, so it is clear that there is no significant difference between the mean scores of idealism with respect to mother's monthly income.

Hence, Hypothesis XIII (h) which states that "There is no significant difference between the mean scores of "idealism" of students studying at higher secondary level with respect to mother's monthly income" is rejected.

INFLUENCE OF SEX ON MENTAL HEALTH

The obtained scores of mental health of boys and girls have been computed and the difference is tested for significance as shown below.

TABLE. 9.75: Showing the Significant Difference Between the mean Scores of Mental Health of Male and Female XI standard Students

Group	Number of Students	Mean	Standard Deviation	Standard Error	Critical ratio	Level of Significance
Male	145	35.1241	5.478	.455	2.82	.01
Female	157	33.2611	6.020	.480		

The calculated table value (2.82) is greater than the standard table value (2.58) at .01 level, so, it is clear that there is significant difference between the mean scores of mental health of male and female students.

Hence, Hypothesis XIV (a) which states that "There is no significant difference between "mental health" of students studying at the higher secondary level with respect to sex" is rejected.

INFLUENCE OF TYPE OF MANAGEMENT OF SCHOOLS ON MENTAL HEALTH

The obtained scores of mental health on the type of management of schools have been computed and the difference is tested for significance as shown below.

TABLE. 9.76: ANOVA Showing the Significant Difference Between the Scores of Mental Health with Respect to Type of Management of Schools

Source	Degrees of Freedom	Sum of squares	Mean Squares	F ratio	Level of significance
Between groups	2	16.1615	8.0807	.2364	N.S.
Within groups	299	10221.5239	34.1857		
Total	**301**	**10237.6854**			

The calculated table value (.2364) is less than the standard table value (3.02), so it is clear that there is no significant difference between the mean scores of mental health of the students with respect to type of management of schools

Hence, Hypothesis XIV (b) which states that "There is no significant difference between "mental healths" of students studying at the higher secondary level with respect to type of management of schools" is accepted.

INFLUENCE OF TYPE OF FAMILY ON MENTAL HEALTH

The obtained scores of mental health on type of family have been computed and the difference is tested for significance as shown below.

TABLE. 9.77: Showing the Significant Difference between the mean Scores of Mental Health with Respect to Type of Family

Groups compared	Number of Students	Mean	Standard Deviation	Standard Error	Critical Ratio	Level of Significance
Nuclear Family	212	34.1273	6.023	.414	0.13	N.S
Joint Family	90	34.222	5.388	.568		

The calculated table value (0.13) is less than the standard table value (1.96), so it is clear that there is no significant difference between the mean scores of mental health of students with respect to type of family.

Hence, Hypothesis XIV(c) which states that "There is no significant difference between "mental health" of students studying at higher secondary level with respect to type of family" as accepted.

INFLUENCE OF BIRTH ORDER OF THE CHILD ON MENTAL HEALTH

The obtained scores of mental health on birth order of the child have been computed and the difference is tested for significance as shown below.

TABLE. 9.78: ANOVA Showing the Significant Difference between the mean Scores of Mental Health with Respect to Birth Order of the Child

Source	Degrees of Freedom	Sum of squares	Mean Squares	F ratio	Level of significance
Between groups	2	.3283	.1641	.5091	N.S.
Within groups	299	96.4035	.3224		
Total	**301**	**96.7318**			

The calculated table value (.5091) is less than the standard table value (3.02), so it is clear that there is no significant difference between the mean scores of mental health of the students with respect of birth order of the child.

Hence, Hypothesis XIV (d) which states that "There is no significant difference between "mental healths" of students studying at the higher secondary level with respect to birth order of the child" is accepted.

INFLUENCE OF FATHER'S EDUCATIONAL QUALIFICATION ON MENTAL HEALTH

The obtained scores of mental health on father's educational qualification been computed and the difference is tested for significance as shown below.

TABLE. 9.79: ANOVA Showing the Significant Difference Between the mean Scores of Mental Health with Respect to Father's Educational Qualification

Source	Degrees of Freedom	Sum of squares	Mean Squares	F ratio	Level of significance
Between groups	2	85.2206	42.6103	1.2549	N.S.
Within groups	299	10152.4649	33.9547		
Total	301	10237.6854			

The calculated table value (1.2549) is less than the standard table value (3.02), so, it is clear that there is no significant difference between the mean scores mental health of students with respect to father's educational qualification.

Hence, Hypothesis XIV (e) which states that "There is no significant difference between "mental health" of students studying at higher secondary level with respect father's educational qualification" is accepted.

INFLUENCE OF MOTHER'S EDUCATIONAL QUALIFICATION ON MENTAL HEALTH

The obtained scores of mental health on mother's educational qualification been computed and the difference is tested for significance as shown below.

TABLE. 9.80: ANOVA Showing the Significant Difference between the mean Scores of Mental Health with Respect to Mother's Educational Qualification

Source	Degrees of Freedom	Sum of squares	Mean Squares	F ratio	Level of significance
Between groups	2	114.6671	57.3335	1.6934	N.S.
Within groups	299	10123.0184	33.8562		
Total	**301**	**10237.6854**			

The calculated table value (1.6934) is less than the standard table value (3.02), so, it is clear that there is no significant difference between the mean scores of mental health of students with respect to mother's educational qualification.

Hence, Hypothesis XIV (f) which states that "There is no significant difference between "mental healths" of students studying at higher secondary level with respect mother's educational qualification" is accepted.

INFLUENCE OF FATHER'S MONTHLY INCOME ON MENTAL HEALTH

The obtained scores of mental health on father's monthly income have been computed and the difference is tested for significance as shown below.

TABLE. 9.81: Showing the Significant Difference between the Mean Scores of Mental Health with Respect to Father's Monthly Income

Group	Number of Students	Mean	Standard Deviation	Standard Error	Critical ratio	Level of Significance
Less than Rs.3000	87	33.3448	6.219	.667	1.48	N.S.
Above Rs.3000	215	34.4837	5.650	.385		

The calculated table value (1.48) is less than the standard table value (1.96), so it is clear that there is no significant difference between the mean score of mental health of students with respect to father's monthly income.

Hence, Hypothesis XIV (g) which states that "There is no significant difference between "mental healths" of students studying at higher secondary level with respect to father's monthly income" is accepted.

INFLUENCE OF MOTHER'S MONTHLY INCOME ON MENTAL HEALTH

The obtained scores of mental health on mother's monthly income have been computed and the difference is tested for significance as shown below.

TABLE. 9.82: Showing the Significant Difference between the mean Scores of Mental Health with Respect to Mother's Monthly Income

Group	Number of Students	Mean	Standard Deviation	Standard Error	Critical ratio	Level of Significance
Less than Rs.3000	275	33.9273	5.898	.356	2.68	0.01
Above Rs.3000	27	36.4815	4.586	.883		

The calculated table value (2.68) is greater than standard table value (2.58) at .01 level, so it is clear that there is significant difference between the mean scores of mental health of students with respect to mother's monthly income.

Hence, Hypothesis XIV (g) which states that "There is no significant difference between "mental health" of students studying at higher secondary level with respect to mother's monthly income" is accepted.

INFLUENCE OF SEX OF SOCIAL MATURITY

The obtained scores of social maturity of boys and girls have been computed and the difference is tested for significance as shown below.

TABLE.9.83: Showing the significant difference between the mean scores of social maturity of male and female XI standard students

Group	Number of Students	Mean	Standard Deviation	Standard Error	Critical ratio	Level of Significant
Male	145	230.9724	13.851	1.150	1.83	N.S.
Female	157	227.9363	15.043	1.201		

The Calculated table value (1.83) is less than the standard table value (1.96), so it is clear that there is no significant difference between the mean scores of social maturity of the students with respect to sex.

Hence, Hypothesis XV (a) which states that "There is no significant difference between "social maturities" of students studying at higher secondary level with respect to sex" is accepted.

INFLUENCE OF TYPE OF MANAGEMENT OF SCHOOLS ON SOCIAL MATURITY

The obtained scores of social maturity of students on the type of management of schools have been computed and the difference is tested for significance as shown below.

TABLE. 9.84: ANOVA Showing the Significant Difference Between the Mean Scores of Social Maturity with Respect to Type of Management of Schools

Source	Degrees of Freedom	Sum of squares	Mean Squares	F ratio	Level of significance
Between groups	2	695.9799	347.9900	1.6535	N.S.
Within groups	299	62926.1293	210.4553		
Total	**301**	**63622.1093**			

The calculated table value (1.6535) is less than the standard table value (3.02), so, it is clear that there is no significant difference between the mean scores of social maturity of students with respect to type of management of schools.

Hence, Hypothesis XV (b) which states that "There is no significant difference between "social maturities" of students studying at the higher secondary level with respect to type of management of schools" is accepted.

INFLUENCE OF TYPE OF FAMILY ON SOCIAL MATURITY

The obtained scores of social maturity on type of family have been computed and the difference is tested for significance as shown below.

TABLE. 9.85: Showing the Significant Difference Between the mean Scores of Social Maturity with Respect to Type of Family

Groups compared	Number of Students	Mean	Standard Deviation	Standard Error	Critical Ratio	Level of Significance
Nuclear Family	212	229.1274	14.740	1.012	0.50	N.S
Joint Family	90	230.0222	14.113	1.488		

The calculated table value (0.50) is less than the standard table value (1.96), so it is clear that there is no significant difference between the mean scores of social maturity of students with respect to type of family.

Hence, Hypothesis XV(c) which states that "There is no significant difference between "social maturity" of students studying at higher secondary level with respect to type of family" as accepted.

INFLUENCE OF BIRTH ORDER OF THE CHILD ON SOCIAL MATURITY

The obtained scores of social maturity on birth order of the child have been computed and the difference is tested for significance as shown below.

TABLE. 9.86: ANOVA Showing the Significant Difference between the mean Scores of Social Maturity with Respect to Birth Order of the Child

Source	Degrees of Freedom	Sum of squares	Mean Squares	F ratio	Level of significance
Between groups	2	.2944	.1472	.6988	N.S.
Within groups	299	62.9771	.2106		
Total	**301**	**63.2715**			

The calculated table value (.6988) is less than the standard table value (3.02), so it is clear that there is no significant difference between the mean scores of social maturity of students with respect to birth order of the child.

Hence, Hypothesis XV (d) which states that "There is no significant difference between "social maturity" of students at higher secondary level with respect to birth order of the child" is accepted.

INFLUENCE OF FATHER'S EDUCATIONAL QUALIFICATION ON SOCIAL MATURITY

The obtained scores of social maturity on father's educational qualification have been computed and the difference is tested for significance as shown below.

TABLE. 9.87: ANOVA Showing the Significant Difference between the mean Scores of Social Maturity with Respect to Father's Educational Qualification

Source	**Degrees of Freedom**	**Sum of squares**	**Mean Squares**	**F ratio**	**Level of significance**
Between groups	2	31.3376	15.6688	.0737	N.S.
Within groups	299	63590.7716	212.6782		
Total	**301**	**63622.1093**			

The calculated table value (.0737) is less than the standard table value (3.02), so it is clear that there is no significant difference between the mean scores of social maturity of students with respect to father's educational qualification.

Hence, Hypothesis XV (e) which states that "There is no significant difference between "social maturity" of students studying at the higher secondary level with respect to father's educational qualification" is accepted.

INFLUENCE OF MOTHER'S EDUCATIONAL QUALIFICATION ON SOCIAL MATURITY

The obtained scores of social maturity on mother's educational qualification have been computed and the difference is tested for significance as shown below.

TABLE. 9.88: ANOVA Showing the Significant Difference between the mean Scores of Social Maturity with Respect to Mother's Educational Qualification

Source	**Degrees of Freedom**	**Sum of squares**	**Mean Squares**	**F ratio**	**Level of significance**
Between groups	2	261.1498	130.5749	.6162	N.S.
Within groups	299	63360.9595	211.9096		
Total	**301**	**62622.1093**			

The calculated table value (.0162) is less than the standard table value (3.02), so it is clear that there is no significant difference between the mean scores of social maturity of students with respect to mother's educational qualirication.

Hence, Hypothesis XV(F) Which States That "There Is No Significant Difference Between "Social Maturity" Of Students Studying At The Higher Secondary Level With Respect To Mother's Educational Qualification" Is Accepted.

INFLUENCE OF FATHER'S MONTHLY INCOME ON SOCIAL MATURITY

The obtained scores of social maturity on father's monthly income have been computed and the difference is tested for significance as shown below.

TABLE. 9.89: Showing the Significant Difference between the mean Scores of Social Maturity with Respect to Father's Monthly Income

Group	Number of Students	Mean	Standard Deviation	Standard Error	Critical ratio	Level of Significance
Less than Rs.3000	87	229.6782	15.657	1.679	0.20	N.S.
Above Rs.3000	215	229.2791	14.098	.961		

The calculated table value (0.20) is less than the standard table value (1.96) so it is clear that there is no significant difference between the mean scores of social maturity of students with respect to father's monthly income.

Hence, Hypothesis XV(g) which states that "There is no significant difference between "social maturity" of students studying at higher secondary level with respect to father's monthly income" is accepted.

INFLUENCE OF MOTHER'S MONTHLY INCOME ON SOCIAL MATURITY

The obtained scores of social maturity on mother's monthly income have been computed and the difference is tested for significance as shown below.

TABLE. 9.90: Showing the Significant Difference between the mean Scores of Social Maturity with Respect to Mother's Monthly Income

Group	Number of Students	Mean	Standard Deviation	Standard Error	Critical ratio	Level of Significance
Less than Rs.3000	275	228.9564	14.606	.881	1.81	N.S.
Above Rs.3000	27	233.8519	13.266	2.553		

The calculated table value (1.81) is less than the standard table value (1.96) so it is clear that there is no significant difference between the mean scores of social maturity of students with respect to mother's monthly income.

Hence, Hypothesis XV (h) which states that "There is no significant difference between "social maturity" of students studying at higher secondary level with respect to mother's monthly income" is accepted.

CONCLUSION

The analysis and interpretation of the data represent the application of deductive and inductive logic in the research process. The data is often classified by division into sub groups and then analysed and synthesized in such a way that hypotheses may be accepted or rejected.

In the succeeding chapter a brief report of the research. Study together with their education implications has been presented.

❐

10

Retrospects and Prospects

"Research is an honest, exhaustive, intelligent searching for facts and their meanings or implications with reference to a given problem. The products of findings of given piece of research should be an authentic, verifiable contribution to knowledge in the field studied"

- P.M. Cook.

This chapter deals with the consolidation of the various findings presented in the previous chapters. Findings are statements of factual information based upon the data anlaysis. Conclusions are answers to the questions raised or the statements of acceptance or rejection of the hypothesis proposed. In this chapter, the researcher deals with the aspects pertaining to the tools used for investigation objectives and hypotheses of the study, based on analysis the major findings arrived at and finally the educational implication together with suggestion for further study.

STATEMENT OF THE PROBLEM

The problem for the study is titled as follows: A study on value conflicts and mental health of students at the Higher Secondary level in relation to their social maturity.

OBJECTIVES FOR THE STUDY

The following objectives are set in the present study.

i. To find out the dimension of value conflict of higher-secondary students.
ii. To identify the level of mental health of higher secondary students.
iii. To find out the level of social maturity of higher secondary students.
iv. To investigate whether the different dimensions of value conflict viz. Fortitude, Self - Reliance, Probity, Affection, Assertion and Idealism exhibit different levels of (ie) low, average and high social maturity among students studying in higher secondary level.
v. To find whether categories of mental health exhibit different levels (ie) low, average and high social maturity.
vi. To find whether there is significant association between value conflict and mental health of students studying at Higher Secondary level.
vii. To find whether there is significant difference between scores of value conflict of students studying at higher secondary level with respect to
    - Sex
    - Type of management of Schools (Government / Government aided / Private).
    - Type of family (Nuclear / Joint)
    - Birth order of the child (1st / 2nd / 3rd / and above)
    - Father's educational qualification (Illiterate / School level / College level)
    - Mother's educational qualification (Illiterate/School level/ College level)
    - Father's monthly income (less than Rs.3000 / above Rs.3000)
    - Mother's monthly income (less than Rs.3000/ above Rs.3000).
viii. To find whether there is any significant difference between scores of fortitude of students studying at higher secondary level with respect to
    - Sex
    - Type of management of schools
    - Type of family
    - Birth order of the child
    - Father's educational qualification
    - Mother's educational qualification
    - Father's monthly income
    - Mother's monthly income
ix. To find whether there is any significant difference between scores of self-reliance of students studying at higher secondary level with respect to

- Sex
- Type of management of schools
- Type of family
- Birth order of the child
- Father's educational qualification
- Mother's educational qualification
- Father's monthly income
- Mother's monthly income

X. To find whether there is any significant difference between scores of probity of students studying at higher secondary level with respect to

- Sex
- Type of management of schools
- Type of family
- Birth order of the child
- Father's educational qualification
- Mother's educational qualification
- Father's monthly income
- Mother's monthly income

xi. To find whether there is any significant difference between scores of love of students studying at higher secondary level with respect to

- Sex
- Type of management of schools
- Type of family
- Birth order of the child
- Father's educational qualification
- Mother's educational qualification
- Father's monthly income
- Mother's monthly income

xii. To find whether there is any significant difference between scores of assertion of students studying at higher secondary level with respect to

- Sex
- Type of management of schools
- Type of family
- Birth order of the child
- Father's educational qualification
- Mother's educational qualification
- Father's monthly income
- Mother's monthly income

xiii. To find whether there is any significant difference between scores of Idealism of students studying at higher secondary level with respect to

- Sex
- Type of management of schools
- Type of family
- Birth order of the child
- Father's educational qualification
- Mother's educational qualification
- Father's monthly income
- Mother's monthly income

xiv. To find whether there is any significant difference between mental health of students studying at higher secondary level with respect to

- Sex
- Type of management of schools
- Type of family
- Birth order of the child
- Father's educational qualification
- Mother's educational qualification
- Father's monthly income
- Mother's monthly income

xv. To find whether there is any significant difference between social maturity of students studying at higher secondary level with respect to

- Sex
- Type of management of schools
- Type of family
- Birth order of the child
- Father's educational qualification
- Mother's educational qualification
- Father's monthly income
- Mother's monthly income

HYPOTHESES

The following hypotheses are set in the present study.

i. The dimension of value conflict of higher secondary students is Idealism in nature.

ii. The level of mental health of higher secondary students is average in nature.

iii. The level of social maturity of higher secondary students is average in nature.

iv. The different dimensions of value conflict viz fortitude, self - reliance, porbity, affection, assertion and idealism will exhibit different levels of social maturity (i.e) low, average and high social maturity among students studying at the higher secondary level.

v. The different categories of mental health (i.e) low, average and high will exhibit different levels of social maturity.

vi. There is significant association between value conflict and mental health of students studying at the higher secondary level.

vii. There is no significant difference between the mean scores of "value conflicts" of students studying at higher secondary level with respect to :

- Sex
- Type of management of schools (Government / Government aided / Private).
- Type of family (Nuclear / Joint).
- Birth order of the child (1st / 2nd / 3rd and above).
- Father's educational qualification (Illiterate / school level / college level).
- Mother's educational qualification (Illiterate / school level / college level).
- Father's monthly income (less than Rs.3000/- above Rs.3000).
- Mother's monthly income (less than Rs.3000 / above Rs.3000).

viii. There is no significant difference between the mean scores of "fortitude" of students studying at the higher secondary level with respect to

- Sex
- Type of management of schools
- Type of family
- Birth order of the child
- Father's educational qualification
- Mother's educational qualification
- Father's monthly income
- Mother's monthly income

ix. There is no significant difference between the mean scores of "self - reliance" of students studying at the higher secondary level with respect to

- Sex
- Type of management of schools
- Type of family
- Birth order of the child

- Father's educational qualification
- Mother's education qualification
- Father's monthly income
- Mother's monthly income

x. There is no significant difference between the mean scores of "probity" of students studying at the higher secondary level with respect to

- Sex
- Type of management of schools
- Type of family
- Birth order of the child
- Father's educational qualification
- Mother's educational qualification
- Father's monthly income
- Mother's monthly income

xi. There is no significant difference between the mean scores of "affection" of students studying at the higher secondary level with respect to

- Sex
- Type of management of schools
- Type of family
- Birth order of the child
- Father's educational qualification
- Mother's educational qualification
- Father's monthly income
- Mother's monthly income

xii. There is no significant difference between the mean scores of "assertion" of students studying at the higher secondary level with respect to

- Sex
- Type of management of schools
- Type of family
- Birth order of the child
- Father's educational qualification
- Mother's educational qualification
- Father's monthly income
- Mother's monthly income

xiii. There is no significant difference between the mean scores of "Idealism" of students studying at the higher secondary level with respect to

- Sex
- Type of management of schools

- Type of family
- Birth order of the child
- Father's educational qualification
- Mother's educational qualification
- Father's monthly income
- Mother's monthly income

xiv. There is no significant difference between mental health of students studying at the higher secondary level with respect to

- Sex
- Type of management of schools
- Type of family
- Birth order of the child
- Father's educational qualification
- Mother's educational qualification
- Father's monthly income
- Mother's monthly income

xv. There is no significant difference between social maturity of students studying at the higher secondary level with respect to

- Sex
- Type of management of schools
- Type of family
- Birth order of the child
- Father's educational qualification
- Mother's educational qualification
- Father's monthly income
- Mother's monthly income

SAMPLE OF THE STUDY

The sample included 302 students drawn from six schools which belong to higher secondary level under Tamil Nadu State Board Syllabus.

TOOLS USED

The following tools have been used in this study to verify the hypothesis.

1. Value Conflict Scale prepared by R.L. Bharadwaj.
2. Mental Health Inventory prepared by Droved and Augustine.
3. Social Maturity Scale prepared by Dr.Nalini Rao.

MAJOR FINDINGS OF THE STUDY

The following findings have been arrived through this study

1. The dimension of value conflict of higher secondary students is idealism in nature.
2. The level of mental health of higher secondary students is average in nature.
3. The level of social maturity of higher secondary students in average in nature.
4. The different dimensions of value conflict viz. fortitude, self - reliance, probity, affection, assertion and idealism will exhibit different levels of social maturity (ie) low, average and high social maturity among students studying at the higher secondary level.
5. The different categories of mental health (ie) low, average and high will exhibit different levels of social maturity.
6. There is significant association between value conflicts and mental health of students studying at the higher secondary level.
7. Students studying in private schools have significantly higher mean scores of 'value conflict' than students studying in government and government aided schools. It is also noted that students whose mother's have college level educational qualification have significantly higher mean scores of value conflicts than the other two groups, whereas gender, type of family, birth order of the child, father's educational qualification, father's monthly income and mother's monthly income have no significant influence on value conflicts among higher secondary students.
8. It is clear that male students have significantly higher scores than female students on `fortitude'. It is also noted that students studying in private schools have significantly higher mean scores than students studying in government and government aided schools. Students whose mother's monthly income is above Rs.3,000 have significantly higher mean scores in fortitude than students whose mother's monthly income is less than Rs.3000 whereas type of family, birth order of the child, father's and mother's educational qualification and father's monthly income do not have any significant influence on fortitude.
9. As far as self - reliance is concerned students studying in private schools are superior in 'self-reliance' than their counterparts, whereas all the other presage variables namely sex, type of family, birth order of the child, father's educational qualification, mother's educational qualification, father's monthly income and mother's monthly income do not influence self - reliance of higher secondary students.

10. In the case of 'probity' of higher secondary students, private school students have scored higher mean scores in probity than the other two groups. It is also noted that students whose mother's college level education are significantly higher in probity than the other two groups. Students whose mother's monthly income is above Rs.3,000 have significantly higher mean scores in probity than their counterparts, whereas gender, type of family, birth order of the child, father's educational qualification and father's monthly income do not influence probity of higher secondary students.
11. Students studying in private schools, students whose mother's have college level education and students whose mother's monthly income is above Rs.3,000 have significantly higher mean scores in affection than their respective counterparts, whereas all the other presage variables, do not have significant influence on `affection' among higher secondary school students.
12. It is noted that students whose mother's have college level education and students whose mother's monthly income is above Rs.3000 are more superior in 'assertion' than their respective counterparts. It is note worthy that assertion of higher secondary students is not affected by any other presage variables of the study.
13. As far as 'idealism' is concerned students studying in government school, students whose father's are illiterate, students with illiterate mother's and students whose mother's monthly income is less than Rs.3,000 have significantly lesser mean scores than their respective counterparts, whereas idealism of higher secondary students is not affected by all the other presage variables undertaken in the present study.
14. It is clear that boy's are superior in 'mental health' than girls. Students whose mother's monthly income is above Rs.3,000 are more superior in mental health than their counterparts. It is also noted that, type of management of schools, type of family, birth order of the child, father's educational qualification, mother's educational qualification and father's monthly income have no significant difference on mental health of higher secondary students.
15. It is clear that the 'social maturity' of higher secondary students is not influenced by any of the following presage variables viz., sex, type of management of schools, type of family, birth order of the child, father's educational qualification, mother's educational qualification, father's monthly income and mother's monthly income.

EDUCATIONAL IMPLICATIONS OF THE STUDY

The students must know the difference between the values and value conflicts. Values play a very important role in the life of an individual and in society. Values are to a large extent, goal-related. Value conflicts results in inconsistent and even anarchic behavior. The educational system should emphasize on the development of fundamental, social, moral and spiritual values and also the consequences of value conflicts, so that the students can build up a confidence with their own personality.

Mental health is to be assessed by how a person thinks, feels and acts, when faved with life's situations. Mental health is how people look at themselves, their lives and the other people in their lives, evaluate their lives, evaluate their challenges and problems and explore choices. This including stress, relating to other people and making decisions. The teachers and parents are responsible for the development of a good mental health.

Family acts as a powerful source of influence on the child's social maturity and other related traits. Social maturity appears to be cumulating and one who is socially adaptive gets greater opportunities to further practice and improve one's social skills. The implications of findings such as those reviewed are that, our education program planned on the theory that there are various stages of development in pupils social maturity. So, contributing to the social development of pupils and helping them to attain social maturity are important. It is the ability or skill with which an individual maintain order and system in his relation with others in the society.

LIMITATIONS OF THE STUDY

The present study has the following limitations.

1. The study is done only in Chennai City.
2. The XI - standard students are taken as the sample.
3. The study is done with 302 samples.

SUGGESTIONS

- This study was concentrated only on XI-standard, similar study could be extended to college level.
- The present study is limited to schools in Chennai City. It could be extended to other schools in Tamil Nadu.
- A comparative study between the value conflicts and mental health, mental health and social maturity can also be conducted in further study.

CONCLUSION

The purpose of the present investigation was to study the relationship among the variables, such as value conflicts, mental health and social maturity. The study is sure to find some usefulness in the field of education and findings of the study can serve as a database for further research.

❐

11

Social Inteligence and Social Maturity Problem and its Perspectives

Emergence of the study

Every difference of environment means a difference in one's habit and one's way of living in so far as these differences create a different environment, a dynamic equilibrium of life is maintained through a processing of constant selections and constant adaptations. The society is not the world but is directly related to every one's life and maturity. The more complex the adaptation with society becomes, the more complex the social maturity and intelligence. Society and environment is essential for development of intelligence, maturity according to the need.

Society is a significant medium where certain quality of life and certain types of activity and occupation are provided with the aim of securing child's development based on the social needs. Since it is a stem of growth characteristics of an adolescent period by which every student should adapt to the society in which we live and to which he is expected to adjust and contribute, the social intelligence and maturity receives importance at the present context.

The conduct of many individual in the society tells about his intelligence and social maturity through which he can respond right according to situations.

At the present age of competitive world, every human being meets a lot of problems in his daily activities. The roots of most of human psychological problems are more socially based than psychologically based. Their problems are not mental illness. It is social incompetence, a lack of social intelligence as well as social maturity. So every human need knowledge about social intelligence and social maturity for leading a very healthy life in this world.

The present study takes a position that social intelligence and maturities are very important to the students who live and grow in the complex social environment. Hence there is a need to find out if there is any correlation between social intelligence and social maturity. Hence the problem emerged to study the two variables social intelligence and social maturity.

Statement of the problem

The title of the problem is as follows: A Study of Social Intelligence and Social Maturity among Arts and Science College students.

Operational Definitions

Social Intelligence

Social intelligence means ability of an individual to react to social situations of daily life. Social intelligence would not include the feelings or emotions aroused in us by other people, but merely our ability to understand others and to react in such a way towards them that the ends desired should be attained. High social intelligence is possessed by those who are able to handle people well. Adequate adjustment in social situations is the index of social intelligence.

VERNON (1933) defined social intelligence as the "Person's ability to get along with people in general, social technique or case in society, knowledge of social matters, susceptibility to stimuli from other members of a group, as well as insight into the temporary moods and underlying personality traits of strangers".

E.L.THORNDIKE (1920) has pointed out that there is an aspect of personality that can be called "Social Intelligence", distinct from, "Concrete" and "Abstract" intelligence,

STERNBERY (1984), defines Intelligence as "Consisting of purposive selection and shaping of an adaptation to real-world environments relevant to one's life".

Social Maturity

Maturity assumes accountability, constantly assesses, judges and takes appropriate decisions. Maturity develops a balanced emotional outlook, helping the individual to accept himself, his talents and limitations and to accept others as they are. It analysis values and internalizes them consistently. It helps towards progressive advancement in spiritual growth, impelling the individual to adapt himself to change and to life without emotional crisis.

ABRAHAM SPERLING (1967) defined social maturity in the following words, "An adolescent should get along with others. He ought to develop self-reliance in matters of taste and ought to develop tolerance of human differences".

NAZARATH MARIA E. WAPLES (1978) defines as, "Maturity is the blossoming of man's character into a unified totality. It discerns the process that contributes to the psychological and physical growth and well being of man".

HENRY E GARRETT (1968) states, "Social maturity is the degree of social participation as measured by child's activities, attitudes and play interests. It is related to physical growth and maturity and to mental ability. Every individual develops his own unique way of adjustment in the society. An individual, since his birth attempts to adjust to his environment".

Importance of Social Intelligence

Social intelligence is at the heart of human happiness and emotional comfort.

Explored further, the reason for unhappiness is the inability to maintain positive human relationships with the society. The result will be depression, fear, confusion and anger, created by the lack of positive human emotions that are critical to the happiness of us all. So social intelligence is very important in human's life that is created to bring the practical technology of skills-based training into the world of human interaction and relations.

Need for Social Intelligence

Although anyone can benefit from social intelligence training, it has been especially successful with the following group.

1. People in high stress jobs.
2. Single or divorced men and women who would like to find and build a healthy relationship.
3. Senior - mid level managers.
4. Workers in a regular contact with public.

Factors of Social Intelligence

The following factors are mostly including in the concept of social intelligence.

Patience, Co-cooperativeness, Confidence level, Sensitivity, Recognitions of social environment, Tactfulness, Sense of humours and memory.

1. **Patience:** Calm endurable under stressful situation.
2. **Co-cooperativeness:** Ability to interact with others in a pleasant way to be able to view matters from all angles.
3. **Confidence Level:** Form trust in one self and one's chances.
4. **Sensitivity:** To be acutely aware of and being responsive.
5. **Recognition of social environment:** Ability to perceive the nature and atmosphere of the existing situation.
6. **Tactfulness:** Delicate perception of the right thing to say or do.
8. **Sense of humours:** Capacity to feel and cause amusement; to be able to see the lighter side of life.
9. **Memory:** Ability to remember all relevant issues; names and faces of people.

Stages of Social Maturity

An individual takes times in his social development. So, we may think of some stages of social maturity according to the physical, mental, emotional and language development of the individual. They are,

- Awareness of the presence of another person.
- Mixing with others.
- Understanding of social relationships.
- Understanding of all the above three things refers to human stages of social maturity.

Social Maturity and its Characteristics

Social maturity is the final expected outcome of social development and socialization, certain characteristics of social maturity are,

1. A socially matured person has a sense of his proper place and role as a member of the social group. He is willing and able to orient himself in the various activities and customs to the group.
2. He is able to assume a reasonable amount of responsibility, to adjust him to the inevitable limitations and restrictions of the community life.
3. He can be original and yet conform to the broad pattern of his social environment.

4. He evaluates social problems not from a purely selfish point of view but has regard to the right opinion of others.
5. He accepts responsibility for his actions, does not indulge in self-pitying.
6. He has a realistic self-concept being conscious of his assets and limitations.
7. He is relatively secure and so open to new experiences, which contribute, to his continuous development.

In short, co-operation, pleasing manner, consideration for others, positive and optimistic outlook on life and social intelligence are signs of socially matured individual.

Importance of Social Maturity

Social maturity has been defined as an indication of willingness and ability to orient oneself in the various activities and customs of the group to make a proportionate contribution to the work to be done, to take a suitable part in the social exchange, to assume a reasonable amount of responsibility and to adjust oneself to the inevitable limitations and restrictions of community life without waste of energy or loss of satisfaction.

Significance of the Study

A new concept social intelligence with its significance is more important for one's daily life. It may be defined as one's unitary ability to know, feel, judge, behave and cooperate with a person's thinking process for behaving in a proper way with the ultimate realization of happiness in him and in others. In view of its wide significance from the individual as well as social angles, it becomes quite imperative that serious efforts should be made for its proper development right from early child hood among human beings.

A person's social intelligence helps him much in all spheres of life. Social intelligence also helps a person to understand and give direction to live a very healthy life.

Social intelligence and social maturity are important for survival, decision making, boundary setting, communication and making unity in society, which are very essential to makes ones life's happy.

Every human being should have the knowledge of good social relationship. The social intelligence makes ones knowledge good in social relationship. Therefore social intelligence and social maturity plays very essential and significant role in humans, who are want to live a happy social life.

Objectives of the study

The following are the objectives of the present study:

1. To find out the level of social intelligence of Arts and Science college students.
2. To find out the level of social maturity of Arts and Science college students.
3. To find out the relationship between social intelligence and social maturity among Arts and Science college students.
4. To find out the significant difference between boys and girls on their social intelligence among Arts and Science colleges.
5. To find out the significant difference between boys and girls on their social maturity among Arts and Science colleges.
6. To find out the significant difference between rural and urban environment on their social intelligence among Arts and Science colleges.
7. To find out the significant difference between rural and urban environment on their social maturity among Arts and Science colleges.
8. To find out the significant difference of social intelligence of Arts and Science college students based on their college type.
9. To find out the significant difference of social maturity of Arts and Science college students based on their college type.
10. To find out the significant difference between government and government aided college students on their social intelligence among Arts and Science Colleges.
11. To find out the significant difference between government and government aided college students on their social maturity among Arts and Science Colleges.
12. To find out the significant difference between nuclear and joint family students on their social intelligence among Arts and Science college students.
13. To find out the significant difference between nuclear and joint family students on their social maturity among Arts and Science college students.
14. To find out the significant difference of social intelligence of Arts and Science college students based on their parental income.
15. To find out the significant difference of social maturity of Arts and Science college students based on their parental income.

Limitations

The present investigation has the following limitations.

1. The investigation is limited to Arts and Science college students.
2. The study is restricted to three colleges.
3. The sample is restricted to 300 students.

CONCLUSION

The problem of the present study has been discussed briefly in this chapter, bringing out the characteristics, importance and objectives of the study etc. A detailed discussion of the related literature follows in the next chapter.

❐

12

Review of Related Literature

The researcher takes the advantage of the knowledge, which has accumulated in the past as a result of constant human endeavour. Research can never be undertaken in isolation of the work that has already been done on the problem, which is directly or indirectly related to study proposed by a researcher. One of the important steps in the planning of any research study is careful review of the research journals, books, dissertations, and other series of information on the problem to be investigated. A review of the related literature must precede any well-planned research study.

Review of the related literature allows the researcher to acquaint him with current knowledge in the field or area in which he is going to conduct his research. The important specific reason for reviewing the related literature is to know about the recommendation of previous researchers for further research, which they have listed in their studies. The present summary of research studies are related to the problem "Social Intelligence and Social Maturity" among Arts and Science college students.

STUDIES RELATED TO SOCIAL INTELLIGENCE

Indian Studies

The study was undertaken by Buch. M.B (1960) for assessing the social intelligence of individuals quantitatively and to study the effect of environmental factors as grade as occupational status of social intelligence. The subjects for the present study of social intelligence were selected on the basis of certain independent findings supported by the content analysis of the available tests of social intelligence. The sub tests included were (1) judgment in social situations. (2) Memory for names and faces. (3) Observation of human behaviors. (4) Recognition of the mental state. (5) Sense of humor. (6) Social Introduction. The major findings indicated that the environmental factors very much influenced the social intelligence of individuals.

Ray. T (1972) aimed at developing test in Bengali for the objective measurement of social intelligence. The final form of the test had eighty items distributed on six subjects corresponding to six different areas of human behaviour namely (1) judgment in social situations. (2) Observation of human behaviors. (3) Recognition of the mental state. (4) Memory for names and faces. (5) Appreciation of humour. (6) Adjustment. The findings revealed that the human behaviour had very significant relationship to social intelligence.

On examining the social interest and attitude of college students and to see how these attitudes will influence their future family organization. Singhai. S (1986) found that the social interests and attitude of adolescent students were adequate, mature and stable. It was found that suitable environment influenced development of healthy social interest and attitude of student.

R. Lenin (2005) conducted an investigation into emotional intelligence and social intelligence of teacher trainees, who were studying under University of Madras. The shamble consists of 293 students from six teacher-training colleges in chennai. It was found that the level of social intelligence and emotional intelligence of teacher trainees is moderate in nature and there is a significant relation between emotional intelligence and social intelligence.

Vootnoori Rajesh (2006) conducted the study, which was analysing the achievement in social science with related to emotional maturity and social intelligence of 308 secondary school students in karimnagar District, Andra Pradesh . It was found that the level of emotional maturity and social intelligence of secondary school students and level of achievement in social science of secondary school students is moderate in nature. It was found that there is significant association between emotional maturity and social intelligence.

Foreign Studies

A study was done by Brar S (1992) to examine the social emotional competence of pre-school children and relationship to intelligence and maturity. A study verifies empirically whether social emotional competence depends on the intelligence and social maturity of young children who were under taken in India. A standardized intelligence test was administered to the children to assess social emotional competence and social maturity. Based on test and observation results, children were categorized into groups of high and low intelligence and into groups of high and low social maturity. Scores for the group were compared with respect to four aspects of social emotional competence: (1) Self-confident (2) Antonomy-dependance (3) Quality of social interaction and (4) coping technique.

A study was done by Gabriellsen, Eric (1992) to examine the role of self-monitoring in the choice of college major. A self monitoring person is an individual who adopts a social orientation so that he can manage self presenting, self monitors are likely to modify their academic choices to fit social situations or others expectations. Data were collected using a four-part questionnaire that explored background, a self-monitoring scale, a personal freedom versus social conformity scale and a friendship scale. Result indicated that self-monitors played a role in selection of college majors. However, data and findings also indicated that the direct influence of close friends was not what most presented self-monitors with regard to choice of major.

Chen-shyuefee, Agens; Michael, William B. (1993) has investigated first order and higher order factors of creative social intelligence with in Guilford's structure -of - intellect model . The study carried out how accurately each of several hypothesized combinations of first- order and higher - order factors reflecting creativity in the social intelligence of 192 high school students described the covariation in selected submatrixes from the total correlation matrix originally analyzed. Results support Guilford,s structure of intellect model.

STUDIES RELATED TO SOCIAL MATURITY

Indian Studies

Ghosh. S (1975) has investigated social maturity of pre school Bengali children of Calcutta city belonging to different social-economic groups. Thirty five, nursery and kinder garden schools were randomly selected from the different regions of Calcutta and 40 pre-school children were selected from each school at random equally distributed in each are group. Data were also collected by using a standardized interview schedule on the mothers of these selected children. The final sample included 1410 cases. The study revealed that sex had very insignificant role in imbibing social maturation. Economic status was insignificant as testimony of ability to enrich the social maturity level.

Rao.N. (1978) conducted a research work on social maturity of high school children in Bangalore city. A sample of 1020 students were chosen from 50 secondary schools in Bangalore. The self-constructed questionnaire was used in this study. The major findings were as follows; (I) positive correlation between social maturity and intelligence (II) positive relationship between social maturities and self-esteem. (III) Girls generally scored higher then boys on social maturity. (IV) There were class differences in social maturity among the children of lower grades. (V) Private school children scored more on social maturity than government schools.

Puranik, S.D (1985) has studied the relationship of social maturity of pupils with organizational climate and teacher's morale in the primary schools of Banglore city. The sample consists of 70 schools 2634 students and 712 teachers. The study indicated the development of social maturity; autonomous climate, private management and unaided students and urban location of schools were most conductive factors. No effect of moral of teachers of both senses was noticed on the development of social maturity of male (or) female students (or) on the students of both sexes even under the influence of organizational climate, school organization and localities.

Asthana, Anju (1989) conducted a study of social maturity among school going children in city of Lucknow. The Objectives were, (I) To study whether social maturity increases with grade level. (II) To study association of intelligence, socio-economic status academic achievement, adult dependence and sex of the child with social maturity. It was found that the

Social maturity increased with inverse in grade level, the growth rate being highest in the first school years. Intelligence, academic achievement and adult dependence were significantly associated with the social maturity of children although adult dependence and a negative association and SES was not found to contribute to social maturity at any of the five grade levels.

Sarojamma, Y.H. (1990) has conducted a comparative study of reading ability and social maturity of over normal and underachievers of standard VIII, the final sample comprised of 476 boys and 524 girls. The social maturity scale by Sathyanarayana and Swadha was used. It was found that, there was significant difference in the reading ability of,

1. Normal and under achievers,
2. Over and normal achievers,
3. Girls and boys,

4. Students having high and low social maturity (f) Students in private and government schools.

The interaction effect of the variables on reading ability, hypothesized were not significant.

Malin, A. J. (1990) conducted a study on the relationship of social maturity with classroom climate and academic achievement. The sample consisted of 1200 students of classes VIII and IX. The tools used were Edwards's social maturity state and achievements test. The research points out students studying in classes IX had higher maturity as compared to students of class VIII. The mean maturity scores of students having low achievement for both classes. Classroom climate and achievement has a significant effort on maturity scores of students of both the class.

Agnihotri, C.S. (1991) has conducted a cross cultural comparative study between tribal and non tribal first generation and traditional learners in relation to their social maturity and educational adjustment. The sample consisted of 113 first generation tribal learners and 108 traditional tribal learners. Social maturity was independent of traditions of learning. The tribal and non-tribal differed in terms of their placements on attribute of social maturity. The traditions of learning were found to be contributing to social maturity. It was found that, the social maturity and educational adjustment were only social ingredients. Psychological characteristics also influenced the social maturity and educational adjustment of children and social maturity was independent of traditions of learning.

Bhushan, A. (1994) conducted a study on social maturity across sex and family vocations. The sample comprised of 200 student teachers from two colleges, equally divided between two sexes. Major variable used were sex values, and family vocations. The tools used for data collections were the form D of value survey. The study highlights, male and female uniformly assigned highest importance to social maturity. Both male and female from service and non-service class had politeness as a subdivision on their maturity.

Foreign Studies

Vora, J.I (1980) in his research work on social maturity of B.Ed., students in Gujarat. The sample size was 855 student teachers from Gujarat University, South Gujarat University and M.S. University. Some of the major findings were (I) The male students were superior to the female students in their social maturity (II) Age had no relation with social maturity (III) The arts students were more socially mature than science students. (IV) The higher socio-economic status had better social maturity.

Saovoluk Thongngamkhom (1983) has investigated the social maturity as a function of some psycho socio-adjustment factors of B.Ed college students of north central region of Thailand. The scale was standardized on a sample of 922 students-including boys and girls. The study states that boys and girls having dominant personality traits were more socially matured than those having submissive personality traits. The two groups of B.Ed., students having high suggestibility and low suggestibility trait did not differ on social maturity. The study revealed that the college students with high SES background were found more socially matured than those of coming from low SES strata. The students having dominant personality trait were more socially matured than those of having submissive personality trait. The students having high leadership personality trait were more socially matured than those of having low leadership personality trait.

Pattramon JumpanGern (1986) investigated the social maturity of teachers, college students of western region of Thailand and found that the teachers - college student coming from urban areas were found to be more matured than those coming from rural areas. Students having good family adjustment were more socially matured than those having poor family adjustment. It was found that the higher secondary students coming from urban areas were found to be more matured than those coming from rural areas. The male higher secondary students were found superior to the female students. The higher secondary students with high SES were more socially matured than those with low SES.

Bancs Ann Leslie (1995) conducted a study on measuring the effect of participation in a peer facilitation project on sixth graders self esteem, social maturity and patterns of social choice. The population chosen for the study was rural mainstream sixth grade students. The sample was tested by sociometric pattern of choice. It was found that some significant difference in social maturity for gender and there was significant relationship between self-esteem and social maturity.

Mulia, R.D (1991). A comparative study of the social maturity of higher secondary students in the contest of their streams, sex and IQs. The objectives were, (I) To study the stream effect on social maturity. (II) To study the sex effect on social maturity. (III) To study the effect of levels of IQs on social maturity. (IV) To study the interaction effect among independent variables on social maturity. It was found that there was no significant relationship in social maturity among students of three streams and between the two sexes, while IQ had main significant effect on social maturity streams and sex and no interaction effect of streams and sex as well as sex and IQs was found significant on social maturity.

Flymin Xavier, J., (2003) attempted a study on social maturity and academic achievement among higher secondary school students. The sample of 300 were taken from government, government aided and private higher secondary schools in Trivandram. The sample were tested by Rao's Social maturity scale. Some of the major findings were (i) Gender has no influence on social maturity (ii) Type of schools had no influence on social maturity (iii) Social maturity and academic achievement are positively correlated.

Mani, M., (2004) did his study on social maturity and adherence to school regulation of higher secondary students. Taken the sample of 300 higher secondary school students studying in 5diffrent schools in Chennai. Rao's social maturity scale was used for administration. Some of the major findings were (I) Gender has significant bearing on social maturity (II) There is significant relationship between social maturity and adherence to school regulations (III) There is significant relationship between social maturity and academic achievement.

Saravanan, K., (2005) attempted a research on social maturity on self-concept among higher secondary school students. The sample of 249 boys and girls who studied XI standard in various schools in Chennai was taken. Rao's social maturity scale was used for administration. Some of the major findings were (I) Social maturity is found to be moderate. (II) Gender has no influence on social maturity. (III) Type of school had no significant difference on social maturity.

CONCLUSION

The survey of related literature has helped the investigator to have clear perspective of the problem chosen for the above review of related literature that very few studies had been carried out using both variables "social intelligence" and "social maturity". Hence the investigator has chosen to study these two variables on college students. The reviews based on Indian and foreign studies, had helped the researcher to frame appropriate hypotheses.

In the light of the literature studied, the third chapter has been designed. ❐

13

Research Design and Methods of Investigation

This chapter gives an overall picture of the design of the study, research tools used for the study, nature and selection of the sample and a brief description of the procedure adopted for the collection of data, in the light of other research studies.

Thyer (1993) defined research design as "a blue print for how research study is to be completed operationalising variables so they can be measured, selecting a sample of interest to study collecting data to be used as a basis for testing hypothesis and analyzing the results".

Research is always directed towards solution to a problem. It is a procedure from known to unknown. The ultimate goal of any research work is to find out the cause and effect relationship between the variables.

Hypotheses

The following hypotheses are set for the present study.

1. The level of social intelligence of Arts and Science college students is moderate in nature.
2. The level of social maturity of Arts and Science college students is moderate in nature.

3. There is a significant relationship between social intelligence and social maturity among Arts and Science college students.
4. There is a significant difference between boys and girls on their social intelligence among Arts and Science College.
5. There is a significant difference between boys and girls on their social maturity among Arts and Science College.
6. There is a significant difference between rural and urban environment on their social intelligence among Arts and Science college students.
7. There is a significant difference between rural and urban environment on their social maturity among Arts and Science college students.
8. There is no significant difference of social intelligence of Arts and Science college students based on their college type.
9. There is no significant difference of social maturity of Arts and Science college students based on their college type.
10. There is no significant difference between government and government aided college students on their social intelligence among Arts and Science college students.
11. There is no significant difference between government and government aided on their social maturity among Arts and Science college students.
12. There is a significant difference between nuclear and joint family students on their social intelligence among Arts and Science college students.
13. There is a significant difference between nuclear and joint family students on their social maturity among Arts and Science college students.
14. There is a significant difference in social intelligence of Arts and Science college students based on their parental income.
15. There is a significant difference in social maturity of Arts and Science college students based on their parental income.

Description of the tools used

To verify the framed hypotheses the following tools and techniques were used in the present investigation.

1. Social Intelligence scale.
2. Social Maturity scale.

SOCIAL INTELLIGENCE SCALE

Description of the tool

This test consists of 54 items and photographs of 12 eminent persons constructed by Dr.N.K.Chadha. This tool deals with 8 factors of social intelligence. They are patience, confidence, cooperativeness, sensitivity, tactfulness, sense of humours, memory, and recognition of social environment.

Administration

The investigator established rapport with the students and explained the purpose of the investigation. The investigator made the arrangements for investigation and informed to the students that they were not being tested, and their responses would be kept confidential in the strict sense. Then the inventory was distributed to the class and the students were asked to record their responses by putting a (X) mark against every statement on the answer sheet. In part V, the list of eminent persons was given. The students were asked to write their names on the answer sheet.

Scoring

In the case of the first four dimensions patience, cooperativeness, confidence, and sensitivity, scores of 1, 2, and 3 were given to three response alternatives. For e.g., in the confidence dimension a score of 3 would indicate a high degree of confidence, a score of 1 a lack of confidence and a score of 2 would reveal moderate confidence. In the other two dimensions (sense of humour and Recognition of social environment) one of three alternatives given is the appropriate response. This response when given was allotted to scores of 1. In the case of the "Tactfulness" dimension the response was awarded a score of "1" the last dimension that of memory was scored "1" or "0" depending on whether or not the subjects response was "right" or "wrong".

SOCIAL MATURITY SCALE

Description of the tool

The maturity outcomes of school going population can best be estimated in the light of paucity of such essential increasing instruments. The social maturity scale was developed by "Dr. Nalini Rao", Department of Education, Bangalore University. The framework for the integrated conceptual virtues of social maturity was adapted from the psychosocial structure.

It was formulated by Green Berger ET.AL. The final form of the questionnaire consists of 90 items know as "Rao's SOCIAL MATURITY SCALE" (RSMS).

Administration

The social maturity scales were administrated to the respondents in groups in the regular classroom situation. The instruction provided on the first page of the scale booklet is self-explanatory. Reading of the instructions by the examiner to the group however ensures better conditions for responding to the items of the scale. The answers were recorded by the respondent on the scale protocol.

The item required completing the scale items are between 45 minutes and one hour classification sought by the student regarding any item is to be handled by the examiner through encouraging the respondents. In this way the administration procedure is carried out.

Scoring

The final form of the questionnaire consists of 90 items. Each item was accorded a four point response speed, the intervals of which are labeled.

- Strongly agree
- Agree
- Disagree
- Strongly disagree

The successive response intervals were subsequently scored as 4, 3, 2 and 1 with the high score represents mature response. There was no right or wrong answers. The answers were checked against the key and point is given for each item ticked as per the key. The total point obtained gives a measure of social maturity.

By this way the scoring is carried out for social maturity.

TABLE. 13.1: Scoring key of the Questionnaire According to the Nature of Items

Nature of item	Strongly Agree	Agree	Strongly Disagree	Disagree
Positive: 17,21,24,26,36,39,41,42,50,51,52,54,56, 57,59,63,74,77,89,90	4	3	2	1
Negative: 1,2,3,4,5,6,7,8,9,10,11,12,13,14,15,16, 18,19,20, 22,23,25,27,28,29,30,31,32,33,34,35,37,38,40,43,44,45,46,47,48,49, 53,55,58,61,62,63,64, 65,66,67,68,69,70,71,72,73,75,76,78,79,80,81,82,83,84, 85,86,87,88	1	2	3	4

Pilot Study

A pilot study was conducted on 50 students to establish the reliability and validity of the different tools used in the present study.

Establishing reliability and validity

The reliability of a test may be defined as the degree of consistency with which the test measures what it does measure. A test score is called reliable to be stable and trustworthy.

The reliability of the tool was calculated using Spearman Brown's formula for split half method.

$$r_{11} = \frac{2r_{hh}}{1 + r_{hh}}$$

r_{11} = Reliability coefficient of the whole test.

r_{hh} = Reliability coefficient of the half test, found experimentally.

SOCIAL INTELLIGENCE SCALE

Reliability

In order to establish the reliability of the social intelligence scale, the split half method was used. The reliability of social intelligence was found to be 0.817. Hence the social intelligence scale is considered as a reliable.

Validity

The index of validity, which is the square root of reliability, was found to be 0.9. Hence social intelligence scale selected for the study was considered to have high validity.

SOCIAL MATURITY SCALE

Reliability

In order to establish the reliability of the social maturity scale, the split half method was used. The reliability of social maturity scale was found to be 0.76. Hence social intelligence scale is considered as a reliable tool.

Validity

The index of validity, which is the square root of reliability, was found to be 0.78. Hence social intelligence scale selection for the study was considered to have high valid.

Main Study

The validated scales were used to collect the necessary data for the main study. The study was carried out on a sample of 300 arts and science college students in the month of November 2006.

The sample was stratified on the basis of type of management viz, Government and Aided colleges and type of location viz, rural and urban environment.

It was also stratified on the basis of the type of college viz, Boys only, girls only and co education.

TABLE. 13.2: The Table Shows the Background Variables of the Samples.

College name	Type of College	College location	Type of management	No of samples
APA arts and science college for boys	Boys only	Urban	Government	90
APA arts and science college for girls	Girls only	Rural	Government	95
St Joseph's College.	Co education	Urban	Government Aided	115

Statistical Techniques used

Suitable descriptive and inferential statistical techniques were used in the interpretation of data to draw out a meaningful picture of results from the collected data. In the present study the following statistical measures were used.

1. Mean

$$X = A + \frac{fD}{f} XI$$

Where,

A = Assumed mean

F = Frequency

D = Deviation from the assumed mean

I = Class interval

2. Quartile Deviation

$$Q_1 = L1 + \left(\frac{N/_4 - CF1}{F1} X1 \right)$$

$$Q_2 = L3 + \left(\frac{3N/_4 - CF3}{F3} X1 \right)$$

$$Q_3 = \frac{Q_3 - Q_1}{2}$$

QD = Quartile Deviation.

Q_1 = First Q D

Q_3 = Third Q D

L_1, L_3 = Lower limit of medium class.

N = Total Frequency.

CF1, CF2 = Cumulative frequency.

F_1, F_2 = Frequency of the medium class.

CONCLUSION

This chapter indicates the details regarding the design of the study, hypotheses, pilot study and statistical techniques used. A detailed discussion of analysis of study and interpretation of the study follows in the next chapter. ❐

14

Analysis and Interpretation of the Data

Research consists of systematic observation and description of the characteristics of properties for the purpose of discovering relationship starts with the description of the measures of the variables and goes on the higher level of statistics analysis. To develop the research plan, processing and analysis of data is necessary .It covers all the technical matters related to research work. This chapter describes the analysis of data and testing of hypotheses that have been framed on the basis of objectives, using appropriate statistical techniques.

The data collected was carefully edited, systematically classified, tabulated, analyzed, interpreted and rationally concluded.

TESTING OF HYPOTHESES

Hypothesis - I

The level of social intelligence of Arts and Science college students is moderate in nature.

TABLE. 14.1: Showing the Level of Social Intelligence of Arts and Science College Students.

Factor	Description	Number of Students	Percentage
Social Intelligence	Low	75	25.00
	Average	143	47.67
	High	82	27.33
	Total	**300**	**100.00**

Interpretation

From the above table it is clear that the level of social intelligence among arts and science college students is average in nature, confirming the hypothesis.

Hypothesis - II

The level of social maturity of Arts and Science college students is moderate in nature.

TABLE. 14.2: Showing the Level of Social Maturity of Arts and Science College.

Factor	Description	Number of Students	Percentage
Social Maturity	Low	78	26.00
	Average	141	47.00
	High	81	27.00
	Total	300	100.00

Interpretation

From the above table it is clear that the social maturity among arts and science college students is average in nature, confirming the hypothesis.

Hypothesis-III

There is a significant relationship between social intelligence and social maturity among Arts and Science college students.

TABLE .14.3: Showing the Relationship Between Social Intelligence and Social Maturity.

Factor	Number of students	Correlation	Level of significance
Social Intelligence and Social Maturity	300	0.79	0.01

Interpretation

From the above table it is clear that there is a relationship between social intelligence and social maturity among arts and science college students. Hence, the empirical hypothesis is accepted.

Hypothesis-IV

There is a significant difference between boys and girls on their social intelligence among Arts and Science college students.

TABLE. 14.4: Showing the Difference Between Boys and Girls on their Social Intelligence.

Factor	Gender	Number of students	Mean	SD	SEMD	CR	L.S
Social Intelligence	Male	150	95.86	15.74	1.29	1.28	N.S
	Female	150	98.01	13.40	1.1		

Interpretation

From the above table it is clear that, there is no significant difference between boys and girls on their social intelligence among Arts and Science college students. Hence, the empirical hypothesis is rejected.

Hypothesis-V

There is a significant difference between boys and girls on their social maturity among Arts and Science college students.

TABLE. 14.5: Showing the Difference Between Boys and Girls on their Social Maturity.

Factor	Gender	Number of students	Mean	SD	SEMD	CR	L.S
Social Maturity	Male	150	236.74	20.65	1.69	2.51	0.05
	Female	150	242.41	18.41	1.50		

Interpretation

From the above table it is clear that, there is no significant difference between boys and girls on their social maturity among Arts and Science college students. Hence, the empirical hypothesis is accepted.

Hypothesis-VI

There is a significant difference between rural and urban environment on their social intelligence among Arts and Science college students.

TABLE. 14.6: Showing the Significant Difference between Rural and Urban Environment on their Social Intelligence.

Factor	Location	Number of students	Mean	SD	SEMD	CR	L.S
Social Intelligence	Rural	95	97.0	13.04	1.33	0.05	N.S
	Urban	205	96.91	15.34	1.07		

Interpretation

From the above table it is clear that, there is no significant difference between rural and urban environment on their social intelligence among Arts and Science college students. Hence the empirical hypothesis is rejected.

Hypothesis-VII

There is a significant difference between rural and urban environment on their social maturity among Arts and Science college students.

TABLE. 14.7: Showing the Significant Difference between Rural and Urban Environment on their Social Maturity.

Factor	Location	Number of students	Mean	SD	SEMD	CR	L.S
Social Maturity	Rural	95	240.16	19.1	1.96	0.35	N.S
	Urban	205	239.31	20.1	1.40		

Interpretation

From the above table it is clear that, there is no significant difference between rural and urban environment on their social maturity among Arts and Science college students. Hence the empirical hypothesis is rejected.

Hypothesis-VIII

There is no significant difference in social intelligence of Arts and Science college students based on their college type.

TABLE. 14.8: Showing the Difference of Social Intelligence based on College Type.

Factor	Source	DF	Sum of squares	Mean squares	F ratio	L.S
Social Intelligence	Between groups	2	1009.15	504.58	2.3787	N.S
	Within groups	297	63000.64	212.12		
	Total	**299**	**64009.80**			

Interpretation

From the above table it is clear that, there is no significant difference of intelligence of Arts and Science college students. Hence the null hypothesis is accepted.

Hypothesis-IX

There is no significant difference in social maturity of Arts and Science college students based on their college type.

TABLE. 14.9: Showing the Difference of Social Maturity based on College Type.

Factor	Source	DF	Sum of squares	Mean squares	F ratio	L.S
Social Maturity	Between groups	2	4661.14	2330.56	6.2	0.01
	Within groups	297	111810.10	376.47		
	Total	299	116471.24			

Interpretation

From the above table it is clear that there is a significant difference of social maturity of Arts and Science college students based on their college type. Hence the null hypothesis is rejected.

Further analysis has been under taken to see group difference in the following table.

TABLE. 14.9(A): Showing Multiple Comparison of the Difference of Social Maturity based on College Type.

Factor	College type	Number of students	Mean	SD	SEMD	CR	L.S
Social Maturity	Boys only	90	233.94	20.04	2.113	2.16	0.05
	Girls only	95	240.16	19.1	1.96		
	Boys only	90	233.94	20.04	2.113	3.47	0.01
	Co education	115	243.50	19.16	1.79		
	Girls only	95	240.16	19.1	1.96	1.26	NS
	Co education	115	243.50	19.16	1.79		

Interpretation

The Arts and Science college students for girls only and co-education college are not having significant difference in their social maturity but all other categories are showing significant differences.

Hypothesis-X

There is no significant difference between government and government aided college students on their social intelligence among Arts and Science college students.

TABLE. 14.10: Showing the Difference between Social Intelligence based on Type of Management.

Factor	Type of management	Number of students	Mean	SD	SEMD	CR	L.S
Social Intelligence	Government	185	95.74	15.10	1.11	1.81	N.S
	Government aided	115	98.87	13.68	1.28		

Interpretation

From the above table it is clear that there is no significant difference between government and government aided college students on their social intelligence among the Arts and Science college students. Hence the null Hypothesis is accepted.

Hypothesis - X I

There is no significant difference between government and government aided college students on their social maturity among Arts and Science college students.

TABLE. 14.11: Showing the Difference between Social Maturity based on Type of Management.

Factor	Type of management	Number of students	Mean	SD	SEMD	CR	L.S
Social Maturity	Government	185	237.14	19.75	1.45	2.75	0.01
	Government aided	115	243.50	19.16	1.79		

Interpretation

From the above table, it is clear that there is a significant difference between government and government aided college students on their social maturity among Arts and Science college students. Hence the null hypothesis is rejected.

Hypothesis - XII

There is a significant difference between nuclear and joint family students on their social intelligence among Arts and Science college students.

TABLE. 14.12: Showing the Significant Difference between Social Intelligence based on Family Type.

Factor	Type of family	Number of students	Mean	SD	SEMD	CR	L.S
Social Intelligence	Nuclear	270	96.38	14.73	0.897	1.99	0.05
	Joint	30	101.97	12.83	2.342		

Interpretation

From the above table, it is clear that there is a significant difference between nuclear and joint family students on their social intelligence among Arts and Science colleges. Hence, the empirical hypothesis is accepted.

Hypothesis - XIII

There is a significant difference between nuclear and joint family students on their social maturity among Arts and Science college students.

TABLE. 14.13: Showing the Difference Between Social Maturity based on Type of Family.

Factor	Type of family	Number of students	Mean	SD	SEMD	CR	L.S
Social Maturity	Nuclear	270	238.76	20.06	1.22	2.16	0.05
	Joint	30	246.9	14.9	2.72		

Interpretation

From the above table, it is clear that there is a significant difference between nuclear and joint family student on their social maturity among Arts and Science college students. Hence, the empirical hypothesis is accepted.

Hypotheses -XIV

There is a significant difference on social intelligence of Arts and Science college students based on their parental income.

TABLE. 14.14: Showing the Difference of Social Intelligence based on Parental Income.

Factor	Source	DF	Sum of squares	Mean squares	F ratio	L.S
Social Intelligence	Between groups	2	7020.88	3510.43	18.29	0.01
	Within groups	297	56988.92	191.88		
	Total	**299**	**64009.80**			

Interpretation

From the above table, it is clear that there is a significant difference on social intelligence of Arts and Science college students based on their parental income. Hence the empirical hypothesis is accepted.

Further analysis has been undertaken to see the group difference in the following table.

TABLE. 14.14 (A): Showing Multiple Comparison of Dfference of Social Intelligence based on Parental Income.

Factor	Parental income	Number of students	Mean	SD	SEMD	CR	L.S
Social Intelligence	<20000	57	89.23	15.19	2.012	2.99	0.01
	20000-50000	150	96.1	14.44	1.18		
	<20000	57	89.23	15.19	2.012	6.22	0.01
	> 50000	93	103.09	11.89	1.23		
	20000-50000	150	96.1	14.44	1.18	3.94	0.01
	>50000	93	103.09	11.89	1.23		

Interpretation

The Arts and Science college students of all the categories are having significant difference in their social intelligence.

Hypothesis: XV

There is a significant difference on social maturity of Arts and Science college students based on their parental income.

TABLE. 14.15: Showing a Difference of Social Maturity based on Parental Income.

Factor	Source	DF	Sum of squares	Mean squares	F ratio	L.S
Social Maturity	Between groups	2	14837.84	7418.92	21.68	0.01
	Within groups	297	101633.40	342.2		
	Total	**299**	**116471.24**			

Interpretation

From the above table, it is clear that there is a significant difference on the social maturity of Arts and Science college students based on their parental income. Hence the empirical hypothesis is accepted.

Further analysis has been undertaken to see group difference in the following table.

TABLE. 14.15 (A): Showing Multiple Comparison of Social Maturity based on Parental Income.

Factor	Parental income	Number of students	Mean	SD	SEMD	CR	L.S
Social maturity	<20000	57	227.56	20.71	2.74	3.78	0.01
	20000-50000	150	238.94	18.84	1.54		
	<20000	57	227.56	20.71	2.74	6.68	0.01
	> 50000	93	247.97	16.41	1.70		
	20000-50000	150	238.94	18.84	1.54	3.81	0.01
	>50000	93	247.97	16.41	1.70		

Interpretation

The Arts and Science college students of all the categories are having significant difference in their social maturity.

CONCLUSION

This chapter summarizes the analysis of data, testing of hypothesis description and discussion of the table. A brief report of the research study together with the major findings and conclusion along with their educational implications has been presented in the succeeding chapter.

❐

15

Summary, Findings & Conclusion

In this chapter, after presenting briefly the statement of the problem and the description of the procedure used in the investigation, the findings and the conclusions are presented. In the light of the findings of the present study, a few suggestions have been proposed at the end of the chapter for further research in this field.

Statement of the Problem

The problem is titled as, "A Study of Social Intelligence and Social Maturity among Arts and Science College students".

Objectives

1. To find out the level of social intelligence of Arts and Science college students.
2. To find out the level of social maturity of Arts and Science college students.
3. To find out the relationship between social intelligence and social maturity among Arts and Science college students.
4. To find out the significant difference between boys and girls on their social intelligence among Arts and Science colleges.
5. To find out the significant difference between boys and girls on their social maturity among Arts and Science colleges.

6. To find out the significant difference between rural and urban environment on their social intelligence among Arts and Science colleges.
7. To find out the significant difference between rural and urban environment on their social maturity among Arts and Science colleges.
8. To find out the significant difference of social intelligence of Arts and Science college students based on their college type.
9. To find out the significant difference on social maturity of Arts and Science college students based on their college type.
10. To find out the significant difference between government and government aided college students on their social intelligence among Arts and Science College.
11. To find out the significant difference between government and government aided college students on their social maturity among Arts and Science College.
12. To find out the significant difference between nuclear and joint family students on their social intelligence among Arts and Science college students.
13. To find out the significant difference between nuclear and joint family students on their social maturity among Arts and Science college students.
14. To find out the significant difference of social intelligence of Arts and Science college students based on their parental income.
15. To find out the significant difference of social maturity of Arts and Science college students based on their parental income.

Hypotheses

1. The level of social intelligence of Arts and Science college students is moderate in nature.
2. The level of social maturity of Arts and Science college students is moderate in nature.
3. There is a significant relationship between social intelligence and social maturity among Arts and Science college students.
4. There is a significant difference between boys and girls on their social intelligence among Arts and Science Colleges.
5. There is a significant difference between boys and girls on their social maturity among Arts and Science Colleges.
6. There is a significant difference between rural and urban environment on their social intelligence among Arts and Science college students.

7. There is a significant difference between rural and urban environment on their social maturity among Arts and Science college students.
8. There is no significant difference of social intelligence of Arts and Science college students based on their college type.
9. There is no significant difference of social maturity of Arts and Science college students based on their college type.
10. There is no significant difference between government and government aided college students on their social intelligence among Arts and Science college students.
11. There is no significant difference between government and government aided college students on their social maturity among Arts and Science college students.
12. There is a significant difference between nuclear and joint family students on their social intelligence among Arts and Science college students.
13. There is a significant difference between nuclear and joint family students on their social maturity among Arts and Science college students.
14. There is a significant difference on the social intelligence of Arts and Science college students based on their parental income.
15. There is a significant difference on the social maturity of Arts and Science college students based on their parental income.

Sample

IRVIN J.LEHMANN defined, "A sample is a smaller number of elements selected from a population and hopefully representative of that population.

The population consists of students who are studying in arts and science colleges.

The investigator randomly selected 300 students from 3 Arts and Science colleges.

Tools used

The following tools were used,

1. Social intelligence scale by Dr.N.K.Chatha.
2. Social maturity scale by Dr.Nalini Rao

Major Findings

The findings arrived at, from the analysis of the data have been presented below,

1. The level of social intelligence among Arts and Science college students is moderate in nature.

2. The level of social maturity among Arts and Science college students is moderate in nature.
3. Students studying Arts and Science College have relationship between social intelligence and social maturity.
4. There is no significant difference between boys and girls studying in Arts and Science College with respect to their social intelligence.
5. There is no significant difference between boys and girls studying in Arts and Science College with respect to their social maturity.
6. There is no significant difference between rural and urban environment Arts and Science college students with respect to their social intelligence.
7. There is no significant difference between rural and urban environment Arts and Science college students with respect to their social maturity.
8. There is no significant difference of social intelligence of Arts and Science college students with respect to their college type.
9. The Arts and Science college students studying girls only and coeducation college are not having significant difference in their social maturity and all other categories are showing significant difference.
10. There is no significant difference between government and government-aided Arts and Science college students with respect to their social intelligence.
11. There is a significant difference between government and government-aided Arts and Science college students with respect to their social maturity.
12. There is a significant difference between nuclear and joint family students on their social intelligence among the Arts and Science Colleges.
13. There is a significant difference between nuclear and joint family students on their social maturity among the Arts and Science Colleges.
14. The Arts and Science college students of all the categories are having significant difference in their social intelligence, based on their parental income.
15. The Arts and Science college students of all the categories are having significant difference in their social maturity, based on their parental income.

Educational Lmplications

Social Intelligence and Social Maturity is an aspect that makes an individual adjusted to the society at large. It is related to the development of the personality of a student. Students studying in Arts and Science colleges are forced to adhere to college regulations as well as social activities. We find that if the students fall in line with the social relationship system and obeying its regulations they may possess a higher social intelligence and social maturity. Therefore for any student social intelligence and social maturity is essential for their daily life.

Hence, the study has a direct impact on the educational practice. The following are some of the major recommendations to be implemented for the social intelligence and social maturity of the students.

- Educators and Administrators should bring about awareness among students to give more importance to develop social intelligence and social maturity.
- Lecturers should provide inspiring leadership to develop social intelligence and social maturity among students.
- Programmes and seminars, which are related to social relationship, are to be arranged in the classroom.

Suggestions for Further Research

- This study was conducted to 300 Arts and Science college students only. To make the study more comprehensive further studies can be conducted on a larger sample.
- This study could be extended to medical, engineering and technical institutions.
- This study could be extended to professionals also.
- This study is confined to a few variables like, gender, location, type of management and type of family, etc., Other variables like, religion, parental qualification, medium of instruction can also be under taken for further research.

❒

16

The Problem and its Perspective

Personality disorders often lack distinguishable characteristics related to an individual's behavior or mannerisms. They can be interpreted as reactions to the problems an individual experiences in everyday life. However, if a person is exhibiting abnormal personality characteristics on a regular basis, without any presence of extraordinary pressure in their day to day existence, the characteristics can be indicative of a personality disorder.

An individual's personality takes shape over the course of ones life. The average person experiments with a multitude of behaviors and expressed characteristics, until they arrive at a predictable pattern of personality expression. A personality disorder, describes consistent behavior by a person that indicates that they have made a poor adjustment to the adaptation of normal, socially acceptable behaviors. These patterns of behavior can result in functional impairment and a distressing alienation from normal society.

The perception an individual with antisocial personality has of society leans toward a dark view, that there is little kindness or social order to be found in day to day life. They believe that aggression and manipulation are skills one needs to succeed in this world. Individuals with this disorder are quick to argue, quick to anger, and have a need to exert control over their environment and the people in it. These individuals often create a personal appearance of congeniality, that masks their mistrust of others and lack of concern for the welfare of other people. When antisocial people are brought into a counseling environment with others, they learn that other people share their experiences, difficulties, and frustrations. The art of sharing their experiences with others helps them to find social acceptance. This coupled with an increased responsibility for their actions are major steps on the road to recovery for those with antisocial behavior disorder.

People with avoidant personality disorder are very uncomfortable with the notion of developing relationships with others. An avoidant is usually shy, quiet and unassuming. They have anxiety around others and have trouble asserting themselves in group settings. They usually have very low self-esteem, which creates a self concept that they are unworthy of being accepted and admired by others.

People afflicted with borderline personality disorder experience a pattern of instability of self-image, interpersonal relationships and mood. Someone with borderline personality experiences mood swings and can alternately exhibit hostile behaviors or withdraw into sullen, depressed states of mind. Their relationships are marked by inconsistency, because the sufferer swings between an over idealized viewpoint of the situation at hand, or they undervalue the significance of the relationships or people in their lives. In the case of the borderline personality, stress can trigger dysphoria, a combination of anxiety, depression, and anger that can rapidly intensify. The borderlines unconventional behavior is a result of their effort to relieve the inner state of distress that is symptomatic of dysphoria.

Individuals with dependant personality disorder cling to those they have relationships with, and subordinate themselves to the people they are involved with. They need instruction from their relationship partners, on even actions and behaviors as individualistic and basic as how to dress, groom themselves, communicate, and their choice of hobbies, interests, and other friends. They also need constant reassurance that their actions are appropriate and acceptable.

Dependent people usually arrange their lives in a way that their lives in a way that their decisions are made for them by parents, spouses, bosses, or friends. They even tend to choose careers that fit into the employment choice recommendations of others. Having excessive dependence on others limits these individuals when it comes time to express their opinion or show initiative.

Individuals with histrionic personality disorder have an acute deep seated need to gain approval from others. They display an insincere and excessive emotionality and their friendships are short-lived in duration. Friends distance themselves from the histrionic person, because they tire of the conceited and manipulative behavior of the person suffering from the disorder.

The histrionic person often has a faulty self-image. They can consider themselves generous and trustworthy when the opposite is true. Their incorrect self-concept is related in many cases to an upbringing characterized by parental physical abuse and emotional neglect. The individual learns to perform for the benefit of others in an effort to win their attention and approval. In the meantime they lose their true sense of self.

The Narcissistic person exemplifies another personality disorder, characterized by the manipulation of others by insincere behaviors intended to win acceptance or praise. The disorder differs from the histrionic in that rather than appearing warm and sociable, the individual evokes a cold and aloof social presence.

They tend to have delusions of grandeur which they incorporate into their self-concept. While maintaining this exaggerated self-concept, they anticipate a public reception appropriate to this deluded sense of personal status. Sometimes the narcissistic person is merely someone who has been hurt in past relationships, and has a need to maintain a self-generating from of self-love. This self-love may be necessary because of a lack of love based relationships in their lives. However, an individual needs to embrace a true self-concept and a high level of unconditional self-love in order to avoid a semblance of narcissistic behavior in the eyes of someone mental health care providers.

Family relationship is a key factor to develop individual's personality. If the home relation is not conducive to the students naturally personality deviation will be excepted. The sample taken for this study in Engineering College Students. In this scenario the investigator has made an attempt to study the influence of family relationship on their personality disorder.

THE CONCEPT OF PERSONALITY

Woodworth (1958) defines personality as the total quality of an individual's behavior as it is revealed in his habits of thought and expression, his attitudes and interest, his manner of acting and his personal philosophy of life. Hilgard defines personality, as the configuration of individual characteristics and ways of behaving which describes as individuals unique adjustment to his environment. Freedom (1918) defines personality as the product of the dynamic and characteristic organization within the individual of psycho-biological structures or systems and their interaction with the environment". An often quoted definition of personality calls it the dynamic organization within the individual of those psycho-physical systems that determine his unique adjustment to his environment. Allport, (1937). Developing further, he proposed that trait model of personality for the first time.

According to Cattell (1961) "Personality is concerned with all the behavior of the individual both overt and under the skin". Trait formulations have provided a prevalent vehicle for psychologist's attempts to describe individual differences and to incorporate person variables in the prediction of human behavior. That is the assumption that personality can be construed as a set of central traits or relatively enduring behavioral predispositions, has largely structured traditional non-psychodynamic personality theory, measurement and research.

Jung, attempted to classify human beings on two behavioral dimensions: extrovert and introvert. His typology is widely known and is most influential among professional workers. The major characteristics of the two types are as follows:

i. Introvert

A person who tends to withdraw into himself, especially, when faced by emotional conflicts and stress in his environment. Introvert individual is shy, avoids people and enjoys to be alone. Scientists and philosophers may be termed as introvert.

ii. Extrovert

In contrast to the introvert type, extrovert person's orientation is towards the external world. He deals people intelligently in social situations. He is conventional, outgoing, social, friendly, and free from worries. Social workers, politicians, business executive may be types as extrovert. These two broad categories have been further classified on the basis of rational and irrational process.

This classification has been criticized on the ground that in general, the different types or classes as suggested by Jung do not exist. On the basis of typical characteristics prescribed for the extrovert and introvert, most of us may belong to both categories at different times and any may be called ambivert. This introduces a complication and hence the type approach does not give a clear classification or description of personality.

THEORIES OF PERSONALITY

In our day-to-day conversation we ascribe traits to our friends and near one's as being honest, shy, aggressive, lazy, dull, dependent etc. Traits may be defined as relatively permanent and relatively consistent general behavior patterns that an

i. Personality Traits

Personality trait refers to those elements that help in the formation of personality. Good defines a trait as a "a characteristic and relatively permanent mode of behavior, the outcome of heredity and environment".

Garrett defines personality trait as, "distinctive ways of behaving more or less permanent for given individual."

Sociability, submission and persistence are some of the personality traits. The personality traits are expressed in ones behavior. The personality traits are unstable in nature. The expression of a trait depends on the situation. Some of the personality traits are as given below:

a. Honesty

In the presence of this personality trait, one behaves honestly, is sincere in his work.

b. Emotional Stability

This personality enables the individual to maintain equilibrium and mental state even in adverse situations.

G.W.Allport (1961), defined a trait, "as a generalized and focalized neuropsychic system with the capacity to render many stimuli functionally equivalent and to imitate and guide consistent forms of adoptive and expressive behavior."

The definition given by Allport (1961) is a comprehensive one. Traits according to him are general and enduring in nature. They are not linked with a small of stimuli. He classified human traits as cardinal traits, central trait, and secondary disposition. Traits differ in intensity and magnitude from individual to individual. They operate in their own environment in a unique manner.

The traits have certain properties. There are some traits which can be measured quantitatively. They are not static in nature. During childhood days they are flexible. With the attainment of maturity they become stable. Even then some variables continue throughout life. Trait is also a mental set. They are organized frames of reference. In the interaction of individual with the environment traits are learned. The personality of an individual consists of the traits like physical, mental, intellectual, social, emotional and spiritual The reaction of this "patterns of traits" to stimuli may not be the same for different personalities in the same situation or even for the same personality in different situations. Consider the variations in emotional response to a frustrating situation such as this a person is waiting to meet a friend, but the friend fails to appear. In this situation, one person is amused, another angry and a third annoyed, and perhaps a fourth indifferent. Furthermore, in the same situation an individual may react in different ways on different days, depending on such factors as his physical well being, his general emotional tone, and his most recent experiences. In short, even if the stimulus is apparently the same, the individual's response to it on different occasions may be highly variable on account of the uniqueness of each personality, or the uniqueness of the pattern of traits in each individual. The personality of each individual is most of the time determined by many factors the biological, sociological and psychological. All the factors sometime determine an individual to develop certain specific qualities. Leadership qualities could also be one among them. The origin of leaderships drawn from different classifications, they can be seen, as executive, elected and self-emerging.

EYSENCK'S THEORY OF PERSONALITY

Eysenck provides a hierarchical type approach to personality. He describes three basic categories of personality at the top of the hierarchy.

Extroversion ↔ introversion, neuroticism ↔ stability, psychotism ↔ normality.

These have been ultimately reduced to two dimensions namely, stable ↔ unstable and introversion ↔ extroversion. Each of these categories involves certain qualities at the next lower of trait level. For example, the traits of an introvert would include such qualities as persistence, rigidity of approach, subjectivity etc. These traits in turn are associated with the next habitual response level.

For example, we may except an introvert to be persistent in tasks like problem solving etc. Generally, the last is the specific response level, which applies to specific tasks in which also the traits involved in the categories would be expressed in diverse degrees. Eysenck's approach is hierarchical with the top indicating types and the lower indicating traits.

EXTROVERSION, NEUTROTICISM AND PSYCHOISM

Eysenck evaluates both structure and dynamic of personality. Structure consists in the organization of specific responses into habits, habits into traits and traits into type dimensions. The main two dimensions are neuroticism and extraversion. Neuroticism was first established as a dimension in large sample of mental patients and then extended to the normal population. Highly neurotic persons are, likely to be dependent poorly organized nervous system, touchy, suggestible and lacking in persistence and so on. Extroversion was also established as a dimension along with neuroticism. Highly extroverted persons are likely to be sociable and lively and to have a good sense of human.

NEUROTICISM AND THE AUTOMATIC NERVOUS SYSTEM

Eysenck has proposed that neuroticisms also reflect emotionality. Neuroticism is a manifestation of certain characteristics of the autonomous nervous system. From a review of numerous pertinent studies, he concludes that these are a close relationship between neuroticism and liable activity of the autonomous nervous system. If such was the case, neuroticism could also be expected to be inheritable some extent inheritable. Neurotic deviations are mild in nature and could be curable. The personality disorders are very much related to psychotic deviation.

DIFFERNET TYPES OF PERSONALITY DISORDER

i. Paranoid Disorder

In paranoid disorder which has an acuate onset and carries a good prognosis. The duration of illness is usually less than 6 months. The common etiology is abrupt change in environment in immigrants paranoia is a disorder with an insidious onset and relatively stable, chronic course. It is characterized by welt systematized delusions. The emotional response and behavior is understandable in the height of paranoid disorder.

Also called delusional disorder, this disorder is characterized by:

Persistent delusions, Persecution, Grandeur, Jealousy.

A hallucination is commonly found among them. As personality disturbance will happen in the area of delusions. In this type of disorder, absence of schizophrenia and mood disorder is common.

ii. Depression

Depression in elderly patients may present as dementia clinically. It is called depressive pseudodementia. Identification of depression is very important as it is treatable. These patients themselves complain of memory impairment, difficulty is sustaining attention and concentration and reduced intellectual capacity. In contrast a patient of dementia does not complain of these disturbances. Infact when confronted of these disturbances. Infact when confronted with memory testing he often confabulates. As depression may often be superimposed on dementia it is at time necessary to give a therapeutictrial with antidepressants.

The number of conditions which can cause dementia is large. But a majority of causes are due to a few common causes namely Alzheimer's diseases, multi-infarct dementia and hypothyroidism.

iii. Manic

One percent of the population is affected by Manic disorder. This disorder tends to occur in episodes lasting usually 3-4 months, followed by complete recovery. The elevated mood can pass through following four stages depending on the severity of manic episode. The euphoria characterized by increased sense of psychological well being and happiness not in keeping with ongoing events. This is seen in hypomania. The elation moderate elevation of mood or feeling of confidence and enjoyment along with increased psychomotor activity. This is classical of manic. The exaltation or severe elevation of mood intense elation with delusions of grandeur. The ecstasy or very severe elevation of mood, seen in delirious or stupor us manic.

Along with these variations in elevation of mood expensive mood may be present, which is unceasing and unselective enthusiasm for interacting with people and surrounding environment. There may be rapid, short lasting shifts from euphoria to depression or anger.

There is increased psychomotor activity ranging from over activeness and restlessness to manic excitement where the person is on the – toe –on –the- go, (i.e., involved in ceaseless a activity). The activity is usually goal oriented and based on external environmental cues. The person is more talkative than usual describes thoughts racing in mind develops pressure of speech uses playful language with punning, rhyming, joking and testing and speaks loudly.

In manic there is marked increase in activity with excessive planning and at times execution of multiple activities. Due to being involved in so many activities and distractibility there is decrease in functioning ability in later stages. There is named increase in sociability even with previously unknown people. Gradually this sociability leads to an interfering behavior though the person does not recognize it as abnormal at that time.

Due to grandiose ideation, increased sociability over activity and poor judgement the manic person is involved in high risk activities like buying sprees reckless driving foolish business investments distributing money and or articles to unknown persons. He is usually dressed up in gaudy and flamboyant clothes although in serve manic these may be poor self-care.

Sleep is usually reduced with a decreased need for sleep Appetite may be increased but later these is usually decreased food intake, due to marked over activity. Insight into the illness is absent.

iv. Anxiety

Anxiety is the commonest psychiatric symptom in clinical practice and anxiety disorders are one of the commonest psychiatric disorders.

Anxiety is a normal phenomenon which is characterized by a state of apprehension or unease arising out of anticipation of danger. Anxiety is differentiated from fear as fear is an apprehension in response to an external danger while in anxiety the danger is largely unknown normal anxiety becomes pathological when it causes significant subjective distress and (or) impairment in functioning trait anxiety is a habitual tendency to be anxious in general and is exemplified by “ I often feel anxious”

State anxiety is the anxiety felt at the present moment exemplified by ‘I feel anxious now’. Persons with trait anxiety often have episodes of state anxiety.

The symptoms of anxiety can be broadly classified in two groups:

THE PSYCHIC SYMPTOMS OF ANXIETY ARE:

Apprehension, poor concentration, un-ability to relax, irritability, initial insomnia, when severe, felling of impending doom depersonalization and dieselization and exaggerated startle response.

THE PHYSICAL SYMPTOMS OF ANXIETY ARE:

Motor tension live trembling, body aches, restlessness, twichings, fatigue, Autonomic palpitations, dysprea, tachycardia, dry mouth, frequency of maturation, dizziness, lump in the throat.

v. Schizophrenia

One percent of the population suffers from schizophrenia. Although this disorder has puzzled philosophers, physicians and general public for centuries, systematic study of schizophrenia is but a century old. To understand what schizophrenia is, it is important to have a brief look at the history of evolution of the concept of schizophrenia.

vi. The Symptons of Schizophrenia Are

a) HALLUCINATIONS, audible thoughts leaving of voice or hallucinatory voices.

Also thought withdrawal, thought insertion, Thought diffusion or broad casting, Made feeling or affect. Made impulses, and Made volition or acts.

These symptoms have been described in detail as they have very often been used for diagnosis of schizophrenia and have influenced future classifications significantly. As mentioned earlier, they are not specific for schizophrenia and may be seen in other psychiatric disorders like mood disorders, organic psychiatric disorders.

Schizophrenia is characterized by disturbance in thought and verbal behavior, perception, affect, motor behavior and relationship to external world. The diagnosis is entirely clinical.

Autistic thinking is one of the most important features of schizophrenia. Here thinking is governed by private and illogical rules.

A pattern of spontaneous speech in which things said in juxtaposition lack a meaningful relationship or there is idiosyncratic shifting from one frame of reference to another. The speech is often described as being 'disjointed'. Thought blocking is a characteristic feature of schizophrenia, although can also be seen in complex partiel seizures (temporal lobe epilepsy).

vii. Hysteric

The word hysteric has been used in so many contexts by psychiatrists, physicians and non-professionals that it no longer has any one meaning. These various contexts are:

Impulsive, uncontrolled behavior.

Manipulative, dramatic, exhibitionistic emotional and (or) seductive behavior.

DEFINITION OF FAMILY

In a time when sociologists at least in the western world-contend that disintegration and deinstitutionalization of the family has led to a growing pluralization of family forms, defining the family is not an easy task. They range from conceiving of the family as a legalized two generational unit of co-residing persons related by blood and or adoption to viewing it as a widely unspecified constellation of persons who of their own volition call themselves a family.

FAMILY RELATIONSHIP

The number of possible relationships within a family increases exponentially with the number of individual family members. In a four-person family, for example these are 11 groupings of family members (six dyads, four triads and one tetrad). These complex patterns of relationships should be kept in mind as some of the major types of relationships should be investigated.

"Home, a centre of love and affection, is the best place for education and the first school of the child". He regarded home as the one indispensable factor in the young child's training, and the mother as the fountain head of all true education. A child sees the high of the day in the home. Family is the first social environment.

THE IMPORTANCE OF HOME

A successful system of education must harness them all to meet the all around educational needs of man. "Home is the eternal school of life". It is one of the important units of society.

IMPORTANT FUNCTIONS OF HOME OR FAMILY

It is often said that home is the first institution of education and the mother is the first teacher of child. Family as the first teacher educates the child in his health habit, speech pattern, basic ideas and the money fold attitudes towards himself and associates. Intact, family provides the foundation on which the future superstructure of the child education in constructed.

As long as the child is depended on his parents they have to work for satisfying his economic needs. They have to provide for his food, clothing, education, recreation and various other needs, where he needs money. Not only this, they have to train him for some vocation or occupation in life. It clearly reveals that home or family has great educational potentialities.

SPECIFIC EDUCATIONAL FUNCTIONS OF HOME

Physical care of the child is the first important educational responsibility of the family. The home provides such necessities as food, clothing, shelter and the medical care to the child. Thus he maintains good health. Physical health also depends upon good health habits such as regular brushing of teeth, proper sleep etc. The family gives early training in these health rules to enable the child to develop sound physical health.

"Sound mind in a sound body" is an age old maximum. Within the home, the family helps the child in his early intellectual development. Language is the most important activity which the child develops in the family.

FAMILY AS AN EDUCATIONAL AGENCY

The family can play a significant role as an educational agency. Since the whole educative influence proceeds from the parents, it is desirable that there should be healthy relationships between parents and other elders in the family. Moreover, the child-parents relationship also matters a lot in the educative process that goes on within the home.

Crow and Crow have rigidly pointed out: "unfortunate is the educational influence of the home in which parents disagree in the parents of the child concerning what constitutes desirable child behavior. The young child should not be led to discover that if one present denies him a desired privilege, he can get it act of the other parents. Relatives should not become a source of comfort for the undisciplined child. In that case the whole education becomes a force and the family cannot achieve anything constructive". They should become models of desirable behavior for the children and should not indulge in anything which may be vicious of anti-educative.

Raymont warns that the division of responsibility must in no way be taken in imply "a rigid separation" of the two. He adds, "The wise parent and teacher will, however, seek to understand

Each others aims and to second each other's efforts, so that the child's education will form an organic whole. Nothing can be more demoralizing to child than lack of unity and harmony in his home life and his school life".

This it is through complementary nature of the home and the school that education of the child becomes or shared responsibility and a joint enterprise. It is an this sense that the teacher is the only true parent and the only true teacher.

WAYS AND MEANS ADOPTED TO SEEK ACTIVE CO-OPERATION BETWEEN THE HOME AND SCHOOL

The first essential thing in the home-school relationship is the parent's interest in their child's education. Crow and Crow have rightly pointed out that the beginning months at school, "constitute an important milestone and a child's life". During this period the parents should take pride in the fact that their son or daughter is now big enough to go to school. At home, the child should be given the feeling that his teacher will be as much interested in his welfare as his own parents are. In fact, during the child's whole school life this feeling should continue and parents should show a sincere interest in the child's activities at school. Parental reports about their children count a lot towards the teacher understands of the child. A complete case history of the child will be of immense use.

All wise parents are interested in their child's work at school. The school can enlist the faith and co-operation of the parents by sending detailed reports of the work of the child to his parents. These reports will invite parents opinion and advice in the well-being of the child. The school can also make suggestions about the child's home, conditions of work, play, rest and food and about his relations with his elders and friends.

Parents visit to the school is an essential condition for co-ordinated effort of the home and the school. The visit will provide occasions and opportunities for home-school co-operation.

ROLE OF PARENT'S EDUCATION

It is a platitude and also a truth that it can be one of the easiest things in the world, to become, and one of the hardest things in the world to be a parent. Sensible parents gave proper replies to children's questions and contribute, to the development of their powers of expression, understanding, conversation and discussion.

"The hand that rocks the cradle rules the world" bears a testimony to the fact that any education is misnomer if there is no pertinent sharing of parents. There is no denying the fact that education does not commence with the alphabet, it begins with a mother's look, with a fathers and of approbation or a sign of reproof, with sister's gentle pressure of the hand or a brother's noble act of forbearance. Hence the starting point of all education is the early life of the child curved out by the genius with the child's need. Parents who themselves are in conflict with their quarrels and tragic scenes are bad company for the child considered mother as a true nurse.

The mother plays an important role in promoting the forward looking tendencies in the growing child. The moral tone and the emotional-atmosphere of the life may have equal reaction on the child's school work. Thus if the home and mother supply the right environment of study, love and affection and provide the child with he opportunity to express himself in freedom, then like a plant, given good soil and sunlight, the child will flourish.

The foundation for education is laid in the home of the child. That is home is the eternal school or in other words, home is a school away from school and school of the parents under the bracing environments of parental proof.

Education is a careless process of modification and corrections. Mother educate children to develop them in to a potential parent. Thus the seed of parenthood at the adult stage. The lamp lighted by another lamp shines lack to the previous one. It is abundantly clear now that parenthood pervades the entire life of the child. To make the life rich and fuller, the image of an ideal home must be visualized. If one has to prepare the list of educators participating in the task of education parents will primarily top the list.

The loving mother and intelligent father have to play their roll in complete harmony and accordance is a home away from home. Home is the base and school forms that future construction. "Home is a place on which the sun shines and home is a place in which the sun stains". The first lesson of citizenship is being learnt at home. There cannot be water light compartments between home and school.

STATEMENT OF PROBLEM

Personality Disorders and Family Relationship among Engineering College Students.

OPERATIONAL DEFINITION

1. **Personality Disorders:** By this the investigator means the scores obtained from Multiphasic Personality Questionnaire constructed and standardized by H.N. Murthy.
2. **Family Relationship:** By this the investigator means the scores obtained from Index of Family Relationship by Walter W Hudson.
3. **Engineering College Students:** By this the investigator means the students who are studying the Bachelor of Engineering after completion of their Higher Secondary education.

DEFINITION OF TECHNICAL TERM USED

1. **Personality Disorders:** Personality Disorders often lack distinguishable characteristics related to an individual's behavior or mannerisms. A Personality disorders, describes consistent behavior by a person, that indicates that they have made a poor adjustment to the adaptation of normal, socially acceptable behaviors.

2. **Family Relationship:** Family, broadly speaking is a single unit of people who live together and share life's basic day-by-day functions. Humanity has demonstrated the need for such a core group, and the need for each individual to grow. These dual, sometimes, contrasting, human needs create the paradox of the family unit, in which exist struggle for separateness and togetherness, difference and similarity, protection and freedom, support and independence.

OBJECTIVES OF THE STUDY

1. To find out the significant difference between boys and girls of Engineering College Students on their personality disorders.
2. To find out the significant difference between personality disorders and Family Relationship of Engineering College Students.
3. To find out the significant difference between boys and girls of Engineering College Students belonging to nuclear and joint family on their personality disorders
4. To find out the significant difference between the students belonging to nuclear and joint family on their Family Relationship.
5. To find out the significant difference on the personality disorders of engineering college students based on their mother's occupation.
6. To find out the significant difference on the Family Relationship of engineering college students based on their mother's occupation.
7. To find out the significant difference of personality disorders among engineering college students based on their parental income.
8. To find out the significant difference of Family Relationship among Engineering College Students based on their parental income.
9. To find out the significant difference on the type of personality disorders of Engineering College Students based on their father's occupations.
10. To find out the significant difference on the type of Family Relationship of Engineering College Students based on their Father's occupation.
11. To find out the significant relationship between home relation and personality disorders of Engineering College Students.

LIMITATIONS

1. This study is limited to investigate among the Engineering College Students
2. A sample of 250 is selected for this study.
3. This study is taken only one college named Thandhai Periyar Engineering College in Vellore District.

CONCLUSION

Family is the first place of education of the child. It plays a vital role in the Personality development of the child. Children of same parents vary in personality and respond to stimuli and environment in different ways. This chapter deals with the overview of the problem, objectives and limitation of the study. The next chapter concerns with the review of related literature.

❐

17

Review of Related Literature

Review of related literature is an important prerequisite to actual Planning and then the execution of any research work. Best (1963) writes "A familiarity with the literature in any problem area helps the students to discover what is already known, attempted methods promising and disappointing, and problems that remain to be solved"

The investigator feels that the study of related literature in acquiring information about the studies done in the field protects against unnecessary duplication, guides in carrying out the investigation successfully and makes him familiar with the steps. In the following pages, a review is made on the studies conducted in India and abroad related to the present study.

NEED FOR SURVEY OF RELATED LITERATURE

Extensive initial reading in a field makes the investigator familiar with the accumulated facts in this field. Study of related literature sensitizes the individual to new avenues in research. It furnished the researcher with indispensable suggestions about comparative data, good procedures, likely methods.

Barg says that review of literature is an important part of the scientific approach and is carried out in all areas of scientific research. It gives scholars the understanding of previous work that has been done. It also provides the means of getting to the frontiers in the particular field of knowledge.

So the investigator has attempted on relevant information related to his work. A number of studies conducted on family relationship and academic achievement are presented in this chapter.

STUDIES RELATED TO PERSONALITY DISORDERS

Johnson and Jeffrey-G. 1996 conducted a study on Psychiatric Symptomatology and Substance Use in Adolescents with Personality Disorders.

The extent to which adolescents diagnosed with one or more Personality Disorders through the Personality Diagnostic Questionnaire-Revised were at an elevated risk of substance abuse was studied with 441 undergraduates. Those with one or more Personality Disorders showed higher levels of psychiatric Symptomatology and substance use.

Hardy and Gillian-E.(1995) conducted a study on Impact of Cluster C Personality Disorders on Outcomes of Contrasting Brief Psychotherapies for Depression.

Study compares 27 depressed clients diagnosed with Cluster C Personality Disorder (PD) with 87 depressed clients without the diagnosis. All clients completed cognitive-behavioral or psychodynamic-interpersonal psychotherapy. Treatment length did not influence outcome for PD clients. PD clients whose depression was also relatively severe showed significantly less improvement after treatment than either PD clients with less severe depression or non-PD clients.

Mills and Anne (1995) conducted a study on a Survey of Current Practice.

Reports findings of a 1993 questionnaire completed by 46 North American art therapists that focuses on the outpatient treatment of multiple Personality Disorder. Includes information on role in diagnosing, fees and third-party payment, and therapeutic activities. Treatment issues include pacing and containment, and managing the client's chronic suicidality.

Fong and Margaret-L. (1995) conducted a study on a Primer for Counselors.

The DSM-IV categorizes 10 Personality Disorders, long-term patterns of personality traits that result in impairment of social and occupational functioning. The author details steps in the recognition and diagnosis of Personality Disorders, with emphasis on using the DSM-IV diagnostic framework.

Kjos and Diane (1995) conducted a study on Linking Career Counseling to Personality Disorders.

Relates Personality Disorders to career development issues and counseling interventions. Case examples suggesting career-focused treatment interventions for dependent, borderline, obsessive-compulsive, and passive-aggressive Personality Disorders are presented.

Morris and Maureen-Batza (1995) conducted a study on the Diagnostic Drawing Series and the Tree Rating Scale: An Isomorphic Representation of Multiple Personality Disorder, Major Depression, and Schizophrenic Populations.

The tree drawings of 80 subjects, who were diagnosed with either multiple Personality Disorder, schizophrenia, or major depression, and a control group, were rated. Patterns were examined and graphs were used to depict results. Certain features were found to distinguish each category. The descriptive statistical findings were both consistent and inconsistent with earlier Diagnostic Drawing Series research findings.

Baltaxe and Christiane (1995) conducted a study on Discourse Cohesion in the Verbal Interactions of Individuals Diagnosed with Autistic Disorder or Schizotypal Personality Disorder.

This study compared high functioning adolescents and young adults with autism (n=8) or schizotypal Personality Disorder (n=9) in use of social language referencing. Both groups had similar rates, types, and patterns of cohesive reference errors, though subjects with schizotypal disorder used cohesive ties of reference more often and more correctly than did subjects with autism.

Trull and Timothy-J. (1995) conducted a study on Borderline Personality Disorder Features in Non clinical Young Adults. Identification and Validation.

Two studies involving approximately 3,500 college students were conducted to establish and validate a self-report method of identifying non clinical young adults with significant borderline Personality Disorder features and to evaluate clinical correlates of this classification across relevant areas of functioning. Results support the validity of the self-report method.

Schroeder and Marsha-L (1992) conducted a study on Dimensions of Personality Disorder and Their Relationships to the Big Five Dimensions of Personality.

Dimensional measures of aspects of Personality Disorders (PD) were developed. Convergence of these measures with the "Big Five" personality factors was studied in 300 general population subjects. Results suggest substantial similarity between the five factors and PD measures, though the latter cannot be entirely subsumed by the Big Five model.

Stevens and Gail-Flint (1994) conducted a study on Prison Clinicians' Perceptions of Antisocial Personality Disorder as a Formal Diagnosis.

Surveyed and interviewed 53 clinicians who work with prison inmates. Results indicated that clinicians used diagnosis of antisocial Personality Disorder liberally among inmates and felt majority of inmates could be so diagnosed. Large minority of clinicians went beyond Diagnostic and Statistical Manual of Mental Disorders criteria and reported looking for characteristics associated with concept of psychopaths.

Waller and Glenn (1994) conducted a study on childhood Sexual Abuse and Borderline Personality Disorder in the Eating Disorders.

Examination of 115 women with eating disorders revealed a secondary diagnosis of borderline Personality Disorder associated with a history of childhood sexual abuse. A model involving background features, precipitants, and immediate and long-term psychological consequences is suggested to explain the link to childhood abuse, and implications for treatment of eating disorders are considered.

Clarkin and John-F (1993) conducted a study on a Comparison of SCID - II BPD and NEO-PI.

Hospitalized female patients with borderline Personality Disorder were assessed for Axis II disorders by the Structured Clinical Inventory for the Diagnostic and Statistical Manual of Mental Disorders (SCID-II) and for personality traits with the NEO Personality Inventory. The relationship of results to social adjustment and the utility of information on pathology and personality traits are discussed.

Weaver,-Terri-L. and Clum,-George-A. (1993) conducted a study on Early Family Environments and Traumatic Experiences Associated with Borderline Personality Disorder.

Assessed childhood trauma experiences (sexual abuse, physical abuse, witnessed violence, early separation) and family environment characteristics of 17 depressed female patients with borderline Personality Disorder (BPD) and 19 without BPD. Significantly, more BPD subjects reported histories of sexual abuse, physical abuse, and witnessed violence. Sexual abuse emerged as only significant predictor of dimensional BPD score.

STUDIES RELATED TO FAMILY RELATIONSHIP

Peters and Scott-Ryan (1995) conducted a study on Family Relations and Writing: Using One to improve the other-an Annotated Bibliography.

Presents a 25-item annotated bibliography of journal articles (published between 1991 and 1994) describing writing and research exercises and approaches for helping students becomes aware of their own families and others.

Lawson and David-M. (1994) conducted a study on Counselor Trainee Early Family Structure and Current Intergenerational Family Relationships Implications for Training.

Investigated counselor trainee's recollections of early family structure and current intergenerational relationships. Found trainees who remained relatively free from "triangling" patterns with parents reported significantly greater spousal intimacy, more individuation from parents, and less triangulation with children and spouses. Reports other results and implications.

Kashubeck,-Susan and Christensen,-Sue-A. (1995) conducted a study on Parental Alcohol Use, Family Relationship Quality, Self-Esteem, and Depression in College Students.

Family relationship quality, not parental alcohol use, predicted levels of depression and self-esteem in 201 college students. Witnessing spousal abuse related to increased depression in adult children of alcoholics, whole poorer family relationship quality was associated with lower self-esteem, suggesting the experience of paternal alcoholism is not uniform among offspring.

Kister and Joanna (1995) conducted a study on Family Relations Resource Guide. A Resource for Teaching the Family Relations Core Course Area of Ohio's Work and Family Life Program.

This resource guide provides those teaching the Family Relations course of the Ohio Work and Family Life Program an overview of the course content, teacher background information, learning activities, and assessment ideas. It has one teaching module for each process competency and each content competency in the Family Relations and Process Competency units of the Occupational Competency Analysis Profile (OCAP). These modules appear in this guide in the same order in which the competencies are listed in the OCAP. The learning activities are written from the students' perspective, but teacher notes are included to assist teachers in conducting activities. The four process modules are as follows: managing work and family responsibilities, solving personal and family problems, relating to others, and assuming a leadership role. The eight content modules cover the following subjects: analyzing the significance of families; nurturing human development; forming one's own family; building and maintaining healthy family relationships; developing family communication patterns; dealing with stress, conflicts, and crises; managing work and family roles and responsibilities; and analyzing social forces affecting families. Each module consists of these components: module overview, including practical problem, process competency, competency builders, and supporting concepts; teacher background information with rationale, background, and list of references; learning activities; assessment (paper and pencil, classroom experiences, and application to real-life settings); and handouts.

McHale and Susan-M. (1995) conducted a study on Links with Family Relations and Children's Well-Being.

Examined patterns of mothers' and fathers' differential treatment of first-born and second-born school-age siblings in 110 families and the links between parents' differential treatment and children's well-being and dyadic family relationships. Found that parental patterns were linked to differences between the siblings' well-being and that younger siblings exhibited greater vulnerability to differential treatment.

Brody and Gene-H. (1994) conducted a study on Family Process in Rural, Two-Parent African American Families.

Examined hypothesis that parental religiosity contributes to organization of rural African American family relationships among sample of 90 African American youths and their married parents. Religiosity was linked with higher levels of marital interaction quality and co caregiver conflict. Associations between religiosity and parent-youth relationship quality were mediated by marital and co caregiver relationships.

Mortimer,-Jeylan-T and Shanahan,-Michael-J (1994) conducted a study on Adolescent Work Experience and Family Relationships.

A 3-year study of 1,000 adolescents and their parents found that student employment has significant effects on family relationships. It fosters separation and individuation, of which parents approve, and diminished family time did not affect the quality of relationships. Boys' work had more positive effects than did girls' work.

Larson and Jeffry-H. (1994) conducted a study on the Impact of Job Insecurity on Marital and Family Relationships.

Examined relationship between perceived stress resulting from job insecurity and marital and family functioning. Data from 111 married couples in which at least 1 spouse was working in insecure job environment showed that job insecurity stress was related in systematic way to marital and family dysfunction and number of family problems reported.

Gentry and Deborah (1994) conducted a study on 1993-Twenty - Fifth Annual National Council on Family Relations Videotape Competition.

Lists and annotates winning entries in 1993 National Council on Family Relations Videotape Competition in categories of substance abuse, aging, social issues, divorce/remarriage, families with special needs, family violence, human development, reproduction and family planning, marital/family issues, mental health, nontraditional families, parenting, sexuality, teenage pregnancy, sexually transmitted disease and Acquired Immune Deficiency Syndrome, and others.

McGuire,-Jacqueline and Earls,-Felton (1993) conducted a study on Exploring the Reliability of Measures of Family Relations, Parental Attitudes, and Parent-Child Relationships in a Disadvantaged Minority Population.

Forty mothers, living in economically disadvantaged inner-city locations completed four parenting questionnaires (Parental Attitudes to Childrearing, Parental Acceptance Rejection Questionnaire, Raising Children, and Conflict Tactics Scale) from two to four weeks apart. Significant test-retest reliability was established for all four measures and internal consistency was similar to published reports.

Whitbeck and Les-B. (1993) conducted a study on Family Relationship History, Contemporary Parent-Grandparent Relationship Quality, and the Grandparent-Grandchild Relationship.

Investigated effects of early family experiences on mediating role of parents for grandparent-grandchild relationship. Findings from parents' and ninth graders' reports regarding 1,138 grandparents revealed that recalled non optimal parent-child relationships between parents and grandparents negatively affected the contemporary parent-grandparent relationship and subsequently affected contact and relationship quality for grandchildren and their grandparents.

Cook,-William-L. and Goldstein,-Michael-J. (1993) conducted a study on Multiple Perspectives on Family Relationships: A Latent Variables Model.

Tested the assumption that social desirability and other factors bias familial self-reports, through the use of a latent variables modeling approach that evaluated rater reliability and bias in mother, father, and child ratings of parent-child negativity. Results based on 78 families demonstrated that family member ratings contained a significant "true score" component that correlated with observer ratings.

CONCLUSION

The chapter mainly concerns with the study of related literature. The next chapter deals with the design and methodology used in this study.

❐

18

Design of the Study and the Method of Investigation

This chapter describes in detail, the design of the study, nature and selection of sample and a brief description of the tools of investigation. It also gives a description of the procedure adopted for the collection of data, for its scoring and classification and finally the proposed statistical treatment of the data for testing the hypotheses that were formulated are explained.

HYPOTHESES

1. There is no significant difference between boys and girls of Engineering College Students on their personality disorders.
2. There is significant difference between personality disorders and family relationship of Engineering College Students.
3. There is no significant difference between boys and girls of Engineering College Students belonging to nuclear and joint family on their personality disorders.
4. There is significant difference between the students belonging to nuclear and joint family on their family relationship.
5. There is significant difference on the personality disorders of Engineering College Students based on their mother's occupation.

6. There is significant difference on the family relationship of Engineering College Students based on their mother's occupation.
7. There is significant difference of personality disorders among Engineering College Students based on their parental income.
8. There is significant difference of family relationship among Engineering College Students based on their parental income.
9. There is significant difference on the type of personality disorders of Engineering College Students based on their father's occupations.
10. There is significant difference on the type of family relationship of Engineering College Students based on their Father's occupation.
11. There is significant relation between home relation and personality disorders of Engineering College Students.

TOOLS AND TECHNIQUES

To test the hypotheses the following tools have been used.

1. Index of family Relations by Walter W. Hudson
2. Multiphasic Personality Questionnaire by H.N.Murthy

INDEX OF FAMILY RELATIONS

Description

The English poet John Donne wrote,"No man is an island; every man is a piece of the continent, a part of the main". For many of us, that continent is our family, those people with whom we share ourselves each day. The family can be a source of great positive energy, encouraging us to try new things and supporting us when our attempts fall short. But for some, the family situation is a source of stress and frustration, pulling energy away from us rather than feeding our needs. These needs that are not met belong to all the family members, for no one is immune to the effects of a stressful family life. Children may show it through physical complaints or school problems, while mom and dad may show the pressure in martial conflicts or behaviors which remove them from home. Both the individual family members and their interview relation rise or fall on the health of the family unit.

For more than thirty years, family researchers have been concerned with the evaluation of the family process. As with any other complex process, attempts have been made to specify what it is in family relationships that can cause problems. Some of the other tests are the results of that work such as martial roles and sexual compatibility, but Dr. Walter Hudson saw the need for a global measure of family satisfaction - an index that went directly to the question, "How do you feel about being a member of this family?" In 1977, he developed the Index of Family Relations as part of his series of tests for use in psychological and social work treatment. It has included because of its straight forward way of evaluating family satisfaction.

TABLE.19.1: Showing the Nature of Statements in the Index of Family Relations

Sl. No.	Nature of Statements	Item Numbers	Marks				
			Never	Very Rarely	Sometime	Often	Always
1.	Positive	1,4,5,8,1415,17,18,20,21,23	1	2	3	4	5
2.	Negative	2,3,6,7,9,10,11,12, 13,16,19,22,24,25	5	4	3	2	1

ADMINISTRATION

The test is administered to those students who had been randomly chosen from the Engineering College Students. The following instruction were given :

- Given below are twenty-five statements regarding family relations
- Five answers are given beside every statement
    1. Never
    2. Very rarely
    3. Some time
    4. Often
    5. Always
- Put a tick mark of the answer which is most suitable in your opinion.

Each statement was read clearly and distinctly so as to enable the students to respond to them with ease. The students were found to be cooperative.

i. Scoring Procedure

The index of Family Relations contains both positive and negative statements. The positive items are those which indicate comfortable family relations among the students. They are the following items: 1, 4, 5, 8, 14, 15, 17, 18, 20, 21 and 23. For the positive statements those who marked NEVER will score one; VERY RARELY will score two; SOME TIME will score three; OFTEN will score four; and ALWAYS will score five.

On the other hand the negative statements indicate difficult family relations. The following items are negative: 2, 3, 6, 7, 9, 10, 11, 12, 13, 16, 19, 22, 24 and 25. For these items those who marked NEVER will score five; VERY RARELY will score four; SOME TIME will score three; OFTEN will score two; and ALWAYS will score one.

To find total score, the total points of positive items and the total points of negative items are added. From this sum, twenty-five points are subtracted. The result is the final score.

ii. Interpreting the Score

Students who score between 30-100 are comfortable with their present Family Relations. A high score on this test indicate a low level of family satisfaction. Students who score from 0 to 29 often report significant problems in relating to their family relations.

MULTIPHASIC PERSONALITY QUESTIONNAIRE

i. Description

Multiphasic Personality Questionnaire was constructed and standardized by Dr. H.N.Murthy. This Inventory can used for the normal category of people, to assess their degree of Personality Disorder because it is assumed that each person has lesser degree of Personality Disorder. It comprise of 100 statements with their response of True or False. The different areas of Personality Disorder like Paranoid, Depression, Manic, Anxiety, Schizophrenia, Hysteric, and Psychopathic can be measured using this inventory. In this inventory high score indicate there is every chance of Personality Disorder and low score indicate less degree of Personality Disorder.

ii. Scoring Procedure

The inventory is scored based on the scoring key given by the Author as for as paranoid is concerned if as person is scores 6 and above the person is having the particular disorder. For Schizophrenia and Depression if a person score 5 and above the person may have Schizophrenia and Depression disorder. For Hysteric the score 4 and above indicate Hysteric disorder. In the same manner for manic also 6 and above scores indicated the person is having the manic problem. Also for the Psychopathic deviation the score 17 and above scores the Psychopathic disorder.

In Anxiety disorder the scores 11 and above shows Anxiety disorder.

PILOT STUDY

A pilot study was conducted to determine the suitability of the tools used in the present investigation. A random sample of 50 students was selected for the study for establishing the reliability and validity.

ESTABLISHING RELIABILITY OF MULTIPHASIC PERSONALITY QUESTIONNAIRE

The reliability of a test may be defined as the degree of consistency with which the test measures what it measures. A test score is called reliable, when we have a reason to believe it to be stable and trustworthy.

RELIABILITY OF MULTIPHASIC PERSONALITY QUESTIONNAIRE

To compute the reliability of Personality Disorder for the sample shown, the Spearman Brown Reliability Formula Method was used. The reliability was computed it was found to be 0.64, showing that the tool is highly reliable.

ESTABLISHING VALIDITY

Validity means ability to produce findings that are in agreement with conceptual or theoretical values. It refers to the success of the scale in measuring what it meant to measure. A test is valid, when it measures truly and accurately the ability or quality one wants to measure. Thus, validity means truthfulness of the test.

i. Validity of Multiphasic Personality Questionnaire

The validity of Index of Personality Disorder was found out by computing the square root of the reliability co-efficient which worked out to be 0.81, clearly reveals that the tool is highly valid in nature.

ii. Establishing Reliability of Family Relations

The reliability of a test may be defined as the degree of consistency with which the test measures what it measures. A test score is called reliable, when we have a reason to believe it to be stable and trustworthy.

iii. Reliability of Family Relations

To compute the reliability of Family Relations for the sample shown, the Spearman Brown Reliability Formula Method was used. The reliability was computed it was found to be 0.83, clearly reveals that the tool is highly reliable in nature.

ESTABLISHING VALIDITY

Validity means ability to produce findings that are in agreement with conceptual or theoretical values. It refers to the success of the scale in measuring what it meant to measure. A test is valid, when it measures truly and accurately the ability or quality one wants to measure. Thus, validity means truthfulness of the test. Intrinsic validity computed by calculating the square root of reliability and it was found as 0.91, clearly reveals that the tool is valid in nature.

STATISTICAL TECHNIQUES

Suitable descriptive and inferential statistical techniques were used in the interpretation of the date to draw out a more meaningful picture of results from the collected data. In the present study the following statistical measures were used:

- Mean
- Standard Deviation
- Critical Ratio
- ANOVA
- Correlation

CONCLUSION

This chapter outlines the design of the present study, the procedure followed and the nature of the sample. It describes the hypotheses to be tested, the tools to be used and the methods of administration and scoring. The method of investigation designed was found to be quite appropriate and effective for the study.

❒

19

Analysis of the Data

This chapter presents the results obtained from the analysis of data collected from the Engineering Colleges in Vellore District of Tamil Nadu, on two variables, namely Personality Disorders and Family Relationship. The data has been subjected to statistically treat and are given in the tabular form.

ANALYSIS OF THE DATA FOR PERSONALITY DISORDERS AND FAMILY RELATIONSHIP

Hypothesis-1

There is no significant difference between boys and girls of Engineering College Students on their Personality Disorders.

From the above table 1 it is observed that the mean scores obtained by the male students in Paranoid, Depression, Schizophrenia, Hysteric tendency and Anxiety are higher than the female students and it is statistically proved. All the other Personality Disorders there is no significant difference occurred Hence hypothesis is partially accepted.

TABLE. 20.1: Showing Mean, S.D and Critical Ratio of Boys and Girls of Engineering College Students on their Personality Disorders

Type of personality	Gender	N	Mean	S.D.	SEMD	CR	LS
Paranoid	Male Female	200 50	6.70 6.17	1.74 1.35	0.12 0.19	2.29	0.05
Depression	Male Female	200 50	4.22 3.82	0.98 0.85	0.69 0.12	2.89	0.01
Manic	Male Female	200 50	6.20 6.28	1.27 0.99	0.09 0.14	0.45	N S
Schizophrenia	Male Female	200 50	6.94 6.02	2.19 1.27	0.15 0.18	3.87	0.01
Psychopathic	Male Female	200 50	13.43 13.36	2.35 2.38	0.167 0.383	0.19	N S
Hysteric	Male Female	200 50	4.87 4.40	1.22 0.72	0.08 0.10	3.50	0.01
Anxiety	Male Female	200 50	9.10 9.76	1.93 1.86	0.147 0.26	2.22	0.05

Hypothesis-II

There is significant between boys and girls on the Family Relationship of Engineering College Students.

TABLE. 20.2: Showing Mean, S.D and Critical Ratio of Boys and Girls of Engineering College Students on their Personality Disorders

Gender	N	Mean	SD	SEMD	CR	LS
Male Female	200 50	72.01 70.68	7.61 7.88	0.539 1.114	1.08	NS

From the above table 2 it is observed that the mean scores obtained by the male students are having better attachment to their family than the female students. But it is not statistically proved hence the empirical hypothesis rejected.

Hypothesis-III

There is no significant difference between boys and girls of Engineering College Students belonging to nuclear and joint family on their Personality Disorders.

TABLE. 20.3: Showing Mean, S.D and Critical Ratio of Engineering College Students

Type of personality	Type of Family	N	Mean	S.D.	SEMD	CR	LS
Paranoid	Nuclear Joint	129 121	6.57 6.63	1.76 1.59	0.155 0.145	0.29	NS
Depression	Nuclear Joint	129 121	4.13 4.14	0.99 0.94	0.087 0.086	0.01	NS
Manic	Nuclear Joint	129 121	6.20 6.23	1.23 1.21	0.109 0.111	0.25	N S
Anxiety	Nuclear Joint	129 121	9.05 9.42	1.97 1.88	0.174 0.172	1.50	NS
Schizophrenia	Nuclear Joint	129 121	6.58 6.93	2.04 2.10	0.100 0.191	1.31	N S
Hysteric	Nuclear Joint	129 121	4.80 4.74	1.14 1.15	0.101 0.105	0.43	NS
Psychopathic	Nuclear Joint	129 121	13.51 13.31	2.25 2.47	0.198 0.225	0.66	NS

From the above table 3 it is observed that type of family has no influence on their Personality Disorders. Hence the empirical hypothesis rejected.

Hypothesis-IV

There is significant influence between the students belonging to nuclear and joint family on their family relationship.

TABLE. 20.4: Showing Mean, S.D and Critical Ratio of Engineering College Students

Type of Family	N	Mean	SD	SEMD	CR	LS
N J	129 121	71.62 71.88	7.55 7.84	0.539 1.114	0.27	NS

It is observed from the table 4 the students belonging to nuclear and joint family has no significant difference on their family relationship and hence the empirical hypothesis rejected.

Hypothesis-V

There is significant difference on the type of Personality Disorders of engineering college students based on their mother occupations.

TABLE. 20.5: Showing Mean, S.D and Critical Ratio of Engineering College Students

Type of personality	Type of Family	N	Mean	S.D.	SEMD	CR	LS
Paranoid	Housewife Employed	186 64	6.51 6.84	1.64 1.76	0.121 0.221	1.32	NS
Depression	Housewife Employed	186 64	4.06 4.35	0.95 0.96	0.070 0.121	2.11	NS
Manic	Housewife Employed	186 64	6.25 6.10	1.25 1.12	0.092 0.141	0.88	N S
Anxiety	Housewife Employed	186 64	9.29 9.06	1.95 1.90	0.143 0.238	0.82	NS
Schizophrenia	Housewife Employed	186 64	6.72 6.84	2.03 2.22	0.149 0.277	0.37	N S
Hysteric	Housewife Employed	186 64	4.80 4.70	1.18 1.03	0.087 0.129	0.63	NS
Psychopathic	Housewife Employed	186 64	13.34 13.62	2.29 2.54	0.168 0.318	0.78	NS

From the above table 5 it is observe that mother's occupation has no influencc on their Personality Disorders. Hence the empirical hypothesis rejected.

Hypothesis-VI

There is significant difference on the type of family relationship of engineering college students based on their mother occupations.

TABLE. 20.6: Showing Mean, S.D and Critical Ratio of Engineering College Students

	N	Mean	SD	SEMD	CR	LS
HW EM	186 64	71.88 7.35	7.87 7.09	0.578 0.887	0.49	NS

From the above table 6 it is observe that there is no significant difference occurred among the students studying in Engineering colleges based on their mother's occupations in their family relationship. So the empirical hypothesis rejected.

Hypothesis-VII

There is significant difference of Personality Disorders among engineering college students based on their parental income.

TABLE . 20.7: ANOVA for the Different Areas of Personality Disorders of Engineering College Students based on Parental Income

Type of personality	Source of Variance	Sum of Squares	Df	Sum of Mean Squares	F-ratio	LS
Paranoid	BSS WSS TSS	1.55 700.64 702.19	2 247 249	0.78 2.83	0.27	NS
Depression	BSS WSS TSS	2.37 229.72 232.10	2 247 249	1.18 0.93	1.27	NS
Manic	BSS WSS TSS	24.09 348.80 372.90	2 247 249	12.04 1.41	8.53	0.01
Anxiety	BSS WSS TSS	1.66 934.88 936.54	2 247 249	0.83 3.78	0.21	NS
Schizophrenia	BSS WSS TSS	2.82 1071.29 1074.11	2 247 249	1.412 4.337	0.32	NS
Hysteric	BSS WSS TSS	6.29 323.16 329.45	2 247 249	3.14 1.30	2.40	0.05
Psychopathic	BSS WSS TSS	20.55 1366.18 1389.73	2 247 246	10.27 5.53	1.85	NS

It is observed that from the above table 7 Manic and Hysteric tendency have significant difference have been acquired, but all the other Personality Disorders there is no significant difference based on their parental income. Thus Empirical hypothesis is accepted for manic and hypothesis tendency and rejected for other areas of Personality Disorders.

Further analysis is done to find out the income group difference for Manic and Hysteric Disorders.

Hypothesis-VIII

There is significant difference of family relationship among Engineering College Students based on their parental income.

TABLE. 20.8: ANOVA for the Different areas of Family Relationship of Engineering College Students based on Parental Income

Source of Variances	Sum of Squares	Df	Mean of Squares	F-ratio	LS
BSS	93.31	2	46.65	0.791	NS
WSS	14569.80	247	58.98		
TSS	14663.12	249			

It is observed that from the above table 8 that there is no significant difference between parental income groups on their family relationship of Engineering College Students. Thus empirical hypothesis rejected.

Hypothesis-IX

There is significant difference on the type of Personality Disorders of engineering college students based on their father's occupations.

TABLE. 20.9: ANOVA for the Different areas of Personality Disorders of Engineering College Students based on Father's Occupation

Type of personality	Source of Variance	Sum of Squares	Df	Sum of Mean Squares	F-ratio	LS
Paranoid	BSS	15.70	3	5.235	1.87	NS
	WSS	686.48	246	2.790		
	TSS	702.19	249			
Depression	BSS	0.871	3	0.290	0.30	NS
	WSS	231.22	246	0.940		
	TSS	232.100	249			
Manic	BSS	20.08	3	6.69	4.66	0.01
	WSS	352.81	246	1.43		
	TSS	372.90	249			
Anxiety	BSS	5.89	3	1.966	0.51	NS
	WSS	930.64	246	3.783		
	TSS	936.54	249			
Schizophrenia	BSS	6.694	3	2.23	0.51	NS
	WSS	1067.42	246	4.33		
	TSS	1074.11	249			
Hysteric	BSS	2.599	3	0.86	0.65	NS
	WSS	326.85	246	1.32		
	TSS	329.45	249			
Psychopathic	BSS	21.71	3	7.23	1.30	NS
	WSS	1365.02	246	5.54		
	TSS	1386.73	249			

It is observed that from the above table 9 for the Personality Disorders areas Manic has occupied a significant difference between the students belonging to fathers who are employed. All the other areas Personality Disorders no significant difference has been required. Thus the empirical hypothesis is accepted for manic area and rejected for other of Personality Disorders.

Hypothesis-X

There is significant difference on the type of family relationship of engineering college students based on their Father's occupation.

TABLE. 20.10: ANOVA for the Different areas of Family Relationship of Engineering College Students based on Father's Occupation

Source of Variances	Sum of Squares	Df	Mean of Squares	F-ratio	LS
BSS	227.46	3	75.82	1.29	NS
WSS	14435.65	246	58.68		
TSS	14663.12	249			

It is observed that from the above table 10 there is no significant difference acquired among the students studying in engineering colleges based on their father's occupations in their family relation. Thus the empirical hypothesis rejected.

Hypothesis-XI

TABLE. 20.11: Showing Correlation Co-efficient of Personality disorders and Family Relationship of Engineering College Students

Type of Personality	Family Relationship	L.S.
Paranoid	0.098	N S
Depression	0.028	N S
Manic	0.111	N S
Anxiety	0.084	N S
Schizophrenia	-0.074	N S
Hysteric	-0.045	N S
Psychopathic	0.036	N S

From the above table 11 it is observe that the computed correction coefficient between Personality Disorders and family relationship show no relationship. From this we can conclude family relation may not show any significant relation with the various type of Personality Disorders.

TABLE. 20.12: Showing Correlation Matrix for the Personality Disorders Scores

	Paranoid	Depression	Manic	Anxiety	Schizophrenia	Hysteric	Psychopathic
Paranoid	-						
Depression	0.3694xx						
Manic	0.2643xx	0.2458xx					
Anxiety	0.0425	-0.03460	0.0359	0.0425			
Schizophrenia	0.0776	0.1152	0.0591	-0.1175	0.0776		
Hysteric	0.0070	0.1296x	0.0466	-0.2413xx	0.3317xx		
Psychopathic	0.0020	0.2193xx	0.1212	0.1210	0.1560x	0.1055	-

Inter correlation between various Personality Disorders have been Personality Disorders have been computed and it is given in the above table 4.11. It is observe from the table 4.12. Correlation between paranoid Vs depression, paranoid Vs Manic, Depression Vs Manic, Schizophrenia Vs Hysteric showed significant relation between these variables positive on the other hand Anxiety and Hysteric shows negative relation. This categories show 0.01 level of significant. The variables Hysteric Vs Depression, Psychopathic Vs Schizophrenia shows positive correlation it is significant level 0.05 level.

CONCLUSION

A brief report of the research study together with interpretation is given here. The conclusion arrived at, along with their educational implications have been presented in the succeeding chapter.

❐

20

Summary, Findings and Conclusion

A brief summary of the study, stating the problem, the objective, the methodology and the major findings are presented in this chapter. The implications of the study are then discussed, suggesting a few areas for further.

STATEMENT OF THE PROBLEM

Personality Disorders and Family Relationship among Engineering College Students.

OBJECTIVES OF THE STUDY

1. To find out the significant difference between boys and girls of Engineering College Students on their Personality Disorders.
2. To find out the significant difference between Personality Disorders and Family Relationship of Engineering College Students.
3. To find out the significant difference between boys and girls of Engineering College Students belonging to nuclear and joint family on their Personality Disorders.

4. To find out the significant difference between the students belonging to nuclear and joint family on their Family Relationship.
5. To find out the significant difference on the Personality Disorders of Engineering College Students based on their mother's occupation.
6. To find out the significant difference on the Family Relationship of Engineering College Students based on their mother's occupation.
7. To find out the significant difference of Personality Disorders among Engineering College Students based on their parental income.
8. To find out the significant difference of Family Relationship among Engineering College Students based on their parental income.
9. To find out the significant difference on the type of Personality Disorders of Engineering College Students based on their father's occupations.
10. To find out the significant difference on the type of Family Relationship of Engineering College Students based on their Father's occupation.
11. To find out the significant relationship between home relation and Personality Disorders of Engineering College Students.

HYPOTHESIS

1. There is no significant difference between boys and girls of Engineering College Students on their Personality Disorders.
2. There is significant difference between Personality Disorders and Family Relationship of Engineering College Students.
3. There is no significant difference between boys and girls of Engineering College Students belonging to nuclear and joint family on their Personality Disorders
4. There is significant difference between the students belonging to nuclear and joint family on their Family Relationship.
5. There is significant difference on the Personality Disorders of Engineering College Students based on their mother's occupation.
6. There is significant difference on the Family Relationship of Engineering College Students based on their mother's occupation.
7. There is significant difference of Personality Disorders among Engineering College Students based on their parental income.
8. There is significant difference of Family Relationship among Engineering College Students based on their parental income.
9. There is significant difference on the type of Personality Disorders of Engineering College Students based on their father's occupations.
10. There is significant difference on the type of Family Relationship of Engineering College Students based on their Father's occupation.
11. There is significant relation between home relation and Personality Disorders of Engineering College Students.

METHODOLOGY

To Verify the hypothesis the following tools were used

1. Multiphasic Personality Questionnaire by H.N.Murthy
2. Index of Family Relations by Walter W.Hudson

These tools were administrated among 250 Engineering College Students.

MAJOR FINDINGS

1. It is observed that the mean scores obtained by the male students in Paranoid, Depression, Schizophrenia, Hysteric tendency and Anxiety are higher than the female students and it is statistically proved table 4.1.
2. It reveals that the mean scores obtained by the male students are having better attachment to their family than the female students. But it is not statistically proved table 4.2
3. It is concluded that type of family has no influence on their Personality Disorders table 4.3.
4. It is observed that students belonging to nuclear and joint family have no significant difference on their Family Relationship table 4.4.
5. It is reveals that mothers occupation has no influence on their Personality Disorders table 4.5.
6. It is found that there is no significant difference occurred among the students studying in engineering colleges based on their mother's occupations in their Family Relationship table 4.6.
7. It is concluded that Manic and Hysteric tendency have significant difference have been acquired, but all the other Personality Disorders there is no significant difference based on their parental income table 4.7
8. Family income has no influence on the home relation of Engineering College Students table 4.8.
9. It is inferred that from the above table 4.9 for the Personality Disorders areas manic has occupied a significant difference between the students belonging to father's who are employed. All the other areas Personality Disorders no significant difference have been required table 4.9.
10. It is concluded that from the above table 4.10 there is no significant difference acquired among the students studying in Engineering Colleges based on their father's occupations in their Family Relationship table 4.10
11. It is found that the computed correction coefficient between Personality Disorders and Family Relationship show no relation table 4.11

Inter correlation between various Personality Disorders have been Personality Disorders have been computed and it is given in the table 4.11. It is observe from the table 4.12. Correlation between paranoid Vs depression, paranoid Vs Manic, Depression Vs Manic, Schizophrenia Vs Hysteric showed significant relation between this variables positive on the other hand Anxiety and Hysteric shows negative relation. This categories show 0.01 level of significant. The variables Hysteric Vs Depression, Psychopathic Vs Schizophrenia shows positive correlation it is significant level 0.05 level.

EDUCATIONAL IMPLICATIONS

Personality refers to the total quality of an individual our education institution or very much involved to development integrity personality. The curricular and co-curricular activities are focused on developing good relationship with the family as well as different social groups. If there is any quality development of personality it create certain Personality Disorders as well as Psychotic deviation as for as this study is concerned main Engineering College Students shows Depression Anxiety, Paranoid and Hysteric tendency, it denotes that these people should have given proper Psychotic guidance. Otherwise their personality development attachment with the family other social groups and community will be effected. Ultimately the society will suffer a lot also engineering colleges which gives counseling will not be an effective one. So the education as well as Psychologist should take effective necessary steps to develop good relationship as well as integrated personality.

SUGGESTIONS FOR FURTHER RESEARCH

1. This study may be conducted among arts and science students.
2. A cross cultural study may be conducted taking the variables personality adjustment behavior among self concept and Family Relationship among women students may be conducted.
3. Personality level of aspiration and Anxiety youngest at the school level may be conduct.

CONCLUSION

The purpose of the present investigation was to study Personality Disorders and Family Relationship among Engineering College Students. The study is sure find some usefulness in the field of education and findings of the study can serve as a database for further research.

❐

Bibliography

1. Arachana (1998).“Intelligence as a function of Religion Gender and socioeconomic status”. *Indian Psychological Review.* 3:153-157.
2. Asheval. G.G (2001). “intelligence as a correlate of achievement in mathematics across Different levels of socio-economic status”. *Indian Psychological Abstracts and Reviews* X(1):186.
3. Asthana. M. (2000). “ General intelligence visual motor perception and memory in rural and urban children. Indian *Education Review*..54(1&2): 94-99.
4. Das, B.C. (1993). “Effectiveness of concept attainment model in terms of teaching competency of pre-service student teachers [perspectives in Education. *Indian Educational Abstracts* (Issue-4) 9(1): 34-35.
5. Das, R.C. et al (1976). A study of effectiveness of micro teaching of teachers dept of teachers education. NCERT. New Delhi (Abridged Report).
6. Kukreti (1994). Job motivation and teacher competency. A correlation and study. Experiments in education. Indian Educational Abstract Issue-2. 22(1): 10-14.
7. Laxmi Thakur (2001).“Effect of Home environment on intelligence and educational aspirations”. *Journal of Education and Psychology.* 59(4):8-15.
8. Maline, P.M. (2003). “ Effect of Intelligence and Mastery learning strategy of instruction of IX standard Pupils”. *Experiment in Education.* XXXI(8):149-153.

9. Panda, S.C. (1996). Effect of competency based instruction in achieving MLL competencies in Grade IV. National council of educational research. *Educational Abstract Issue*-6.

10. Prabha, I . and Gupta, Monika(2000)."Effect of sex, Intelligence and socioeconomic status on the achievement of students in Computer Education". *India Psychological Abstracts and Reviews.* III(2).

11. Renuga. N (2003). A study on intelligence and creativity among XI standard Arts and Science Students in chennai city " M. Ed Thesis, Madras University

12. Sadhya Giri Rajan (1985). Competency and personality. Motivation and profession perception of college teachers. Fourth serve of research in education 1983-1988. Volume-11.

13. Shamala, S.K. (1998). Enhancing teaching competency through integration of arts education for effective language teaching at the primary stage. *National council of educational research and training. Indian educational* Abstract Issue-5.

14. Sharma. A and Kumar, H (1999). Birth order and intelligence", *Indian Psychological Review.* 52(6): 85-93.

15. Singhal (1996). Teacher's self-efficacy and competency for improving quality of primary school. National council of educational research and training. *Indian Educational Abstracts Issue*-6.

16. Sinha, S.P and Bvibha (1998). "Intelligence and Vigilance Performance as related to lead Exposure among children", *Indian Psychological Abstracts and Reviews.* VIII(1):183.

17. Srivastsa.R.k (1999). A correlation study of intelligence and academic achievement of High School pupils. *The Progress of education.* XXI(10):218.

18. Thamilmani.P.(1990).Teacher competency and teacher personality in relation to Achievement of High School. Students in science *V Survey of Educational Research* 11:19-26.

19. Bharadwaj, R.L and Mithas, V.J (2003). "Evasion of Fortitude value assumptions along with associated conflict". *Indian Psychological Abstracts and Reviews,* Vol.X(1), pp.35 - 41.

20. Bharadwaj, R.L (1998). "Percieved parenting of Rejection Acceptance and Adolescents value conflicts". *Indian Psychological Review,* Vol.LI, pp.256 - 266.

21. Bhushan A. (1994), conducted a study done on the social maturity across sex and family vocations, M.B. Buch, *The Educational Research,* Volume II.

22. Chakabarthy, Subhra, Brown, Gene and Gillbert, Arthur, H.J.R. (2002). "Evaluation of Rahim's Organisation Conflict Inventory - II as a measure of conflict handling styles". *Psychological Reports,* Vol. XC(2), pp.327.
23. Chamberlin, Susan, R (1998). "The strategies of self - control used by personnel who work with adolescents *"Dissertation abstract"*.
24. Ciarrochi, Joseph, said Terri, Deame, Frank . P (2005), when simplifying life is not be bad. The link between rigidity, stressful life events and mental health in an undergraduate population *British Journal of Guidance and counselling,* V33 n2 p.185 - 197.
25. Coleman, J.C. (1976) Abnormal Psychology and Modern Life Bombay D.B. Taraporawala and Sons.
26. Commons, Mandy, Demello, Lesley, R (2000). "The effect of parental divorce and remarriage and the experience of familial conflict on young adult offspring adjustment". *Indian Psychological Abstracts and Reviews.* Vol.X(2), pp.11 - 18.
27. Constantine et al (2004) exploring indigenous mental health practices, the roles of heals and helpers in promoting well being in people of colour. *Journal of counseling and values.* v 48 n2 p.110 Jan.2004.
28. Davidson, G.C, Neale, J.M. (1988) Abnormal Psychology. *New York, John Wiley & Sons, Inc.*
29. Dhand, Harry (University of Saskatchewan, Canada), Sansanwal D.N., Singh, A.K. (1993). "Value clarification of undergraduate students, A cross cultural study". *Indian Educational Review,* Vol.XXVIII (2-3-4) pp.21.
30. Journal of American College of Health (2005). "The mental health needs of today's college students, challenges and recommendation". Helder publications, *Helen Dwight raid education foundation,* V53 n4 p.157, Jan - Feb. 2005.
31. Kathuria M (1974). "Personality determination of vocational maturity and cancer inducivenes". *Dissertation abstracts.*
32. Magdalin, Sujaritha and Parvathi, S. (2002); "Development of adolescents moral value questionnaire". *Journal of Psychometry,* Vol. XV(1) pp.29 - 36.
33. Malin A.J. (1990). A study on the relationship of social maturity with class room climate and Academic Achievement. Third survey of Research in Education Buch. M.B. 547-53.
34. Mulia, R.D. (1991), *Journal of Education and psychology,* volume 48 p.145.

35. Myers.D.G. (1964). "The science of Educational Research". *Eurasia Publishing House, New Delhi.*
36. Pattraman Junpangerh (1986); "Social maturity of higher secondary students in Thailand". *Dissertation Abstract International.*
37. Rao N.A. (1968). "Reports Social Maturity of Children, M. B. Buch", *Third Survey of Research in Education* (p.305).
38. Roy, Ramashray (CSDC Delhi), 1991; "Conflicts, conflict resolution and human needs theories". *Indian Psychological Abstracts and Reviews,* Vol.I (1), pp.77.
39. Sales, Esther, Greeno, Catherine, Shean, M. Katherine et al., (2004). "Maternal caregiving strain as a mediator in the relationship between child and mother mental health problems". *Social work Research* V. 28, n4 p.211, Dec.2004.
40. Saovaluk Thongamkhom, (1983), Conducted a study on social maturity as a function of some psychosocial adjustment factors of higher secondary students. Fourth Survey of Research in Education Buch, M.B. Volume 1 (p.261).
41. Sarojamma, Y.H. (1990) A comparative study of reaching ability and social maturity of over normal and under achiever of standard VIII, Fourth survey of Research in Education, Buch, M.B. Volume 2, (p.111)
42. Srivastava, Ashok, K. (NCERT, New Delhi), 1999. "Culture and human values continuity and change in the Indian Society". *Indian Educational Review*, Vol.XXXII (2), pp.69 - 91.
43. Sudha, B.G., and Lakkamma (1994). "Assertive Communication of X Standard urban and rural students in relation to their self - esteem and socio - economic status". *Experiments in Education,* Vol.XXII (4), pp.80 - 87.
44. Thinklin. T, Ridell. S, Wilson, A (2005). Support for students certain mental health difficulties in higher education. The student's prospective. *British Journal of Guidance and Counselling.* V33, n4 p495 - 512.
45. Timofeev, Mikhael, I (St. Petersburg Technical U, Inter - Branch Institute of Advanced Training, Russia) (1993); "Irrational beliefs and conflict - handling orientations". *Journal of Rational Emotive and Cognitive Behaviour Therapy,* Vol.II (2), pp.109 - 119.
46. Young, Robert, B and Elfrink, Victoria, L. Kent State V), (1991). "Essential Values of Student affairs work". *Psychological Abstracts,* Vol.LXXVIII, pp. 1678.
47. Abram M Sulsky, Gary James Schmidt (2002-2003) Silent welfare, Understanding the world of intelligence, Bratteys INC.

48. Abraham Sperling (1967) Definition of social maturity, Vikas publications, NewDelhi.
49. Adhiseshiah, W.T.V. and Pavanasam, R. (1974) Sociology in theory and practice, Shanthi Publishers, NewDelhi, p 38.
50. Adler, A. (1939). Social Interest: A Challenge to Mankind, New York: Putnam.
51. Baues Ann Leslie (1995) measured the effect of participation in a peer facilitation project on sixth grades self esteem, social maturity and patterns of social choice. Ph.D, Kent state university.
52. Bhusan.A (1994), conducted a study done on the social maturity across sex and family vocations, Buch, M.B,the educational research, Volume II.
53. Crandall, J. (1981). Theory and Measurement of Social Interest, New York: Columiba University Press.
54. Cuber, J.F. (1995). Sociology, New York: Appleton Century.
55. Cron Bach, L.J. and Gleser, G.C(1954). Review of the study of behaviours; Pcychometric, 19, 329 - 333
56. Downie, N.M and Heath, R.W (1970). Basic statistical methods, New York: Harper and Row.
57. Esther N Goody (1995), "social intelligence and interaction" published by Cambridge University.
58. Harry Elmer Barnes (2004). History and social intelligence, Kessengar publishing.
59. Henry I Garrett (1968), general psychology, Eurasia publishing house Pvt. Ltd., New Delhi, p 88.
60. Ghosh S (1975); A study of the social maturity of Bengali children, applied psychology, Calcutta University.
61. Guilford, J.P. (1967). The Nature of human intelligence, New York: Mcgraw Hill.
62. Guilford, J.P. and Hopener, R. (1971). The analysis of intelligence New York: Mcgraw Hill.
63. Hunt.T.(1928).The measurement of social intelligence, Journel of applied psychology, 12, 317 - 334.
64. Nicholas Humphrrey (2003). The Later Eye social intelligence in Evaluation.
65. Pattraman jumpengern (1986); Social maturity of higher secondary students in Thailand, dissertation abstract international.
66. Piaget, J.1947. The psychology of intelligence.
67. Pintner, R. and Upshall, C.C (1928). Some results of social intelligence.
68. Rai, B.C. (2001), Social psychology, prakashan kentra, lucknow p.29

69. Sarojamma Y.H (1990). A comparative study of reading ability and social maturity of over normal and underachievers of standard V11. Ph. D., edu. Bangalore University.
70. Schacter, Richard, T (1983), sociology, mc graw _ hill, inc. New York, p. 328.
71. Stern, w. (1914). The psychological methods of testing intelligence.
72. Thorndike, E.C (1920). The measurement of intelligence, New York; teachers college Columbia University.
73. Pintner, R. and Upshall, C.C (1928). Some results of social intelligence.
74. Bailkeri, K. N. (1983): Effect of self- Instructional Remedial Micro Teaching course on the Instructional Competency of in service secondary school mathematics teachers.
75. Bhalwankar, A. G. (1984): A study of Reliability and Validity of the process appraising scale of teacher effectiveness.
76. Balachandran, E. S. (1981): Teaching effectiveness and student evaluation of Teaching, Ph.D., Education, Madras University.
77. Coates, T. I. and Thoresen (1976 spring): Teacher anxiety, A review with recommendation, Review of educational research 49(2), pp.159-184.
78. Cooper, C. Marshal, J. (1976): Occupational sources of stress. A review of the literature relating to coronary heart disease and mental ill health Journal of occupational Psychology, pp.11-28.
79. Cox, T. Mackay, C. J.Cox, S. Watts, C.and Brockley (1978): Stress and wellbeing in schoolteachers psycho-physiological response to occupational stress. Paper presented to the Economic Society Conference, Nottingham University England.
80. Dohrenwend, D. et. al (1981): Stress in the community a report to the president's commission on the accidents at three-mile land. Annual of the New York Academy of Sciences 365, 159-174.
81. Dac, R.C. Passi, B K. and Singh, A. (1982): Effectiveness of different strategies of integration of teaching skills in developing general teaching competency of student's teachers department of teacher education, NCERT.
82. Davis, H. (1964): Evaluation of current practices in evaluating teacher competency, in B. J. Biddle and J. Ellance (Eds). Contemporary research on teacher effectiveness, New York, Holt, Rinehart and Winston.
83. Donald, M. Medley (1982): Teacher Effectiveness" Encyclopedia of Educational Research, Education Harold. E. Mitzel, Vol. 4. Mac millan publishing &Co., New York.

84. Fimian, M. J. and Santoro, T.M. (1983): sources and manifestations of occupational stress and reported by full item special education teachers. Exceptional children, pp. 540-543.
85. Gupta, N. and Beehr, T.A. (1973): "Job stress and employee behavior", Organization behaviors and human performance, pp. 373-387.
86. Girdano, D.E. and Everly, G. S. (1979): Controlling stress and tension, Englewood cliffs, N.J. Prinetice hall.
87. Greenwood, G.E. Olejuik, S. F. and Parkoy, F. W. (1990): Relationship between four teacher efficiency belief patterns and selected teacher characteristics. Journal of research and development in education,23 (2), 102-106.
88. Gupta, S. (1981): A comparative study of Socio-Economic background problems and professional behavior of men women teachers in co-education Institutions at different levels in the state of Haryana, Ph.D., Education, Kurnool University.
89. Gupta, U. (1981): job involvement and need patterns of primary school teachers in relation to teaching effectiveness Ph.D. Education, All Universities.
90. Hodge, J. and Marker (1978): assuring teacher stress; beneficial task for administrator, American secondary Education, 8(4).
91. Joseph schwrzwaldet at stress reaction of school age children to the Bombardment by send missiles journal of Abnormal Psychology 1993, Vol. 102, No.3, 404-410.
92. Kaiser, J.S. and Polezynski, J. J. (1982): Educational stress sources, reaction, preventions. Poe body journal of education 10.
93. Kessler, R. C. Price, R.H. and Wortman, C. B. (1985): social factors in phycho pathology, stress support and coping process, annual review of psychology 36, 531-572.
94. Kryiacane and Suteliffe, J. (1977): Teacher Stress; A review educational review 29.
95. Kryiacau, C. and Sutclifee, J. (1978): Teacher stress; Prevalence, Source and Symptoms, British journal of educational psychology 48.
96. Lazarus,S. Folkman (1984): Stress appraisal and coping, New York Springer publishing company.
97. Lislie Sovoy (1990): "Source of stress on trainee lectures for further and higher education". Journal for Higher education summer (1990).
98. Vene, M.R. (1985): A study of some of the personality components of creative student teacher in relation to their competency towards teaching.

99. Yogendra Kumar and Rattan Lai (1980): Use of micro-teaching in improving general teaching competency of in service teachers.
100. Arnett, J.J. (1999): Adolescent storm and stress, Reconsidered. American Psychologist, pp. 317-326.
101. Folkman, S. and Lazarus, R. S.(1985): If it changes it must be a prosess: Study of emotion and coping during three stages of a college examination. Journal of personality and social psychology, 48, 150-170.
102. Lazarus, R. S. (1993): Coping theory and research: Past, present and future. Psychosomatic Medicine, pp.234-247.

❑❑❑